Young Children Learning

Young Children Learning

edited by

Tricia David

P·C·P
Paul Chapman
Publishing Ltd

Paul Chapman Publishing Ltd
A SAGE Publications Company
1 Oliver's Yard, 55 City Road
London EC1Y 1SP

SAGE Publications Inc
2455 Teller Road, Thousand Oaks
California 91320

SAGE Publications India Pvt. Ltd
B-42 Panchsheel Enclave
PO Box 4109
New Delhi 110 017

British Library Cataloguing in Publication data
A catalogue record for this book is available from the British Library

Printed on paper from sustainable sources

Typeset by Anneset, Weston-super-Mare, Somerset
Printed digitally and bound in Great Britain by
Biddles Limited, King's Lynn, Norfolk

Contents

Acknowledgements

As Editor, my first acknowledgement must be to the authors who have contributed to this book and to their families for sustaining them, when they needed space in order to write in an already over-worked life! We all acknowledge the role played by our students and other colleagues at Canterbury Christ Church University College and in the wider world of education, from preschool to university level, for without their debate and challenge our own thinking would be limited. Our publishers, especially Marianne Lagrange, have been ever patient and helpful and Louise Duff invaluable for her secretarial skills.

Canterbury Christ Church University College is a developing, vibrant community of learners, set geographically in a position to influence and be influenced by other learners in this large county of Kent and beyond – for we are a 'quick hop' from mainland Europe. The College has been recognised as a leading teacher training institution and so, as teacher educators, we seek in this and the companion publication, *Teaching Young Children*, to share some of our ideas and to encourage the debate and disagreement which are the signs of a strong and healthy democracy. In particular, within that debate, we want parents, educators, teachers, politicians and policy makers to discuss what education is for and what childhood is for – and to explore the meaning of some of the responses to these questions.

Tricia David
Canterbury
June 1998

The authors

Until recently **Dr Richard Bailey** was a Senior Lecturer in the Department of Education at Christ Church University College. He is now in the Department of Science and Technology Education at the University of Reading, where he teaches in the area of Physical Education. His primary research interests concern the contributions the biological sciences can make to education, especially in the early years. Current projects include the evolutionary nature of children's play and children's physiological responses to physical activity.

John Cornwall is a Senior Lecturer, Education Consultant and Psychologist. With a teaching career spanning 18 years and being a former headteacher of an independent school, John is now a consultant, researcher and the author of two books on choice and opportunity in the education system for pupils with disabilities. He is currently researching into violent behaviour and is working with schools and other organisations on the 'human elements' in education, such as stress management, assertiveness and teamwork. John is Director of Personal and Organisational Services (PodS).

Tricia David has worked as a teacher and headteacher in nursery and primary schools, as a researcher, community educator, playgroup tutor, and teacher trainer. She is now a Professor of Education at Canterbury Christ Church University College, with particular reference to the early years. Tricia is currently chairing the Kent Nursery Partnership Training Subgroup and finds this exciting multi-professional mix contributes to her own reflection and development, as part of an international network of researchers in the early years field. She also has a vested interest in Kent's nursery developments, having two grandchildren in the county. At present Tricia's main research energies are focused on the comparative Early Literacy Links project (funded by the Esmée Fairbairn Foundation), editing the *International Journal of Early Childhood* and preparing to edit a new international yearbook of early years research papers.

Rita Headington is widely known for her publication aimed at helping classroom assistants to understand early mathematics, *Supporting Numeracy* (David Fulton, 1990). She worked as a primary school teacher and in an advisory capacity before joining the Maths Education team, as a Senior Lecturer in Primary Education, at Canterbury Christ Church University College. Rita's keen interest in the relationship between home and school has been maintained through her work in mathematics and assessment.

Martine Jago gained an MA in modern Languages at St Anne's College, Oxford and a Postgraduate Certificate in Education (Primary Phase – Language Specialism) from Homerton College, Cambridge. Until 1995, Martine was the Deputy Headteacher of a primary school in Hertfordshire, with responsibility for early years education and for the European Dimension. Martine is nearing the end of the third and final year of study for her PhD, at Canterbury Christ Church University College, where her field of interest is the teaching of modern foreign languages in the early years of primary education. In autumn 1998 Martine took up an appointment as Research Fellow with the Esmée Fairbairn funded Early Literacy Links project at the College, where she is also a tutor for the Early Childhood Studies degree programme.

Angela D. Nurse has a first degree in history but trained as a teacher. Much of her teaching has been with very young children with special needs, mainly in inner London and Kent. Before coming to Canterbury Christ Church University College as a Senior Lecturer, she worked in an advisory capacity with teachers and colleagues in the other statutory services and within the private and voluntary sectors. Angela has worked extensively with parents, often in their own homes. She now directs the Early Childhood Studies degree programme at Canterbury and is a Registered Nursery Inspector and Vice-Chair of the governing body of her local school. Her new role as a grandmother, however, brings into sharper focus all the work she has done with very young children!

Sacha Powell spent over twelve months living and studying in the People's Republic of China and in Taiwan. She worked for several years at the British Academy, where she was responsible for links with China. Sacha is currently a research student in the Department of Education at Canterbury Christ Church University College and her thesis is intended to explore the lives of very young children in the

China of today, a topic which is enhanced by what she is learning from her own small daughter and son.

Mike Radford is a Principal Lecturer responsible for taught higher degrees in the Education Department at Canterbury Christ Church University College. His background is in philosophy and psychology and his interests are in epistemological issues in educational research. He has a particular interest in the nature of knowledge in the context of the arts and in religious education and the concept of aesthetic and spiritual development.

Christopher Robertson has had extensive experience of teaching pupils with physical disabilities but has also worked with pupils with severe learning difficulties and multiple learning difficulties. He was formerly a lecturer with a specialism in the area of physical disability at the London University Institute of Education and is now Senior Lecturer in the Special Educational Needs Research Development Centre at Canterbury Christ Church University College.

Judith Roden qualified as a teacher in 1975 and has studied at the Universities of Wales and Liverpool. Although she is experienced in teaching all age groups, Judith has a particular interest in the early years. She is currently the Year 3 Coordinator for the undergraduate initial teacher education programme and Primary Science Team Leader at Canterbury Christ Church University College.

Keith Sharpe was Head of Primary Initial Teacher Education at Canterbury Christ Church University College. He is now Professor and Head of the Department of Education at Liverpool University. Keith has held a range of teaching and senior management posts in primary and middle schools. He has published on issues in curriculum and methodology and has a particular interest in the teaching of Modern Languages. His research has focused on comparative education studies within Europe and he has been recently engaged in a large scale, ESRC-funded project comparing the attitudes and achievements of ten and eleven year old pupils in England and France.

Beryl Webber was a Senior Lecturer at Canterbury Christ Church University College before taking up an appointment with the new Medway Authority. She was responsible for the coordination of assessment across the primary phase teacher education courses. Beryl has worked closely with SCAA/QCA in the development of National Baseline Assessment and has a particular interest in children learning mathematics.

1

Changing minds: young children learning

Tricia David

More than ever before politicians of all parties are beginning to take an interest in educational provision for children in their earliest years. Not only is daycare for working mothers high on the agenda, as women overtake men as a proportion of the workforce, but evidence that early learning promotes children's later achievements (e.g. Ball 1994; Shorrocks 1992; Schweinhart and Weikart 1993) is at last recognised by top levels of government.

In our two collections, *Young Children Learning* and *Teaching Young Children*, by authors who are or who have been tutors at Canterbury Christ Church College, we are exploring the ways in which we all need to open our minds and reflect on learning and teaching, and their relationships to each other, during the first two 'cycles' of children's education careers – the preschool and early primary phases, between birth and eight years. Although much evidence about the most effective pedagogy for younger children has been available for some time, there is a tendency to revert to 'old', supposedly tried and tested, more visibly teacher-directed ways of working, whenever threatened, either by outside judgements, or by fears of 'loss of control'. However, we might heed Gardner's (1993) remark, that we need to throw out limiting old assumptions and respect the flexibility, creativity, adventurousness, resourcefulness and generativity of the young mind.

Young children thinking and learning

As Audrey Curtis, Iram Siraj-Blatchford and I pointed out in the wake of Alexander, Rose and Woodhead's (1992) report *Curriculum organisation and classroom practice in primary schools* (David *et al.* 1992), no programme of teaching can be successful if we do not take into account the characteristics of young children and how they learn (Edwards and Knight (1994) provides an excellent, longer survey of this topic).

The first eight years of life cover an important period of change and development in children's thinking and in their ability to make sense of the world. Most of the information we have about learning in early childhood has been provided by developmental psychologists rather than by educational researchers, since many of the major research projects in primary education in the UK have focused on the years between seven and 11 (Key Stage 2). While many of the projects carried out by researchers who have not themselves been teachers of young children provide important insights, teachers of younger children have also had to interpret the relevant research evidence from developmental psychology, rather than assuming that educational research pertaining to older children could be adapted (for a fuller discussion see Aubrey *et al.*, forthcoming, and David, 1998).

During the twentieth century, a key question has been: is young children's thinking qualitatively different from that of adults or is it simply lack of experience which produces unexpected replies to our questions? For decades the issue of how children learn has exercised the minds of educators, philosophers, sociologists and psychologists. Behaviourist psychologists like Pavlov, Thorndike and Skinner had an important influence upon the ways in which children were taught prior to the 1950s and there was much emphasis upon rote learning and the need for 'intermittent schedules of reinforcement' – irregular periods of practice.

Gradually it was realised that traditional learning theories, based upon principles of stimulus and response, could not account for all aspects of children's learning and educators turned to the ideas of Piaget (1971) and Susan Isaacs to help them understand how children learn. Piaget saw children's intellectual development as a process of change with the children learning through active interaction with the environment. Piaget argued that a young child's thinking is qualitatively different from the adult's. Meanwhile, Isaacs, who did not always agree with Piaget, as is evidenced in her own publications (for example, Isaacs 1929), recorded detailed observations of children to provide powerful insights into the holistic nature of children's learning.

Although there is recognition that Piaget's theories were never intended to inform pedagogy, his views that children's understanding depends upon their stage of development became embedded in teachers' assumptions and this has been criticised, partly because it is important for teachers to challenge the ideas on which they base their approaches and partly because Piaget's own assumptions and research methods have been evaluated.

Twenty years ago Margaret Donaldson (1978) suggested that young children's inability to carry out correctly some of the Piagetian tasks was due to their failure to understand what was required of them, that they were tricked by the language, rather than unable to complete the task. She argued that all learning takes place within a particular context and if the child's expectations, based upon previous knowledge of the world, are different from the teacher's expectations then the child will 'fail'. So, in Donaldson's view, communication problems between adult and child can create a situation in which the child is doomed to failure. The adult needs to know how to access what the child already knows, to understand the child's point of view and language. In particular, in order to help the child move from a context bound situation to disembedded thinking we need to 'put ourselves in the child's shoes'. If we know what children have already experienced, we are more likely to understand where their amazing ideas, sometimes misinterpretations, come from.

A simple example of this occurred when I was watching the sea and some ships with my two year old grand-daughter, Coralie. I pointed out what I thought was a buoy with a flag on top but she claimed it was a little boat.

TD.   Oh well your eyes are better than mine, Coralie, it must be a boat, if you say so.

C.   A potato? (Laughing) It's not a potato!

TD.   (Also laughing) Oh no, silly Nana, of course it's not a potato!

Of course, that was the first time Coralie had heard anyone use the expression 'If you say so' and because she was concentrating on peering out to sea, she did not fully hear what I had said.

In another example, a two year old was looking at an alpabet book with her mother.

M.   Oh look, an apple. Apple begins with 'a' (sounded out).
       (In a chatty tone) What d'you think orange begins with?

C.   Peeling.

– a wonderful, logical answer to a question which in literacy terms was meaningless to a child with no real understanding of the detail of literacy – though she is already very aware of some aspects of the 'big picture' (Purcell-Gates 1996), more relevant at this early stage.

Donaldson and her colleagues also pointed out that learning will be inefficient if it lacks meaning for the child and action and problem solving are therefore important aspects of the learning process, as indicated by much research including Wood *et al.* (1976) and Sylva (1976). They argued that concrete experience is crucial in helping children towards abstract thinking. Their research, and that of many others, has demonstrated that children do not learn as successfully if they are simply told or shown what to do rather than given the opportunity to experiment for themselves.

Similarly, language has a fundamental role to play in the development of learning and understanding. For Bruner (1983) and Vygotsky (1978), language, communication and instruction are at the heart of intellectual and personal development. In talking the adult acts as facilitator, providing the 'scaffolding' which enables the child to make sense of her world. The child who cannot solve a problem or memorise an experience on her own, may well be able to do so with the help of an adult.

Bruner developed Nelson's (1986) idea of the adult as 'scaffolding' the child's learning and Vygotsky invented the term 'zone of proximal development' to describe the gap between what a child is able to do alone and what that child can attain with the help of someone more knowledgeable. Through language and social interaction adults transmit the knowledge and values of their culture to children. Generally, it is adults who effect this transmission of societal and cultural values, though there are recorded examples of other children providing the appropriate 'scaffolding' (Azimitia 1988) and much of David Wood's recent work has explored the ability of young children to take on the role of 'peer tutor'. Vygotsky argued that 'cooperatively achieved success' is fundamental to learning. The instruction which the more knowledgeable person gives to another with lesser skills enables learning to take place. Furthermore it has been found that when children collaborate on a problem solving task, they are more likely to reach a solution than if they tried to solve the problem alone (Forman and Cazden 1985).

Cooperative learning takes place effectively in many play situations. By playing together and trying out new ideas and combinations of skills, children are able to come to understand many of the skills and behaviours that are expected of them by the adult world. Bruner has argued that it is in the play situation that young children can come to test their ideas and knowledge in innovative combinations, independently from the adults whose role has been that of structuring the play opportunities. Sylva *et al.* (1980) stressed the value of children working in pairs and pointed out that higher levels of complexity in play and language were to be found in these situations.

Although learning is an interactive process, best facilitated by the appropriate intervention of adults, there are other factors which need to be considered which may affect children's learning. Motivation is one important factor. Activities which stem from the child's interests and therefore produce intrinsic motivation are more likely to lead to effective learning. This is probably one of the reasons why rigid instruction programmes like the Bereiter and Englemann (1966) were less successful with Headstart children in the USA than the guided play situations advocated by the High/Scope programme (Weikart *et al.* 1971), a curriculum which is 'invisibly' structured by highly trained professionals. In fact, recent reports of the follow-up to the American Head Start Programmes (Sylva 1998) are demonstrating even more powerfully the long term impact of different types of pedagogy experienced in the early years. Not only the economic gains make sense (seven dollars saved from the national purse for every dollar spent in early childhood because of reduced crime, teenage pregnancies, unemployment, and mental health problems among the children who followed the High/Scope programme), the High/Scope graduates actually contribute more to the national 'good' in adulthood by being positive, autonomous, working citizens. Additionally, they had achieved better scores in early literacy during their primary education phase than their more formally taught peers.

Other relevant factors concerning early learning include memory and recall and concentration. Piaget argued that the child's ability to memorise material is a function of age, and there is no doubt that young children have difficulties in recalling information accurately. However, it seems that children have most difficulty in concentrating and recalling when the task does not match their understanding. The 'problem of the match' is one of the most difficult challenges for the educator. Children in the three to seven years age group are very unlikely to have developed mental strategies like rehearsal, or to be able to organise their thoughts about what they already know, recalling their knowledge in a meaningful way in order to use it for new learning experiences. For this reason the adult acting as facilitator will be, among other things, 'memory bank', 'prompt', 'sounding board', and 'supporter'. It is through this type of modelling that children begin to use metacognition – the ability to reflect on their own thinking and learning.

So the question 'How do children learn?' still requires further study but there is sufficient evidence to show that learning is most effective when children are *actively* involved and not passive recipients of information. The adults' vital role is in transmitting the knowledge and values of different cultures in a context which is familiar and meaningful, but challenging, using appropriate pedagogy.

Where learning is based on first-hand experience, the teacher structures certain activities so that children may explore and experiment (see for example the HMI publications DES 1987, 1989a, b, c, d, 1990a). Then, teachers, acting as facilitators, build on that relevant experience and offer a further range of experiences, depending on their assessment of the child's learning needs. This may range from direct, didactic teaching, to the encouragement to represent, interpret, evaluate, and transform (or be creative with) ideas about those experiences. We have evidence about the experience and development of the role of teacher as 'facilitator', or 'mediator', which is based on Vygotsky's work (1978) from, for example, Wood *et al.* (1980), Desforges and Cockburn (1987). Adult intervention in learning which is child-centred is aimed at helping each child make sense of a new learning situation, or activity, by building on the individual child's existing knowledge and previous experience.

Experienced child-centred practitioners use meaningful questioning, explaining and 'telling' as consistent and essential techniques to be adopted in the process of learning. Such strategies are not inconsistent with the adoption of play as the main vehicle for learning in early years settings (see the chapter by David and Nurse in *Teaching Young Children*. Children may label some school activities as 'play'. Indeed, play with or without an adult's participation may form part of the pattern of a child's day in the early years, but research has shown that even in reception classes deemed to offer 'good practice' by three local authorities, four-year-old children actually played for only 8 per cent of their day (Bennett and Kell 1989). In a later study Bennett *et al.* (1996) researched the pedagogy of early years teachers who professed to teach through play. They found that 'teachers need a more conscious pedagogical knowledge based on greater concerns with how quality of mind in young children can be cultivated' (p. 31). Their research was intended to provide:

> a more rigorous analysis of the relationship between play and learning. Play acts as an integrating mechanism which enables children to draw on past experiences, represent them in different ways, make connections, explore possibilities, and create a sense of meaning . . . It integrates cognitive processes and skills which assist in learning. Some of these develop spontaneously, others have to be learnt consciously in order to make learning more efficient. We would like all children to become successful learners.
>
> (Bennett *et al.* 1996, p. 153)

Young children seem to have dispositions to learn different things, they are not simply bundles of biological urges slowly being transformed, as they pass through universal pre-set stages of development, until they become fully formed humans as adults. On the contrary, once we have decided what kind of society we want, it is in everyone's interests to pay attention to the impact of policies on young children and those who share their lives, even those policies which appear irrelevant to early childhood, and it is perhaps one of the responsibilities of early childhood educators to act as advocates for young children by ensuring policy makers and parents have access to new ideas and research information.

It seems likely that we, as a nation, underestimate the learning capacity of children in these first years of life, because of our assumptions and accepted notions about young children. Received wisdom about very young children in UK society, or established 'regimes of truth' (Foucault 1977), have resulted in our having one of the worst records of nursery provision in the European Union and even 'lifelong education' plans propose the start at three years of age.

The New Labour government's White Paper *Excellence in Schools* (DfEE 1997) devotes a whole chapter to 'A sound beginning', yet here there seems to be a failure to grasp the importance, in learning terms, of the years before three. The idea of babies and young children as people with the capacity to learn and the need to relate to others in meaningful ways, not as objects or possessions who should be mainly restricted to their own homes with only their own mothers for company, is hopefully at last being recognised and funding made available for a 'Sure Start' programme, beginning when a baby is three months old (Ghouri 1998). Parents need support and information to help them in their role as the primary educators of their very young children and this is what the new programme aims to provide.

In the light of American and other evidence (Andersson 1992; Barnett and Escobar 1990; Sylva 1994), such as that from the High/Scope longitudinal study (Schweinhart *et al.* 1993), it seems that spending on the early years is a sound investment. Research has shown that if we want children's early experiences to have beneficial effects in terms of their emotional stability, present contentment and later achievements, we need to pay attention to certain key factors (Field 1991). Those key ingredients include:

- the development of self-esteem in young children;
- investment in young children;

- stable childcare arrangements ensuring children interacted with a limited number of familiar carers each day;
- low staff turn-over;
- good training;
- and low adult:child ratios. (Raban 1995).

Together with other evidence about the importance of affective aspects related to learning (Roberts 1995), 'emotional intelligence' (Goleman 1996) has become a high priority. The foundations of robust emotional health and the ability to relate well to others seem to be laid during these very early years. Only recently has the powerful influence of the emotions on learning been more widely acknowledged in Western/Northern thinking about education. The Age of Enlightenment split between body and mind, emotion and reason has not always served us well, especially in the field of education of young children, since early childhood involves so much more overtly the imperatives of the emotions and bodily functions. This is not to say young children and their educators cannot be rational but that 'pure' rationalists have behaved as if the tip of the iceberg were the iceberg.

We have reaped many benefits as a result of the scientific and industrial advances which have come in the wake of the Age of Enlightenment but it has also been responsible for the erosion of people's contact with the land and the rhythms of the cycles and seasons of nature. We are slowly realising our responsibility to the earth and our need to live in harmony with nature rather than seeking domination. Perhaps as a nation, we may have to undergo an equivalent realisation with respect to babies and young children. Children can only develop the qualities listed by Raban (above) and the emotional intelligence advocated by Goleman if the adults to whom we entrust them can engender those feelings of confidence and self-worth. The adults, whether parents or educators, can only undertake such a task if they have the necessary resources and feel valued in their turn.

Our beliefs about early childhood and the place of young children in society impacts upon policy and practice. Although we cannot know for certain what their lives in the twenty-first century will be like, we need to ask ourselves what, if anything, we hold as a vision of education which will equip these very young people for a post-industrial, 'high-tech' world, where environmental, health and other global concerns are likely to be even more acute than they are today (David *et al.* 1992). Decisions about curriculum reflect the values, the ideology, underpinning a society. There are fears that the Desirable

Outcomes (SCAA 1996) and a narrow system of baseline assessment at age five has contributed to an over-emphasis on literacy and numeracy at the expense of children's other powers. It is also suspected that the Literacy and Numeracy 'hours' are likely to add to this pressure to over-formalise provision for children at a time when they should be laying foundations for lifelong learning, including the National Curriculum.

The two books bring together tutors whose specialisms cover primary, special and early years education. Apart from the publications by the Goldsmiths' team (for example, Blenkin and Kelly 1992), until recently there have been relatively few books which attempted to provide such an inclusive view of thinking about the education of children aged up to eight years and the three sectors (under-fives, five to 11 and special education) have had more or less separate networks and knowledge/research bases.

So in the first three chapters Angela Nurse, Rita Headington, Beryl Webber and I have tried to provide an introduction which not only raises some of the issues concerning common strands in all children's education, but which recognises the centrality of parents and carers and of the kinds of assessments made of children. The next three chapters, by Richard Bailey, Christopher Robertson and John Cornwall, relate to children's well-being, both physically and mentally, while the four that follow, by Mike Radford, Keith Sharpe, Judith Roden and Martine Jago are largely concerned with cognitive aspects of children's development and learning. The chapters in the final section of this book consider spiritual and religious education of young children; young children as citizens and the ways in which different societies' expectations of children impact on the children themselves and the kind of early education made available to them. It is in the final chapter, by Sacha Powell and I, that readers are urged to reflect on the implications of children's place in society and how educators contribute to the upbringing of the young learners who will manage that society in the twenty-first century.

Changing minds

So in the chapters which follow, the writers begin from the premise that young children's development and learning is a fascinating and important topic, that children are, from the moment of birth, actively learning, trying to 'make sense' of their world. We write about the years of life when the foundations of later learning are being laid and brain growth is at its most rapid. Most importantly, these are the years in which attitudes to learning and to oneself as a learner are formed.

Learning is embedded in a familiar context and on experience. Later success depends upon continuity, upon being able to make sense of new learning because it relates to what has gone before, with language as 'the connector'.

There is currently a hightened tension between the traditions of the nursery education sector and primary school education, particularly influenced by the top-down, subject-oriented nature of the National Curriculum and Government advisers with only secondary school teaching experience. This has resulted in both a 'battle for pedagogies' and inappropriate formalisation and didactic teaching in many settings for children aged between birth and eight years. By exposing this 'battle', which is not only about curriculum but also about the culture, assumptions, epistemologies and beliefs held by those working in the two sectors, and by engaging in discussion, we can evaluate both sets of assumptions and beliefs, sharing our knowledge bases, and we can perhaps articulate a new more appropriate, inclusive culture, language and pedagogy for these two 'first cycles' of education.

If, as a child, you experience loving, meaningful, instructive responses from those around you, you not only learn from modelling, you are able to respond to other learning situations in positive, daring ways, because you know 'at your centre' that you are valued. Changing minds is not only about the cognitive processes of learning, it is about changing hearts and values too.

References

Alexander, R., Rose, J. and Woodhead, C. (1992) *Curriculum Organisation and Classroom Practice in Primary Schools* London: HMSO.

Andersson, B.E. (1992) Effects of daycare on cognitive and socio-emotional competence of thirteen-year-old Swedish school children *Child Development* 63 p. 20–36.

Aubrey, C., David, T. and Thompson, L. (forthcoming) *Researching early childhood education: methodological and ethical issues* London: Falmer Press.

Azmitia, M. (1988) Peer Interaction and Problem Solving: 'When are two better than one?' *Child Development* 59, 1, p. 87–96.

Ball, C. (1994) *Start Right: the importance of early learning* London: RSA.

Barnett, W.S. and Escobar, C.M. (1990) Economic costs and benefits of early intervention. in S.J. Meisels and J.P. Shonkoff (eds) *Handbook of Early Childhood Intervention* Cambridge: Cambridge University Press.

Bennett, N., Wood, L. and Rogers, S. (1996) *Teaching through play* Buckingham: Open University Press.

Bennett, N. and Kell, J. (1989) *A good start?* Oxford: Blackwell.

Bereiter, C. and Englemann, S. (1966) *Teaching Disadvantaged Children* New Jersey: Prentice Hall.

Blenkin, G and Kelly, A.V. (1992) *Assessment in Early Childhood Education* London: Paul Chapman.

Bruner, J. (1983) *Child's Talk* New York: Norton.

David, T. (ed) (in press) *Researching early childhood education: European perspectives* London: PCP/Sage.

David, T., Curtis, A. and Siraj-Blatchford, I. (1992) *Effective Teaching in the Early Years* Stoke-on-Trent: Trentham Books.

DES (1987) *Primary Schools: some aspects of good practice* London: HMSO.

DES (1989a) *The Teaching and Learning of History and Geography* London: HMSO.

DES (1989b) *The Education of Children under Five* London: HMSO.

DES (1989c) *The Teaching and Learning of Science* London: HMSO.

DES (1989d) *The Teaching and Learning of Mathematics* London: HMSO.

DES (1990a) *Starting with Quality* (Rumbold Report) London: HMSO.

DES (1990b) *The Teaching and Learning of Language and Literacy* London: HMSO

Desforges, C. and Cockburn, A. (1987) *Understanding the Mathematics Teacher* London: Falmer.

DfEE (1997) *Excellence in Schools* Cm3681 London: The Stationery Office.

Donaldson, M. (1978) *Children's Minds* Glasgow: Fontana.

Edwards, A. and Knight, P. (1994) *Effective Early Years Education* Buckingham: Open University Press.

Field, T. (1991) Quality infant daycare and grade school behaviour and performance *Child Development* 62 p. 863–70.

Forman, E. and Cazden, C. (1985) 'Exploring Vygotskian perspectives in education: the cognitive value of peer interaction' in Wertsch J.V. (Ed) *Culture, Communication and Cognition: Vygotskian Perspectives* New York: Cambridge University Press.

Foucault, M. (1977) *Discipline and Punish* London: Allen Lane.

Gardner, H. (1993) *The Unschooled Mind* London: Fontana.

Ghouri, N. (1998) Advisers attack Ofsted early years role, *Times Educational Supplement* no. 4280, 10 July 1998, p. 8.

Goleman, D. (1996) *Emotional Intelligence* London: Bloomsbury.

Nelson, K. (1986) *Event knowledge: structure and function in development* Hillsdale NJ: Erlsbaum.

Piaget, J. (1971) *Science of Education and the Psychology of the Child* London: Longmans.

Purcell-Gates, V. (1996) Stories, coupons and the TV guide: relationships between home literacy experiences and emergent literacy knowledge *Reading Research Quarterly* 31, 4, p. 406–428.

Raban, B. (1995) *Early childhood years – problem or resource.* Inaugural Lecture: Melbourne University, Australia, 27 July 1995.

Roberts, R. (1995) *Self-esteem and Successful Early Learning,* London: Hodder & Stoughton.

SCAA (1996) *Nursery Education Desirable Outcomes for Children's Learning on entering compulsory schooling* London: SCAA.

Schweinhart, L.J. and Weikart, D.P. (1993) *A Summary of Significant Benefits:*

the *High/Scope Perry Preschool Study through Age 27* Ypsilanti MI: High/Scope Foundation.

Schweinhart, L.J., Weikart, D.P. & Toderan, R. (1993) *High quality preschool programs found to improve adult status* Ypsilanti MI: High/Scope Foundation

Shorrocks, D. (1992) Evaluating Key Stage 1 Assessments: the testing time of May 1991. *Early Years* 13, 1, p. 16–20.

Sylva, K. (1976) 'Problem Solving in young children' in J. Bruner, A. Jolly and K. Sylva (eds) *Play: its role in development and evolution* Harmondsworth: Penguin.

Sylva, K. (1994) 'A curriculum for early learning. Appendix C', in C. Ball *The Importance of Early Learning*, London: RSA.

Sylva, K. (1998) *Too formal too soon?* Keynote address to the Islington Early Years Conference, London, 9 July 1998.

Sylva, K., Roy, C. and Painter, M. (1980) *Child Watching at play group and nursery school* London: Grant McIntyre.

Vygotsky, L. (1978) *Mind in Society* Cambridge MA: Harvard.

Weikart, D., Rogers, L., Adcock, C. and Mclelland, D. (1971) *The Cognitively Oriented Curriculum* Urbana USA: ERI.

Wood, D., Bruner, J. and Ross, G. (1976) The role of tutoring in problem-solving *Journal of Child Psychology and Psychiatry* 17, 2, p. 89–100.

2

Balancing the needs of children, parents and teachers

Angela D. Nurse and Rita Headington

All animals are equal but some animals are more equal than others
(George Orwell: *Animal Farm* 1945)

The triangular relationship of parents, children and teachers in schools alters as the social, economic and governmental standing of the nation fluctuates. We hope to demonstrate in this chapter why this happens and to put forward the view that for schools to maintain their purpose and vitality it is essential that the role of the three elements in this relationship are identified and equally balanced, though children should appear at the apex of this equilateral triangle and be supported by a firm base. The concept of a triangle is, on the surface, simple but the singular terms at each angle can lead our thinking into the wider significance of community, institutional and professional interests, as well as exploring what the fundamental needs of each participant are, particularly children. The concept of this threefold relationship is not entirely new. The title, and content, of Margaret Henry's book *Young Children, Parents and Professionals* (Henry 1996) supports our proposal, as does the celebrated work of Loris Malaguzzi, encapsulated in *A Charter of Three Rights* (Malaguzzi 1993). This symbolic representation is used by Sue Robson in exploring the 'potentially powerful relationship' between home and school (Robson and Smedley 1996). The idea of partnership is strengthened and redefined in the Labour Government's first policy document on education, *Excellence in Schools* (DfEE 1997a):

> Excellence can be achieved only on the basis of partnership. We all need to be involved: schools, teachers and parents are at the heart of it . . . Everyone has a part to play.

Along with nursery education, the use of calculators in schools and numerous other shibboleths of current educational controversy, the role

13

and place of parents in their own children's schooling has not been opened up to balanced, critical, debate. Educational debates on such a scale in the UK are generally avoided. The prevailing view within the British psyche holds that education is only a quasi-profession. Other rivals for the title have an air of mystique and a body of knowledge not easily accessed by those without the educational keys to the door. That these keys are 'educational' does not seem to have been acknowledged by and large, with family background, wealth and influence playing a greater role in our national sentiment. This state of affairs hinges on the belief that it is easy to teach. All of us have been through various forms of schooling and the majority of us have survived and, indeed, achieved certain standards. As we have experienced it, we feel we can do it – though many of us have survived medical and surgical interventions but few of us would be confident enough to repeat them without extensive training. The irony, however, is lost when we are faced with the onslaught of recent events in the world of education, such as an attempt to shorten the length and breadth of an education degree, making it specific to the practical skills required in the classroom for implementing the National Curriculum. The notorious 'Mums' Army' affair was the public pinnacle of this aspect of recent national and governmental downgrading of the profession, culminating in a collective outcry against deprofessionalisation which is rarely seen emanating from such a weary workforce.

Politics: recent, past and present

We have not yet achieved any consensus, in the UK especially, as to the nature of the 'education' we should as nations provide, particularly during those first 'five precious years'. A simplistic attitude to public services, not just education, prevailed during the 1980s and quickened in the 1990s. The 'market economy' philosophy and purchaser-provider split in the provision of services were imposed as political ideologies which attempted to rationalise systems far too complex to simplify in this way. Will Hutton has reviewed how this ideology has affected the structure of the UK, including education. He highlights a number of factors which are 'undermining the notion of a universal education system in which everyone has a stake, and where individual educational needs can be met by local structures' (Hutton 1997, p. 86). He cites systematic underfunding, the growth in the private sector and competitive tendering among these.

This has occurred at a time when our notion of a stage in our lives, commonly defined by innocence and freedom, is under attack from early initiation into adult pursuits, either through greater access to the wider world via the media and information technology or through the earlier and earlier introduction of more formal and academic schooling which is adult initiated and led.

Parents are quite frequently mystified by the confusion that results from the plethora of opposing views from governments and professionals in conflict. The emphasis on an early start lest we miss the gravy train denies all the research and good practice established here and in other European countries. This has stressed the value of a thorough understanding of developmental stages and needs, then planning the programme for each child according to what we, as parents or professional educators, recognise as the way in which each child learns and what he or she needs to know next (Bruner 1977; Vygotsky 1978). Many fundamental insights, not only from research and cross cultural studies but also from history, are missed or negated. The great creative minds of the past have rarely emerged from schools but have been the result of a freedom to think and concentrate on a passion, led by a mentor or in close co-operation with a like mind. The recognition that great thoughts radiate from a relaxed mind, rather than one that is bombarded with facts chosen by others, needs greater attention (Claxton 1997). Bruner, early in his career, divided learning from thinking (Bruner 1959). Learning was seen as passive, while thinking was the active use of knowledge, internalised to create something new:

> Let us not judge our students simply on what they know. That is the philosophy of the quiz program. Rather, let them be judged on what they can generate from what they know – how well they can leap the barrier from learning to thinking.
>
> (Bruner 1959, p. 77)

Bruner's statement goes to the heart of the conflict over the nature of the National Curriculum and, especially, what form of 'curriculum' there should be for our youngest children, if any. In his foreword to *The Learning Age: a renaissance for a new Britain* (DfEE 1998), the current Secretary of State for Education, David Blunkett states that 'learning throughout life can build human capital by encouraging creativity, skill and imagination. The fostering of an enquiring mind and the love of learning are essential for our future success.' Yet for those of us resisting the imposition of a skills-based, 'checklist' approach to teaching and assessing the development of our youngest children, Blunkett's statement does not seem to apply to those in their earliest years of learning. Long-standing friends and colleagues, now heads of very successful nursery schools, have described themselves as 'dinosaurs' in danger of extinction because of their commitment to the kind of good practice which fosters just these qualities in young children.

For the many working parents, school has often been seen to conflict with family interests and to be an instrument of confinement and control. The entrenched suspicion on both sides, parents versus schools, has deep roots and ones which have been exploited thoroughly by recent governments, fearing our loss of national supremacy and responding to it in panic mode. As Bastiani (1994) sets out 'from a political point of view, parents have became an important lobby and a key sounding board for educational purposes'. In this way suspicion between parents and professionals has been reinforced.

History

More insights into our current state of ambivalence about the nature and purpose of education can be gained through exploring the history of the relationship between parents and schools. Views on the nature and extent of childhood have changed over time and have been pieced together from literature and art. Children have been viewed as innocent or, conversely, inherently evil until taught otherwise. As far as we can surmise, children were thought to be miniature versions of adults and therefore, in poorer families at least, capable of adult tasks in as far as their physical growth allowed. The notion that children's ideas about the world and their thought processes are radically different from those of adults stem mainly from observation and research in the nineteenth and twentieth century (Piaget 1952; Vygotsky 1978: Bruner 1966). The impact of these psychologists, among others, as well as philosophers (Rousseau, Locke) and noted early childhood educators (Pestalozzi, Macmillan, Montessori, Isaacs) have helped us to create and define a period of life that is special. Although we are in danger of making sweeping generalisations, there seems to have been a shift in the parent–child relationship, from an economic interdependence to a situation which has a social and emotional basis. In Margaret Henry's words, as parents 'our primary role is to advance the interest of those beings we have brought forth' (Henry 1996). In secular times, the investment we have in our future is through our children.

The impact of parents' involvement in their children's education and their relationships with schools is clouded in the mists of time and the class structure of Britain and much of the western world. In

Britain, the 'school', as we now accept it, is a relatively recent phenomenon. Until the nineteenth century 'education', rather than 'schooling', was much more the result of what individual parents were able to provide than a national expectation. The class structure ensured that certain values were transmitted across the generations, maintaining a male-oriented, hierarchical system. The Church, part of this power structure as well as a traditional provider of schooling, protected and reinforced its place by selectively passing on knowledge to those who would maintain its position. Parents, if wealthy enough, could choose to tutor at home or pay for public schooling. In both scenarios, parents could be assured generally that the knowledge passed on to their offspring would respect and match their values and culture. The growing middle-class aped their betters and perpetuated the system, supporting the schools which provided their sons with entry into the promised land. Parents loomed large in the reality of many children's and young people's lives. Not respecting their authority threatened a future of poverty and alienation, witnessed in the miserable lives of many around them (from whom their own wealth often sprung) and mirrored in the stories of the time. Anthony Trollope's long saga, *The Way We Live Now* (1875), underlines the machinations of parents desperate to maintain and improve their wealth or social standing using their children as collateral and fully prepared to bludgeon them into acceptance.

At the other end of the social scale, parents were much more concerned with survival. Children supported their families through work, whether by contributing their labour and skills to family industry within the home, caring for younger siblings or, later, through paid employment outside the home, with the proportion of family income secured by child labour becoming greater as industrialisation proceeded (Cunningham 1995). Although, as life became more complex, many did achieve improvements in status through educational achievement, as more and more call was made for those who could read and write, the social structure of the country was kept in place by inherited interests and the established Church. Some children progressed through the commitment of enlightened employers who provided basic schooling for their employees' offspring but these were few and far between. Industrialisation, trade and the expansion of the colonies offered new opportunities for those with motivation and energy and a greater need for those who had reading, writing and arithmetic skills. The power structure in the colonies was often not so much based on class and inherited wealth but on aptitude and tenacity. To place ourselves within the sentiment of the time, a universal entitlement to an elementary education could be seen as the recognition, for the first time, that children were a valuable asset in maintaining a nation's power and prosperity. It must also have threatened those with power already. The ability to read and gain knowledge beyond what was given aurally, and so more selectively, must have been viewed with trepidation.

There has never been a time when all parents have been in agreement with what all schools have had to offer their children. The establishment of universal education diminished the power of all parents to determine what their children learnt, particularly for those who had no capacity to opt for any other route to knowledge. Although schooling may have had its advantages when not compulsory – as a means for social progress, to inculcate religious knowledge and values, as a 'baby-sitting' service – once the 'right' to schooling was imposed across the western world, it was resented by both parents and children (Cunningham 1995). Secular education was resented by the churches (Horn 1989). The status quo was preserved for those who had always been able to pay for their own children's schooling but the roots of the duality of modern British children's educational experiences (private versus state) matured then.

The development of a universal right to education has crystallised the situation into what has seemed lately almost warfare between those who teach and those who are within the system, particularly in those old established nations which have witnessed their power and authority diminish in a new world order. The vitality and speed of the progress made in the developing economies of what was once labelled the 'third world' has shocked and undermined the confidence of those who were once so sure of their place at the apex of the world hierarchy. Instead of learning the lessons of history and viewing change as a chance to revitalise tired nations, scapegoats have been sought and the one most often identified has been the school.

If we take 1944 as the starting point for reviewing more recent aspects of parent–school relationships, there has been a series of coming together and parting in a pattern which resembles an hour-glass. The year 1944 witnessed the first chink in a system which had been, for those within the state sector, often paternalistic and dictatorial. An element of choice now existed for the most determined parents to opt to educate their children at home. For those lacking the confidence or skills to fight the system schools dominated. Heads and teachers in a more hierarchical society held sway and both parents and children respected and feared their power. Traditional acceptance of the idea that teachers knew best was reinforced by the mythical white lines across many a school playground beyond which a parent dare not stray unless summoned (Docking 1990). There seemed to be no role for parents beyond fulfilling their legal responsibilities to ensure their children attended school.

By the 1960s, however, parental involvement in the playgroup movement and a number of influential research reports (Douglas 1964) were beginning to open up the question of parental influence on children's educational achievement. The much maligned Plowden report (DES 1967) moved the argument on dramatically by accepting and openly stating that parental attitudes, rather than wealth or status, were the foundation stones of good pupil achievement.

Although what is mainly remembered by the public and professionals alike is Plowden's commitment to a 'child-centred' approach, the Committee's recommendations were based on research findings and offered a balanced approach to the relationship between children, parents and schools. Among the recommendations which are significant for our proposition are more parental and community involvement, an expansion of nursery education and delaying admission to primary school until six or seven. This has again been recommended in the report of the RSA committee chaired by Sir Christopher Ball (Ball 1994). At the time, however, and in the intervening years the message of Plowden has been misunderstood and re-interpreted by professional educators who view the outcome as a loss of influence and control and by governments, and thus the public, as the cause of national educational failure and the breakdown of discipline and respect within British society. In effect, a report which should have brought parents and schools together pushed them further apart as the philosophy that Plowden was expounding was not shared.

Most western countries by this time had consolidated state education systems and had had sufficient time to view the effects critically. Throughout the 1960s and early 1970s, particularly in the USA but rapidly spreading here, influential thinkers and writers in the field were analysing and criticising mass education (Goodman 1971; Illich 1973, 1976).

Ten years after Plowden, in a study called School management and government, the Royal Commission on Local Government revealed that only twenty counties or county boroughs had any parental representation on governing bodies (Lowe 1997). Also in 1977, the Taylor Committee made recommendations for reforming and restructuring governing bodies which now appear radical and ahead of their time. It aimed to increase their role and authority, suggesting that they should set out the broad aims of individual schools and monitor the staff as they then devised the means to put these aims into practice. A proposal for some control of the school's finances was added to the end of the report (Lowe 1997). Representation on the governing body was to be balanced with equal numbers selected from the LEA, the school staff, parents and the community. Initial and on-going training was to be provided by the LEA. Some of these recommendations were incorporated into the 1980 Education Act, but a change of government restricted their impact to extended parental and teacher representation. Nevertheless, the plethora of legislation throughout the 1980s and into the 1990s has seen the gradual implementation of the Taylor Committee's recommendations in full. Alongside other legislation which has opened up the inner world of the school to parental and community scrutiny, the extension of the power and influence of the governing body has met with mixed emotions, often anger and despair. Where the relationship works well, governing bodies recognise their role as a critical friend in supporting schools and do so skilfully. In those areas where parents do not feel confident and have other priorities, or where community issues cut across those of the school, then the ability of parents to work with the teachers is curtailed and relations can become hostile. Even in schools with good parental support, the annual meeting to discuss the governors' report to parents is generally noted as an occasion when governors outnumber parents. Lowe (1997, pp. 160–1) documents graphically the effect of increased parental influence in schools:

> First, it confirmed the shift towards that consumerism which was becoming so marked a feature of the system: schools were now obliged to listen to and, to some extent, were fashioned by their more vocal and committed parents. While this may have been in many ways a good thing, what was less desirable was that this process gave undue influence to schools in middle-class areas where there was little difficulty in recruiting parents who were often well connected within the local professions and who knew how to lobby effectively and how best to organise. This was not the case in the inner-city areas where parents were often too busy pursuing other more immediate concerns to be able to contribute effectively to school management and were less likely to be able to win resources for their children's school. This situation was a gift to the better-off suburbs.

Specific legislation

Forster's Education Act 1870, which heralded compulsory state education, made provision for school boards to ensure attendance but they were not compelled to do so, though later Acts strengthened this aspect. More recent Education Acts, however, have reinstated the right of parents to opt to educate their children 'at home', though this has often been made difficult and met with social and administrative disapprobation. This was enshrined in the Education Act 1944 where the term 'education otherwise' was coined, and again in Section 7 of the Education Act 1996 which states:

> The parent of every child of compulsory school age shall cause him to receive full-time education suitable:
>
> a)   to his age and aptitude, and
>
> b)   to any special educational needs he may have, either by regular attendance at school or otherwise.

It seems that, even though children are being admitted to school at an increasingly younger age, more and more parents are opting to educate children at home, particularly at the primary stage. A variety of reasons exists, but the overwhelming ones seem to be a reaction to an overloaded National Curriculum, large classes with little personal contact time with a teacher and general dissatisfaction with a loss of control over what children are taught. In the UK, Education Otherwise was founded in 1977 to support parents educating their children at home and has seen a steady growth in membership and the number of self-help groups around the country. The development of information technology helps not only in providing children with access to new knowledge but also keeps such families in touch with each other and close to sources of support and advice.

Local management of schools, introduced alongside the National Curriculum and Grant Maintained Schools by the Education Reform Act 1988, was welcomed by the majority of head teachers as it gave greater choice and flexibility in financial decision-making. It has led, however, to many more management and administrative responsibilities for which few were originally trained. By reducing the power of local education authorities, the ability of the community to influence the character and content of schools within its area has declined. Since 1986, greater power has been given to governors, including parent governors, without defining exactly where the boundary lies between their duties and the professional responsibilities of the staff of the school. Rather than discussing with professional staff and parents how they would like to see the school function as a part of the community (and in some places it is now only the school which holds the community together), governors are bogged down with ensuring the National Curriculum is followed precisely, monitoring school development plans, stretching inadequate budgets to fit and maintaining the fabric of the building.

Recent educational legislation has legitimised parents' rights within the system, but so far has done little to define their responsibilities. Both editions of the Parent's Charter (DES 1991; DfEE 1994) clearly delineated 'rights' without defining 'obligations'. The right to a state school of their choice, a right to information about their children's individual progress and to the academic results of all state schools have been promised. The right to 'choice' is emphasised, but a small increase in choice for some has led to a decrease in choice for the many who cannot exercise that choice. The idea of 'partnership' was extended in the updated version to include a paragraph on discipline. This was added to homilies on attendance, completion of homework and volunteering to share skills and interests with the school. Any idea of parents having a greater part to play in imparting knowledge and skills and helping their children to use these effectively is not discussed nor acknowledged.

Almost in direct contradiction to the sentiments of the education legislation, one of the main tenets of the Children Act 1989 establishes that parents have responsibilities and not just rights. This Act parallels the formulation of the United Nations Convention on the Rights of the Child in 1989 which placed children at the top of our equilateral triangle. Another major principle of the Act states that the child's welfare is paramount. Although this Act is seminal in UK legislation, bringing together a number of other pieces of law which involve children, the full scope and impact of it has not yet been appreciated. Particularly it has not yet been recognised, nor fully understood by education departments, that it applies to 'services provided by the local authority', not just social services departments. As with much UK legislation, it is enabling rather than prescriptive and interpretation depends on the outcome of court cases. Nevertheless, it heralded a new venture in British education where the interests of children could supersede those of family or state.

Role of parents

Home-school relationships are never easy, because we have not defined what this whole concept means and agreed what it involves. It means something different for each teacher and for each set of parents: often the expectations and types of relationship vary with individual children in a family. It is important to recognise that educators' relationships are different with either parent. Writing specifically about parents who have children with special needs, Blamires *et al.* (1997, p. 18) point out:

> It is often assumed that when two parents are involved with their child's education they speak with one voice and present a united front ... there is seldom any recognition of the fact that two people faced with what may be the most life-changing, emotionally demanding events of their lives as parents may not react in unison and may not have identical perceptions of the problem or its solution.

Over the past decade a number of authors have viewed the situation critically and have outlined the factors we need to consider and where future research is needed (Bastiani 1994; Keating and Taylorson 1996; Bastiani and Wolfendale 1996; Bastiani 1997). The part played by parents and teachers in this relationship are not the same, but are equally important and should be recognised as of equivalent worth. Atkin *et al.* (1988) have produced a comprehensive model of home-school relationships which charts the influences of each, starting with the parents' intimate knowledge of their own child in contrast with a teacher's knowledge of many children. John Sayer (in Wolfendale 1989) talks of the boundaries of parental and professional responsibility for education but recognises the need for schools to move in new ways, If schools are organised as centres for community learning, 'partnerships' need to be fostered

> to the full meaning of partnership ... with all the shared sense of purpose, the mutual respect and the real dialogue between parents, pupils and professionals that can be a basis for continued negotiated learning beyond school.
>
> (in Wolfendale 1989)

Not only will parents bring varying skills and experiences into school but will also have different goals for and expectations of their children and of themselves. Often the expectations of the teacher or school can be at odds with those of the parents. As teachers, we are sometimes faced with parents whose values or educational or professional achievements are removed from our own. One of the most undermining experiences we can have is when a parent's expectations of his or her offspring are vastly disparate from our own. One of the most neglected areas of initial teaching training has been working with other adults and in particular with parents. New National Curriculum-focused initial training programmes have, if anything, made the situation worse. Beresford and Hardie in Bastiani and Wolfendale (1996) suggest the skills needed by teachers include:

- listening to parents,
- planning,
- organising and facilitating groups,
- communicating appropriately with adults,
- negotiating,
- counselling, and
- managing volunteers.

They go on to stress that teachers feel unprepared for this important aspect of their work by their initial training and consequently tend to deal with it reluctantly or avoid it altogether. As a result teachers 'can appear patronising, didactic and insensitive to parents' own experiences and needs'.

For many women, and now more men, the school forms the focus of their own friendship groups and can be the heart of their community. This is especially so when families are far away and people have migrated to new areas, and particularly new housing estates, in search of work or promotion. With a large proportion of women now working up until the birth of their first child, the workplace has often formed the basis of friendship groups rather than the neighbourhood in which they live. The isolation and depression the loss of friendship may cause can persist until children are admitted to nursery or school. Nurseries and especially schools in the UK are not seen primarily to have a social function beyond 'socialising' young children into the wider world. The primary role now of statutory schooling, at least, is to transfer to our children a body of knowledge and a set of clearly defined skills. The advent of the National Curriculum has sanctified this role. There are fears that the introduction of the *Desirable Outcomes for Children's Learning* (SCAA 1996) at five years of age, as well as the development of Baseline Assessment schemes which chart children's accomplishments on entry to school, are again prescribing a preferred body of knowledge for children whose formal achievements can easily be checked and ticked off a list. This denies the complexities of young children's learning and the varying time-scales in their acquisition of knowledge and competencies. It celebrates outcomes rather than processes. It also disadvantages those who have special needs or are from backgrounds where experiences in the early years do not prepare children for 'schooling' in a way acceptable to those who oversee our system. Children who have not attended preschools or are from certain ethnic or class backgrounds run the risk of being further disadvantaged. In these circumstances, parents who are more confident, or perhaps angrier, have often taken matters into their own hands. Parents from minority backgrounds have inaugurated and supported supplementary schools to maintain their own language and culture or, more importantly, to redress their children's perceived educational disadvantage within the state system. In the period from the end of the Second World War until the Education Act 1981, many parents whose children had special educational needs fought the system which denied them influence or choice in where their children were sent to school. We run the risk of stamping levels on children at the very beginnings of their school careers which will stay with them for life. We have known for a long time that children respond to teachers' expectations of what they can achieve (Rosenthal and Jacobson 1968 in Delamont 1976 (pp. 55–6)).

As we have mentioned before, Education Otherwise, the association formed in 1977 to support parents choosing to educate their children at home, has seen a steady growth in membership and the number of self-help groups around the UK is increasing. The development of information technology helps not only in providing children with access to new knowledge but also keeps such families in touch with each other and close to sources of support and advice.

Training

The whole question of training to work with young children, and also with their parents, is crucial once an agreed philosophy has been established. The routes into working with young children are varied and the status of 'educators' in the UK spans the spectrum from those with no qualifications at all to degree level and beyond. Currently it is impossible to qualify purely as a nursery teacher. To allow this may well split the profession and break the continuity of practice from pre-statutory provision to Key Stage 1 of the National Curriculum. The emphasis on the National Curriculum, however, and the introduction of set competencies, now standards, for newly qualified teachers have resulted in few initial training courses offering thorough nursery training. The knowledge and skills, like child development, essential to successful early years practice have been neglected. Denise Hevey and Audrey Curtis (in Pugh 1996) review teacher training for the early years and emphasise the need for management and leadership skills and the ability to work with parents and professionals from other disciplines. They conclude that 'such training is not developed within the current initial training programmes'.

The huge variety in the length and quality of training to meet the needs of this age group are clearly tabulated by Oberhuemer and Ulich

(1997). At a time when most European countries have been moving towards an all-graduate teaching profession, there have been fears in England and Wales (though not in Scotland where training to teach very young children was extended in 1994) that we are about to remove that status from the teachers of the very young. The 'Mums' Army' affair heightened our very real anxieties but the general undermining of our professional expertise, of which this was a symptom, comes from within the profession as well as from outside. So often this aspect of the teaching profession has been seen to be professionally easier and delegated to the margins. One reaction to the paucity of high level, academic as well as practical, training in this area has been the introduction of a number of interdisciplinary Early Childhood Studies degree programmes (Taylor and Woods 1998) which can lead on to vocational qualifications in teaching or social work, as well as offering a number of other career options within the early childhood sphere.

Questions need to be asked about all the other adults employed in nurseries or classrooms, whether on a salaried or voluntary basis. The growth in class size in the UK, coupled with the lower age of admission and inclusion of many more young children with special needs, has seen a huge increase in classroom assistants 'assigned to tasks previously thought to be within the domain of teachers' (Moyles and Suschitsky 1996). They may have been committed parent helpers and are often initially employed to support children with special educational needs especially those with a statement. Many of these people have been employed with little previous experience beyond their own families and with few opportunities for training in situ. Janet Moyles has now researched this whole area with Wendy Suschitsky (1996) for the Association of Teachers and Lecturers. Until this, the role of the classroom assistant had rarely been defined. Their recommendations raise specific questions about the cost-effectiveness of Specialist Teaching Assistants (STA) courses currently available and include proposals for schools to undertake audits of assistants' responsibilities and duties, matching these to the help teachers actually require. A documented skills audit could serve to enrich and extend the curriculum as well as highlighting areas of knowledge and expertise within the whole staff. Parents have a right to expect that those who teach their children are appropriately trained and prepared for each particular age-group. The absence of widespread revolt over conditions in many early years settings, where numbers, space and equipment do not match need, testifies to complacency amongst the nation's parents or a complete misunderstanding of how young children develop optimally. Only the parents of children with special educational needs seem to question the knowledge and experience of those entrusted with their children's education, often the classroom assistant. If a classroom assistant with little prior knowledge were expected to teach 'A'-Level Mathematics there would soon be a huge outcry. Yet the education of our youngest children is in many ways more important as attitudes, habits and ways of learning are being set for a lifetime.

The school or nursery can also be a route into employment and a stepping stone to further or higher education for those who start as classroom assistants or become involved as parent governors. Confidence is regained, forgotten skills revived and new ones developed. The end goal for many is not only teaching, but women especially have gone on to create new careers for themselves in arenas where good interpersonal, organisational and administrative skills are required. The government is advocating employment for young mothers (though we hope there will be choice in this and greater, good quality, childcare support for those who decide it is appropriate for them). Schools can have a part to play in this aspect of life-long learning, encouraging and supporting parents to rediscover their skills and play an important part in their communities.

Conclusion

If we are to instigate a new era of parent-school relationships in the interests of the child, and then ultimately the national interests, an open discussion must take place about this relationship and there must be a drawing together of the different factions and a new realisation and acceptance of the roles and responsibilities of each player. Research evidence and the experiences of other countries must be taken into account, not piecemeal, but carefully considered and selected to fit our needs. This concept is not radical. Twenty-five or more years ago, theorists were attempting to identify educational themes, such as thinking skills, creativity and adaptability to change, that overlay and exceeded the more narrow facts-based curriculum with which we have become all too familiar:

> The basic functions of all education, even in the most traditional sense is to increase the survival prospects of the group . . . survival in a rapidly changing environment depends almost entirely upon being able to identify which of the old concepts are relevant and which are not. . . What we are saying is that 'selective forgetting' is necessary to survival.
> (Postman and Weingartner 1971, p. 195)

At a time when patterns of work are changing drastically, people seem loathe to let go of the old idea of full male employment. This causes society great anxiety over youth unemployment, particularly amongst young men. The proportion of our lives spent in work, and especially in one secure form of employment, is declining. Responsibilities within homes are altering as a greater part of the family income is earned by women, especially working mothers. Yet these factors rarely seem to be taken into consideration when the role of education is discussed and the form of schooling is decided. Jobs and full employment underline governmental and parental choices, with the idea that there will always be progress. As professional and managerial people we want our children to do at least as well as us educationally, or even better, and are rarely satisfied when their choices are not ours and they settle for something deemed 'less'. The idea that there will continue to be general progress is rarely challenged. As the millennium approaches, we stand at a point in history where we view rapid change within our own lives as the norm, forgetting that for centuries change like this had not been perceived over several lifetimes. The idea of change, for the good, is rarely questioned nor is the resulting underemployment of millions of people who have not been taught to use their time effectively and enjoyably.

A debate needs to be initiated and freely argued, without the acrimony and partisan jealousies that often surround such discussions. Assumptions, policies and practices need to be re-examined and re-interpreted, particularly those which led, for instance, to the reduction in the age when formal schooling now starts in UK, in comparison with most other countries, following the early introduction of an academically formal National Curriculum. Long-term investment which enables early years provision to match what is known throughout the world as good practice, as well as meeting the needs of communities and parents, will pay for itself in coming generations of people who are at ease with themselves, self-sufficient and thinking (Schweinhart, Barnes and Weikart 1993a). Good examples of dynamic and inspiring early years provision have been provided in the UK by the Soho Community Centre, Pen Green and other combined nursery centres and in Europe where the work of the Reggio Emilia centres in Italy is well known (Gura 1997). These centres not only maximise the children's natural desire to learn, they extend educators' thinking and involve parents fully in policy-making, day-to-day administration and teaching. They can provide opportunities for parents to gain confidence and widen their own educational horizons within the security of an environment they know well and trust. This supports the government's commitment to 'life-long learning'. In the Foreword to the Green Paper (1998), the Secretary of State for Education, David Blunkett, writes:

Learning is the key to prosperity – for each of us as individuals as well as for the nation as a whole. Investment in human capital will be the foundation of success in the knowledge-based global economy of the twenty-first century.

In summary, 'changing minds' in the context of parent-teacher relationships involves a complete reappraisal of the *raison d'être* of schools within our society. The debate needs to be broadened beyond the 3Rs. Taking on board well-funded research findings, responding to parental and community needs and meeting the challenges of changes in society can reinvigorate our provision for our youngest children. Some risks need to be taken. The prospect is exciting.

Issues

1. Who is primarily responsible for our youngest children's education? Who should play a role in their education? What form should their 'education' take? Where should it take place?
2. How do we use research to inform our decision-making? Is there anything more we need to find out before decisions are made?
3. What are the training needs of those working with young children? What form should training take? What should be included?

References

Athey, C. (1990) *Extending Thought in Young Children: A Parent–Teacher Partnership*. London: Paul Chapman.

Atkin, J., Bastiani, J. and Goode, J. (1988) *Listening to parents: an approach to the improvement of home-school relations*. London: Croom Helm.

Ball, C. (1994) *Start Right: the importance of early learning*. London: RSA.

Bastiani, J. (1989) *Working with Parents: A Whole School Approach*. Windsor: NFER-Nelson.

Bastiani, J. (1994) *Your Home-School Links*. London: NEP.

Bastiani, J. and Wolfendale, S. (ed) (1996) *Home–School Work in Britain: review, reflection and development*. London: David Fulton Publishers.

Bastiani, J. (ed) (1997) *Home–School Work in Multicultural Settings*. London: David Fulton Publishers.

Blamires, M., Robertson, C. and Blamires, J. (1997) *Parent–Teacher Partnership: Practical Approaches to Meeting Special Educational Needs*. London: David Fulton Publishers.

Blunkett, D. (1998) The Learning Age – A Renaissance for a New Britain, House of Commons, London: Green Paper.

Bruner, J. S. (1959) *Learning and Thinking in Problems and Issues in Contemporary*

Education: An Anthology from the 'Harvard Educational Review' and 'Teachers College Record' (1968). Illinois: Scott, Foresman & Co. pp. 70–77.

Bruner, J. (1966) *Towards a Theory of Instruction.* London: Harvard University Press.

Bruner, J. (1977) *The Process of Education.* London: Harvard University Press.

Bruner, J. and Haste, H. (ed) (1990) *Making Sense: The child's construction of the world.* London: Routledge.

Claxton, Guy (1997) *Hare Brain Tortoise Mind.* London: Fourth Estate.

Cohen, A. (ed) (1988) *Early Education: The Parents' Role.* London: PCP.

Cunningham, Hugh (1995) *Children and Childhood in Western Society Since 1500.* London: Longman.

Delamont, S. (1976) *Interaction in the Classroom.* London: Methuen.

Department of Education and Science (1967) *Children and their Primary Schools* (The Plowden Report). London: HMSO.

Department of Education and Science (1977) *A new partnership for our schools: The Taylor Report.* London: HMSO.

Department of Education and Science (1991) *The Parent's Charter: You and Your Child's Education.* London: DES.

Department for Education (1994) *Our Children's Education: The Updated Parent's Charter.* London: DfE.

Department for Education and Employment (1997) *Early Years Education: A summary of the Government's plans for excellence in the early years.* London: DfEE.

Department for Education and Employment (1997a) *Excellence in Schools.* London: DfEE.

Department for Education and Employment (1997b) *Excellence for all children: Meeting Special Educational Needs.* London: DfEE.

Department for Education and Employment (1998) *The Learning Age: a renaissance for a new Britain. A summary.* London: DfEE.

Docking, J. W. (1990) *Primary schools and Parents.* London: Hodder & Stoughton.

Douglas, J. W. B. (1964) *The Home and the School.* London: MacGibbon and Kee.

Drummond, M. J. (1990) Conference address, London: Roehampton Institute of Education.

Elder, G. H. Jr., Modell, J. and Parke, R. D. (ed) (1993) *Children in Time and Place: Developmental and Historical Insights.* Cambridge: Cambridge University Press.

Goodman, P (1971) *Compulsory Miseducation.* Middlesex: Penguin Books Ltd

Gura, Pat (ed) (1997) *Reflections on Early Education and Care.* London: BAECE.

Henry, Margaret (1996) *Young Children, Parents and Professionals.* London: Routledge.

Horn, Pamela (1989) *The Victorian and Edwardian Schoolchild.* Gloucester: Alan Sutton.

Hutton, Will (1997) *The State to Come.* London: Vintage.

Illich, Ivan (1973) *Deschooling society.* London: Penguin.

Illich, Ivan (1976) *After Deschooling, What?* London: Readers and Writers Publishing Co-operative.

Keating, I. and Taylorson, D. E. (1996) The Other Mums' Army: Issues of Parental Involvement in Early Education. *Early Years* Vol 17, No 1, Autumn.

Lowe, Roy (1997) *Schooling and Social Change 1964–1990.* London: Routledge.

MacKinnon, D, Statham, J and Hales, M (1995) *Education in the UK: Facts and Figures.* London: Hodder & Stoughton/OU.

Malaguzzi, L. (1996) *The Hundred Languages of Children.* pp. 214–15.

May, Trevor (1987) *An Economic and Social History of Britain 1760–1970.* London: Longman.

Mead, Margaret (1961) Questions That Need Asking in *Problems and Issues in Contemporary Education: An Anthology from the 'Harvard Educational Review' and 'Teachers College Record' (1968).* Illinois: Scott, Foresman & Co. pp. 41–45.

Moyles, J. (with Suschitzky, W.) (1996) *Jills of All Trades . . . ? Classroom Assistants in KS1 Classes.* London: Association of Teachers and Lecturers and University of Leicester.

Moyles, J. (with Suschitzky, W.) (1997) *'The Buck Stops Here. . . !' Nursery Teachers and Nursery Nurses working together.* The Esmée Fairbairn Charitable Trust and University of Leicester.

Munn, P. (ed) (1993) *Parents and Schools: Customers, Managers or Partners?.* London: Routledge.

Oberhuemer, P. and Ulich, M. (1997) *Working with Young Children in Europe.* London: Paul Chapman.

Orwell, George (1945) *Animal Farm.* London: Secker & Warburg.

Piaget, J. (1952) *The Origins of Intelligence in Children.* London: Routledge & Kegan Paul.

Postman, N. and Weingartner, C. (1971) *Teaching as a Subversive Activity.* Middlesex: Penguin Books Ltd.

Pugh, G. (ed) (1996) *Contemporary Issues in Education.* London: Paul Chapman.

Reggio Children (1996) *The Hundred Languages of Children.* Reggio Emilia: Reggio Children.

Robson, S. and Smedley, S. (1996) *Education in Early Childhood.* London: David Fulton.

Rosenthal, R. and Jacobson, L. (1968) *Pygmalion in the Classroom.* New York: Holt, Rinehart and Winston.

Schools Curriculum and Assessment Council (1996) *Desirable Outcomes for Children's Learning.* London: DfEE/SCAA.

Schools Curriculum and Assessment Council (1996) *Baseline Assessments: Draft Proposals.* London: SCAA.

Taylor, J. and Woods, M. (eds.) (1998) *Early Childhood Studies*: An Holistic Introduction. London: Arnold.

Trollope, Anthony (1875) *The Way We Live Now.* London: Chapman & Hall.

Vygotsky, L. S. (1978) *Mind in Society.* London: Harvard University Press.

Wolfendale, S. (ed) (1989) *Parental Involvement: Developing Networks Between School, Home and Community.* London: Cassell.

Woodhead, M., Light P. and Carr, R. (eds) (1991) *Growing up in a Changing Society.* London: Routledge/OU.

3

Assessment: the key to learning

Beryl Webber

Reflecting on the development of the centrality of assessment as an integral part of the teaching and learning process, it is essential to make reference to the far sighted Report of the Task Group on Assessment and Testing produced for the DES in 1987. They stated their position with clarity and based their recommendations on sound principles for teaching and learning, their starting point was based on the following five propositions:

- A school can function effectively only if it has adopted clear aims and objectives, ways of gauging these and comprehensible language for communicating the extent of those achievements to pupils, their parents and teachers, and to the wider community, so that everyone involved can take informed decisions about future action.

- Promoting children's learning is a principal aim of schools. Assessment lies at the heart of this process. It can provide a framework in which educational objectives may be set, and pupils' progress charted and expressed. It can yield a basis for planning the next educational steps in response to children's needs. By facilitating dialogue between teachers, it can enhance professional skills and help the school as a whole to strengthen learning across the curriculum and throughout its age range.

- The assessment process itself should not determine what is to be taught and learned. It should be the servant, not the master, of the curriculum. Yet it should not simply be a bolt-on addition at the end. Rather, it should be an integral part of the educational process, continually providing both 'feedback' and 'feedforward'. It therefore needs to be incorporated systematically into teaching strategies and practices at all levels. Since the results of assessment can serve a number of different purposes, these purposes have to be kept in mind when the arrangements for assessment are designed.

- Any system of assessment should satisfy certain general criteria. For the purpose of national assessment we give priority to the following four criteria:
  - the assessment results should give direct information about pupils' achievement in relation to objectives: they should be criterion-referenced;
  - the results should provide a basis for decisions about pupils' further needs: they should be formative;
  - the scales or grades should be capable of comparison across classes and schools, if teachers, pupils and parents are to share a common language and common standards: so the assessments should be calibrated or moderated;
  - the ways in which criteria and scales are set up and used should relate to expected routes of educational development, giving some continuity to a pupil's assessment at different ages: the assessments should relate to progression.
- Our recommendations have been composed in the light of these. Unless the criteria are met, the potential value of national assessment in assisting learning and supporting the professional development of teachers is unlikely to be realised.

(TGAT 1998, Introduction)

These propositions will be examined and reflected upon with the benefit of nearly a decade of experience since the implementation of the National Curriculum.

Starting as it did by legislating for Key Stage 1 pupils, many teachers of young children had the opportunity to consider the teaching and learning of a defined set of knowledge, skills and processes which were to be assessed at or towards the end of the key stage. For the first time in the history of English and Welsh education system teachers were being told what to teach and when to make assessment judgements. In other words they were to be made accountable.

Schools had to plan for the implementation of the curriculum subjects as they became statutory. They needed to learn and understand the language of assessment and undertake criterion referenced assessment based on statements of attainment which they were required to interpret and agree. They also had to undertake the administration of the National Curriculum Tasks and Tests with six/seven year old children. Schools needed strong and supportive management to implement these changes and to overcome the resistance and concerns of many of the staff.

Those schools where aims and objectives were defined found the process difficult because there were often conflicts with, as they saw it, a nationally imposed set of teaching requirements and their aims and objectives designed to reflect the needs of the pupils in the school.

The first national test materials reflected a curriculum which was complicated, extensive and, in the main, untried for such young children.

In 1992 *Curriculum Organisation and Classroom Practice in Primary Schools – A Discussion Paper* was published by the DES. There was a reference to the 1991 National Curriculum assessment results:

> The National Curriculum assessment results have to be interpreted with great caution since the assessment procedures, including the administration of the standard assessment tasks, were still at a fairly early stage of development. They involved some 43,000 Year 2 teachers making National Curriculum assessments for the first time.
>
> (DES 1992, para. 2–6)

In its short life since 1991, the National Curriculum has undergone two revisions including a shift in the assessment model from criterion referenced statements of attainment to performance related level descriptions. For assessment purposes this has meant a complete rethink by teachers, who had only just become familiar with the criterion referenced model interpreted by very many schools to mean a massive burdensome recording system based on extensive tick lists.

There has been a major shift from a model requiring evidence of competency for each criterion within the attainment targets, to a 'best fit' model which describes a range of performances with level descriptions read and interpreted by teachers making judgements based on their own professional knowledge of the performance of all the pupils in their class.

The revision to the curriculum has meant a major shift from small steps of progression, identified as the statements of attainment, to a whole key stage programme of study in which teachers can decide on the order and depth of study required by their pupils and at what stage. This has given schools a greater flexibility in their curriculum provision.

Resources can be better shared if cohorts of children follow a similar programme which has been planned by a team of teachers working together. There is a more consistent approach to the teaching across different classes within the same age range.

This should also include a more consistent interpretation of pupil performance. Teacher assessment should be the fundamental cornerstone for raising standards in schools. Planning from assessment outcomes is integral to a programme of study that is planned to reflect the needs of a particular group of pupils with a collaborative approach to the planning, implementation and assessment of progress.. The question 'Where to now?' needs to be answered by future learning programmes reflecting the identified needs. Could teachers have come to this model without the restrictive first attempt at a nationally imposed curriculum and assessment procedures?

In 1994, in *A Fair Test* Gipps and Murphy reviewed the properties of assessment:

> Formative and summative assessment have different properties; for example, for summative assessment, consistency across tasks and markers is important, since we need some confidence that it can be used to make comparisons between individuals, schools, LEAs, etc. For formative assessment, consistency is less significant, informality tends to be a feature content and construct validity are much more important than reliability.
>
> (Gipps and Murphy 1994, pp. 260–1)

It has taken several years and a review of the National Curriculum for schools to come to this understanding.

Early Years teachers have the advantage of the programmes of nationally organised training, the local debate and the research evidence to inform their understanding of conceptualisation and articulation of an area of learning that was defined as the intuitive understanding of pupil progress. Teachers were concerned that their judgements were not consistent with teachers working in other schools with different interpretations of the curriculum provision and assessments judgements made. By giving equal status to teacher assessment and end of key stage test results, Sir Ron Dearing has endorsed the professionalism of teachers and acknowledged that there are two distinct purposes for assessment as defined by Gipps and Murphy in 1994.

Schools should plan assessment to be at the heart of the learning programme. The model can be described by the following sequence of events.

1. A school considers its aims, policy statements and the statutory requirements.
2. It decides what the pupils are to learn and how to identify success criteria for all pupils.
3. Schemes of work are developed based on pupil needs and the statutory requirements.
4. Plans are drawn up to enable learning to happen. These are based

on what pupils know, understand and can do. Starting points are identified.

5. Learning is managed in each of the classrooms. This is when learning is explained and opportunities are created to assess the learning.

6. Evidence is gathered. Pupils and teachers decide what will be recorded. Feedback, discussion and marking are integral elements of this decision.

7. Next steps in learning are considered. Plans for future curriculum programmes are considered. The assessment information is used to inform the learning paths and work is matched to reflect the needs of the individual.

This is a model familiar to teachers of nursery or reception aged children. In many cases there has been prior contact with providers and/or parents. There are also many children who are not known to the teachers. They are sometimes working with very little prior knowledge of the child, for a variety of reasons, such as a child who has recently moved into the locality and there is no contact with school until the child arrives on the first day of term.

8. The Early Years Unit considers its aims, policy statements and the statutory requirements.

9. They refer to the Desirable Outcomes to decide what the children are to learn and how to identify success criteria.

10. Children's needs are identified by home visits, prior records, pre-attendance visits to the school allowing the teacher to undertake some observation of the new entrant and ongoing discussion with parents/carers.

11. Plans are drawn up to enable learning to happen. These are based on what pupils know, understand and can do. Starting points are identified. These are shared with the other adults working in the classroom.

12. Learning is managed in each of the Early Years classes. This is when learning is explained and opportunities are created to assess the learning.

13. Evidence is gathered. This is usually by observation and discussion with the child. Children and teachers discuss what has been learnt. Feedback and discussion are integral elements of this discussion. Children are encouraged to consider what they have achieved.

14. Next steps in learning are considered. Plans for future curriculum programmes are considered. The assessment information is used to inform the learning paths and work is matched to reflect the needs of the individual.

There are stages to the assessment model used by teachers of young children to enable them to know the learning needs of each child. This model has been created from observations, discussions and interviews with teachers, parents and children. It is referred to as the On-Entry Model of Assessment which precedes and includes the National Baseline Assessment procedures completed within the first seven weeks after a child enters the primary school.

On-Entry Model of Assessment

Stage 1: Impressions

The teacher uses all the documentary evidence to obtain a 'feel' for the child.

Stage 2: Forging links

The teacher makes contact with the child and begins to develop a relationship. This enables the child to feel secure in the new environment. During this period of relationship building the child may begin to demonstrate achievement. This information adds to the teacher's general 'feel' for the child.

This stage can take varying amounts of time depending on the confidence and maturity of the child, and the ability of the teacher to gain the child's trust.

Stage 3: Providing experiences

This follows on from the 'settling in ' period. The child can experiment with a range of curriculum options provided by the teacher. At this stage the child is beginning to make decisions regarding preferred activities.

Stage 4: Analysing preferences

It is through observation of the child at stage 3, reference to prior records and discussion with the child that the teacher judges what sort of assessment programme is required. Activities which will highlight individual achievements can now be planned.

Stage 5: Directing experiences

At this stage, specific activities are planned and implemented. For some of the day the child is now being directed to these activities. During this time the baseline achievements are beginning to be noted by the teacher in an informal way.

Stage 6: Formal assessment

At this stage, the teacher begins to introduce formal Baseline Assessment. The teacher now records each child's achievement according to the baseline model which has been adopted by the school/LEA.

Stage 7: A baseline has been established

This is the stage when all the assessment findings are collated and the teacher discusses the outcomes with the child's parents/carers.

Stage 8: Revisiting

Before finalising planning the teacher may need to make further informal assessments of an individual child in order to confirm a specific area of achievement. This may be necessary if the parents' view of the child's ability in a specific area differ from the findings of the Baseline Assessment. Alternatively the teacher may feel that the child's ability in a specific area is not reflected by the baseline score. This decision would normally be based on the teacher's prior informal assessments, and their general 'feel' for the child. Once any additional assessments have been made the teacher plans an appropriate programme of study.

These stages are illustrated by the case study of Eleanor who started part time education in her local primary school in the year the National Baseline assessment was being piloted by the teachers in her school.

The case study has been built up from a series of school visits , discussion with the teacher, access to prior and current records and discussion with her parents. The name of child has been changed to ensure anonymity.

Stage 1: Impressions

Eleanor had visited her class on three occasions during the Summer term. She had met her teacher, NNEB nursery nurse, other members of her class and had explored her classroom. The teacher had noted that Eleanor played alongside other children, that she had a good concentration span, enjoyed stories and had a good singing voice. Preschool records were with the parents and to be handed over at the beginning of the Autumn term. Eleanor and her parents had a meeting with the teacher in the week before she started school. During this meeting Eleanor was able to confidently talk about the pictures she had drawn and the picture sequencing she had done.

Stage 2: Forging links

After a few days the teacher noted that Eleanor was fairly comfortable in school and was happy to talk about the games she was playing. The teacher noted: 'Eleanor enthusiastically told me the names she had given to all the plastic play people.'

After about a week Eleanor began to greet the teacher when they met in the morning and she usually had some news to report. The teacher felt that this was a good sign that Eleanor was settling in well.

Shortly after this Eleanor told her mum that she had to bring a yellow toy to school in the morning. The parents reported that Eleanor always remembered what she had been told by her teacher and that she was very keen to fully participate in school life.

Stage 3: Appropriate target setting

At this stage the teacher began to widen the children's options, giving them more choice. She also changed some of the existing choices, for example, by putting bubbles in the water and setting out printing rather than painting with a brush. During this time the teacher observed the children and made a mental note of the preferences they seemed to have in their tasks they undertook. She noted that Eleanor seemed to prefer opportunities to role play.

Stage 4: Analysis of the preferred tasks

More focused observation of Eleanor revealed that she always chose the imaginative types of activity. Her favourite was the role play area and she especially enjoyed dressing up. She also joined in with all the singing and rhymes the teacher taught the class, memorising new songs and rhymes very quickly. She also liked to sing to an audience and was happy to have her voice recorded on to tape. The teacher noted that Eleanor was good at making up games when playing with plastic interlocking play people and was quite creative, giving each person a character and using them in an appropriate way.

Stage 5: Consolidation

The teacher now created opportunities to make more focused assessments. She asked the children to work with her at a certain time during the day. She set up counting activities and worked individually with children. During this time she noted that Eleanor had a fairly good grasp of number conservation and counting. She was able to tell a story using the pictures in a book.

Stage 6: A Baseline has been established

It was at this stage that the teacher undertook the formal baseline assessment. The school had agreed to pilot the Local Education Authority's model which was based on the SCAA Baseline Scales. She recorded the scores according to the given criteria.

Stage 7: Formalised assessment

Once the scores had been collated the teacher noted that there were some areas in which Eleanor had been unable to achieve a high score. These were recognising initial sounds and one to one correspondence and numeral recognition. However, from previous observations she believed that Eleanor was fairly confident in her number knowledge and understanding but she was somewhat hasty when counting. This was discussed with the parents. Both parents and teacher felt that Eleanor did need a programme to develop her numeral recognition but that her one to one correspondence could be supported at home because it had been noted that Eleanor could conserve numbers to four with ease. The teacher agreed to re-assess this area of concern before planning a programme of study. The teacher was also able to tell the parents that although Eleanor had been unable to re-tell a familiar story she felt that she had good evidence from her informal assessments to support her judgement that this was not an area of concern for Eleanor despite her score on the baseline assessment.

Stage 8: Revisiting

One to one correspondence had been verified and Eleanor had a solo singing part in the Christmas production. At the end of term the teacher reported to the parents that Eleanor could recognise most initial sounds and she had begun to recognise whole words and attempt to write them.

This model was developed during the Autumn term 1997 when Eleanor started part time education in the Reception class at her local school. Eleanor is now 4 years and 8 months old and started full time education in January 1998.

TGAT anticipated that national assessment schemes would be multi-purpose. In the review of the curriculum and its assessment arrangements in 1996, Sir Ron Dearing was the chairman of the Schools Curriculum and Assessment Authority when parity was given to teacher assessment and end of Key Stage National Curriculum tests. There was a clear statement made in the test guidance to teachers sent to all schools with the Key Stage 1 test arrangements for 1996 defining the purposes of the two strands of the end of key stage assessment arrangements.

Table 3.1 highlights the differences in specific areas: curriculum, range of evidence, timing and future needs.

Table 3.1. School Assessment Folder Key Stage 1 (SCAA 1996).

Teacher Assessment	*National Curriculum Tasks and Tests*
End of key stage Teacher Assessment judgements are based on achievements in all aspects of the subject over the whole key stage.	Test results are based on short tests which only sample some aspects of the subject.
Teacher Assessment judgements are based on a variety of evidence (oral, written, observed) in a range of contexts on a number of occasions.	Tests are structured, written assessments giving limited opportunities for children to demonstrate what they know, can do and understand.
Teacher Assessment is an integral and ongoing part of everyday work.	Tests are externally timetabled. Some children may perform better or less well in timed tests than they do in everyday classroom work.
Teacher Assessment identifies achievement over time.	Tests are a snapshot of attainment at a particular moment in time.
Continuous Teacher Assessment informs future learning by identifying areas for development. Its major purpose is to recognise achievement and define next steps.	The tests are designed to establish, at 7 and 11, how children are progressing against national targets.

National Baseline Assessment schemes differ from the end of key stage tests. Teachers are expected to plan the curriculum as a result of the assessments. The assessments cover not only English and mathematics but also personal and social development. However, it is not mandatory to ascribe a score to the latter as only language and literacy and mathematics are required to provide numerical outcomes for value-added purposes. Science is a desirable learning outcome in the goals for children under school age (Desirable Learning Outcomes SCAA 1996). It is subsumed under the title of Knowledge and Understanding of the World, the intention of which is to provide a foundation for later achievement. However, although assessed at the end of the key stages, teacher assessment at Key Stage 1 and national curriculum tests at subsequent key stages, science is not an assessment requirement on entry into school. This reflects the national thrust to improve the levels of achievement in literacy and numeracy. The numerical scores from the assessments in English and mathematics are intended to provide the base for value added purposes.

The progress of every child entering the primary school at four/five years can now be tracked until leaving school at sixteen or eighteen years old. For the first time in the history of English and Welsh education there will be year on year national data on the prior school knowledge and understanding of speaking and listening, reading, writing, numeracy and other aspects of mathematics including shape space and measures, for every child living in England or Wales.

This could be a force for good. Parenting courses could be developed more widely and include modules such as 'Learning to Play with Your Child' and 'The Importance of Talking, Listening and Reading to Your Child', which have been available for years on a limited scale. A national debate could be initiated to discuss and raise the status of Early Years provision and maybe children aged 0 to 4 would finally have a voice that would be heard. This is an opportunity for all educators to grasp.

The value added purpose of the National Baseline Assessment models is a cause for concern. Teachers fear that pressure may be put upon them to suppress the score of the assessments so that the school is seen to make a difference. Monitoring and moderation procedures will be needed to allay the fears of these teachers. As Gipps and Stobart (1993) predicted in *Assessment: A Teachers' Guide to the Issues*:

> National curriculum assessment results are going to be used to evaluate school performance.
>
> (Gipps and Stobart 1993, p. 37)

There is also a message of hope for primary schools with regard to parents seeking a school for their child.

> it is worth remembering two points. The first is that not all parents are able or willing to choose a school that is not the nearest one, so only some parents will make use of the assessment-based evaluation or performance indicators. Second, many parents are not looking for assessment results as the main or only criterion for choice of school. Particularly, at primary level, parents are likely to be looking for a friendly, happy atmosphere, approachable staff, a supportive caring environment and an all round approach to education, as well as evidence that the academic standards are good.
>
> (Gipps and Stobart 1993, p. 37)

There is no reason to believe these criteria will change with the implementation of baseline assessment procedures and data analysis.

Another difference between Baseline Assessment and the other national assessment tests is that there is an expectation that the curriculum provision will be based on the results of the assessment information. This is due to the timing rather than the purpose of the assessments. All other national assessment tests are completed at the end of a stage and are intended as a snapshot of performance in some aspects of the programmes of study to summarise the pupil's achievement before moving on to the next key stage. In most cases it is the quality of teacher that is addressed when a detailed item analysis of end of key stage test results is completed. The cohort of children has moved to other schools or departments making it difficult to communicate these findings to the next teacher.

If the baseline model can prove that by planning from assessment improves the quality of learning for these pupils, then the debate on timing for other national curriculum tests should be opened, particularly testing at Key Stages 1 and 2, as it comes at the end of both key stages and could be moved to the beginning of the next stage. If this is impossible for sound educational reasons then the next school or teacher should be provided with all scripts for close scrutiny before embarking on programmes of study. This reflects one of the six proposals made by TGAT.

There are other differences between national assessment requirements and Baseline Assessment. Baseline results must be shared with parents/carers within the first term.

The National Framework for Baseline Assessment had an accreditation criterion which was a requirement for all scheme providers.

It states that a scheme provider must demonstrate:

- explanation of outcomes of assessments to parents. As a minimum, this should include the opportunity for a discussion between parents and their child's teacher within a term of the child being admitted to school.

(SCAA 1997)

All national assessment results must be communicated directly to parents. At no other stage during the period of compulsory education, is it a requirement for teachers to face parents in an interview situation to report on the assessment outcomes. At all key stages the results are communicated to parents in a written form. This raises the issue of direct accountability. There is pressure on the teacher to ensure that the judgements are sound and are supported by evidence and that they are able to communicate these results clearly in a way that is understood by the parents/carer and that enables them to feel they are partners and can make further contributions to the education of their child. It also gives parents/carers an opportunity to provide evidence of performance in the home environment which, in some cases, may differ from school performance. As seen in the case study of Eleanor, parents can make an input to the curriculum planning and provide teachers with reasons to revisit the assessments made during the seven week Baseline Assessment period. This would be for the purposes of curriculum planning only, not to alter any Baseline Assessments. It should be viewed as an opportunity to plan for a more finely tuned curriculum reflecting the needs of the child and with agreement of both teacher and parent/carer.

It can be seen that some of the proposals are implicit in the baseline model of assessment. Schools need clear aims and policies supporting the practice for entry procedures. These need to be supportive for the staff and enabling for the children. Schools need to ensure they can respond to the prior achievement and provide 'feedforward' curriculum opportunities to secure a good foundation of provision that enables the child to progress in a secure and appropriate, yet challenging environment. In *Value Added Indicators for Schools* (SCAA 1997), value added is defined as:

the progress made by children over a given period. The progress made by an individual child or group of children (a teaching group, a class or school cohort) is compared with the average progress made by a larger sample of children. One way in which that progress can be measured is by measuring the attainment of all the individuals in the sample at the start and then again at the end of the period.

(SCAA 1997)

There are two distinct purposes to the Baseline Assessment:

1. National and local accountability
2. Improving the quality of the provision based on a more thorough focused assessment procedure.

Assessment should be considered integral to the learning process and at the 'heart' of learning. The external value added purposes of Baseline Assessment must not intrude upon the main purpose to inform future teaching/learning programmes that are based on an assessment made as the child starts the statutory, formalised stage of education.

Issues

1. How does Baseline Assessment differ from the end of key stage national curriculum tests?
2. Consider the development of the On Entry Assessment model and relate this to your own experiences when working with a new cohort of children.
3. Analyse a whole school assessment policy, making reference to the TGAT proposals. In your opinion, are they enshrined in the policy?

References

DES (1987) *National Curriculum: Task Group on Assessment and Testing – A Report.* London: HMSO.

DES (1992) *Curriculum Organisation and Classroom Practice in Primary Schools. A discussion paper.* London: HMSO.

Gipps, C. and Stobart, G. (1990) *Assessment. A Teachers' Guide to the Issues.* London: Hodder & Stoughton.

Gipps, C. and Murphy, P. (1994) *A Fair Test? Assessment, achievement and equity.* Buckingham: Open University Press.

School Curriculum and Assessment Authority (1996) *Nursery Education. Desirable Outcomes for Children's Learning on entering compulsory education.* London: SCAA.

School Curriculum and Assessment Authority (1996) *School Assessment Folder.* London: SCAA.

School Curriculum and Assessment Authority (1997) *The National Framework for Baseline Assessment. Criteria and procedures for the accreditation of Baseline Assessment schemes.* London: SCAA.

School Curriculum and Assessment Authority (1997) *Value Added Indicators for Schools. Consultative Paper: Primary.* London: SCAA.

4

Play, health and physical development

Richard Bailey

Or children with bare feet upon the sands
Of some ebbed sea, or playing on the streets
Of little towns in Connacht,
Things young and happy.

(Padriac Pearse, Last Lines 1916)

Young children make up the most physically active group in society. Relative to most adults, children spend a large part of their days moving. An observation of nursery or primary school playtimes reveals most children are physically playing for a large part of the period, whether they are chasing a ball, or chasing another child, or skipping, or dancing, or the million and one other activities that we all recognise as normal, healthy behaviour in infants. In fact, relatively high levels of physical activity among children of all cultures suggests that it is almost certainly an expression of a natural tendency towards movement, that seems to reach its peak in the early years.

This chapter aims to survey the existing research literature on children's physical activity and physical play, and their connection with levels of health. It goes on to suggest ways in which parents, teachers and the wider community can encourage and support children's participation in physical activities and play.

Health, physical activity and play

Physical play is the first and most frequently occurring expression of play in young children (Hutt 1979). In light of the fact that all children in all observed cultures (as well as a large number of other species) play, that children will play without encouragement, and that much exhibited play cannot be accounted for by imitation, it is not inconceivable that there is some sort of 'play instinct' (Fagen 1981).

Certainly, there is a long tradition of ethological research indicating that play is, in part, an opportunity to learn, train and prepare for later life, but what sort of life? One consequence of the recent emergence of an evolutionary psychology is a growing understanding that our minds and our bodies are adapted for the environment in which we evolved, our 'ancestral environment': much more a nomadic, hunter-gatherer existence than the modern television and motor car culture; an environment in which activity and physical exertion were not so much a recreation as a determining factor in survival. Now, there are uncountable consequences of this apparently simple recognition (see, for example, Barkow *et al.* 1992, and Pinker 1997), but with regards to the matter at hand, it is important to acknowledge the inevitable conclusion that our ancestors' very existence was dependent upon developing high levels of physical activity and fitness. Play, it seems, evolved as a process by which the body was prepared for the challenges likely to befall it, occurring at a stage of life when there was time and support structure necessary for such an investment. Of course, it is not being suggested that this is the only function of play; it is common for adaptations to supply a variety of benefits to the organism. Nevertheless, physical training and preparation for adulthood, with their direct connection with survivability, would seem to be functions of some significance. Characteristically high levels of physical activity among young children (in comparison with adults) would seem to be a predictable consequence of this predisposition.[1]

A consequence of the above argument is that one would expect certain benefits to accrue from physical play in young children, benefits that contribute to success within the physical environment. Paediatric research is beginning to identify numerous health and fitness gains associated with physical play and general physical activity, both for the present condition of the child and the future, including the following:

Physical activity and play
- help regulate body weight
- lead to increased bone density and mineralisation
- favourably influence body fatness
- lead to improved ability to use fat for energy
- help regulate blood pressure
  (sources: HEA 1997; Armstrong and Welsman 1997; Malina and Bouchard 1991; Fentem *et al.* 1988).

Others have pointed to the contribution that physical play and physical activity make to wider aspects of 'quality of life' such as those associated with mental and emotional health. Dishman (1986), for example, reviewed a range of sources, and found regular physical activity to be associated with a reduction in anxiety, stress and mild to moderate depression, with benefits across all ages and both genders. Further findings suggest that a physically active lifestyle is associated with improved self-esteem and self-concept (Gruber 1986), and with the ability to deal comfortably with everyday challenges and pressures (HEA 1997).[2]

There is further evidence of the benefits of regular physical activity for adults, and for its role in the prevention of illness and disease (for example, HEA 1997) and, of course, common sense supports the view of the Royal College of Physicians (1991), that physical activity is a habit best acquired during childhood: children have the most time and enthusiasm, as well as being generally open to guidance and positive influence. Sallis and Patrick's (1994) consensus statement concludes that:

> There is substantial evidence that regular physical activity produces multiple beneficial physiological and psychological outcomes during adolescence. The strength and consistency of these findings lead to recommendations for all adolescents to be physically active on a regular basis.
>
> (Sallis and Patrick 1994, p. 314)

How healthy are children?

Based upon the information given so far, one would expect a positive answer, especially in relation to children's physical health. After all, a substantial literature has amassed suggesting a strong relationship between physical activity and health. Moreover, it has been argued that there are reasons to believe that children are 'naturally' active. Therefore, children should be healthy. Unfortunately, however, matters seem not to be so satisfactory. Some researchers have started to raise concerns regarding children's current levels of health, and low levels of physical activity have been identified as a major contributory cause, prompting Armstrong (1990, p. 13), a leading UK exercise physiologist, to describe the current levels and patterns of physical activity as 'cause for concern'.

Concerns for health and low levels of activity are usually directed at adults, with images engendered of more habitually sedentary lifestyles; certainly, the vast majority of Health Education literature and broadcasting would suggest that it is with adults that problems of ill-health lie. However, a number of studies have begun to highlight that serious health risks associated with a sedentary lifestyle are felt among all age groups, including the youngest. Moreover, if it is the case that there is a marked decrease in activity with age (for example, cf. Heartbeat Wales 1987), a further cause for concern becomes apparent.

So, despite the suggestion of a natural predisposition towards physical activity in the early years of life, evidence would seem to indicate that current levels of activity are inadequate to ensure health gains in young children. Hypokinetic diseases (disease related to a lack of physical activity) are being witnessed in increasingly younger children, including coronary heart disease, obesity, hypertension (high blood pressure), hypercholesterolemia (high blood cholesterol), osteoporosis (brittle bones), diabetes, back pain, postural problems, stress, anxiety and depression (Biddle and Biddle 1989). Each can lead to a reduced quality of life and some are life-shortening.

Coronary heart disease is the major cause of death in most Western countries; in England, it is associated with 26 per cent of deaths and 35 million lost working days (Department of Health 1992), and mounting evidence is beginning to suggest that it may have its roots in early childhood. A number of studies are beginning to paint a disturbing picture. One study based in Northern Ireland, for example, found that over 69 per cent of 12 year olds had at least one modifiable risk factor for CHD, with 14 per cent exhibiting three or more risk factors (Boreham *et al.* 1992).[3] In his review of the literature on atherosclerosis (the fatty build-up on the walls of the arteries), McGill (1984) concluded that, 'we can say with certainty that coronary atherosclerosis has its origins in childhood, at least by age 10 and possible earlier' (p. 451). Disturbingly, the age of ten years may be too conservative a figure: signs of the onset of CHD have been identified in children as young as three years of age (Holman *et al.* 1958). So, Morris' warning may be stark, but it seems accurate:

> For lack of exercise, we are bringing up a generation of children less healthy than it could be, and many of whom are likely to be at high risk in later life of serious disease and shortened life expectancy.
> (Morris, in Sports Council 1988, p. 3)

Children are active, but many are not active enough for a healthy lifestyle. Moreover, children may be active, but not in a way that is health promoting (Biddle and Biddle 1989). Mason's (1995) extensive study found that almost all six to 16 year olds surveyed took part in some sort of sport, both in and outside school, although there was a large variation in the amount of activity undertaken. On the other hand, studies carried out by one team question even this; their observational studies of primary-aged and pre-school children, 'contradict the common perception of children being very active' (Baranowski *et al.* 1987; cf. DuRant *et al.* 1993). As will be seen later, in order for exercise to promote short-term fitness gains and enhance long-term health and well-being, children should regularly take part in activities of varying intensity, a number of days a week. The actual levels of physical activity in young children are notoriously difficult to measure; many of the standard procedures used with adults, such as self-reporting, measuring energy intake, heart rate monitoring and observation, can be inappropriate and problematic with infants. For this reason, most researchers have tended to focus upon secondary aged pupils (cf. HEA 1997, pp. 26–7). Nevertheless certain patterns of activity during the pre-school and primary years are beginning to emerge that support the previously expressed concerns.

There seems to have been a general reduction in children's levels of activity during recent decades. One study compiled and compared data on eating habits over 50 years and found that despite there being no change in body mass, there was a significant decrease in food intake (Durnin 1992); the only conceivable explanation for this phenomenon would seem to be a reduction in energy expenditure, in other words, activity. Other studies have used different procedures to arrive at a similar point. Sleap and Warburton (1992; 1994) have carried out a number of studies of primary children's activity levels, and found that many children experience no health-related exercise during their day; in one case, only 14 per cent of the sample had any sustained period of moderate to vigorous activity for at least twenty minutes (Sleap and Warburton 1992). Armstrong and Bray (1991) found similar results, including the finding that a quarter of girls and a fifth of boys did no exercise of proper intensity lasting ten minutes or more, during the entire three days they were recorded. This last finding was corroborated by Bailey *et al.*'s (1995) observational study of the level and tempo of activity for 6–10 year olds. The medium duration of activity of any level was just 15 seconds, with that of intense activity lasting three seconds! Armstrong and Welsman (1997, p. 114) neatly summarised a number of findings: 'children spend most of their time engaged in activities of low intensity interspersed with very short bursts of high intensity physical activity'.

Whatever happened to physical play?

The obvious question arising from these findings is: what has happened to bring about this decline in physical activity? Partly because of the pace of some changes in our culture, and partly because these changes are felt by all of us, not just children, most people could point to some of the contributing factors in declining levels of physical activity.

Television and other media, of course, play a role. The average child in the United Kingdom spends about 20 hours a week watching television (Central Statistical Office 1994). This need not be a detrimental factor, since media have an enormous potential for encouraging certain behaviours, and they could promote lifelong physical activity as much as they seem to promote the sedentary enjoyment of trivia. Moreover, when the media do portray physical activity, it is usually competitive sports, focusing upon a very narrow range, and upon elite performers.

Research into this area is somewhat limited. It is common sense to assume that increased television viewing will reduce levels of physical activity, since time watching soap operas or game shows is time not being active.[4] Surprisingly, some studies have suggested a weak link between television viewing and inactivity, specifically studies of adolescent girls (Robinson *et al.* 1993), a group with generally low levels of habitual activity and for whom both physical activity and television viewing are relatively minor factors in their lives, and of 3–8 year olds (DuRant *et al.* 1994), for whom parental pressures and concerns might play a role. Nevertheless, most research supports the common sense position, namely, that there is a negative correlation between television viewing and physical activity (Williams and Handford 1986) and physical fitness (Tucker 1986).

Changing transport patterns is another factor that seems to negatively effect children's levels of physical activity. Between 1975 and 1991, there was a doubling of the proportion of children taking car journeys to school (Central Statistical Office 1994). This relates, to some extent, to parents' increased fears regarding children's safety. Many parents have weighed the benefits of walking to school, shops and so on, against the perceived costs to personal safety, such as hazardous road conditions and threats to personal safety by assault. This has resulted in many deciding in favour of car travel, despite the possible consequences to long-term health.

Hillman (1993) analysed these trends in terms of 'independent mobility', that is, children's freedom to take part in outdoor activities, and found that there had been a decline with time. His survey of 7–11 year olds found a significant reduction in independent mobility between 1971 and 1990. For example, only one quarter of that group were allowed to use their cycles on the road in 1990, compared with two thirds in 1971, and four times as many children in 1990 were driven to school than in 1971. A further dimension of Hillman's research related to gender. Boys were allowed far more independent mobility than girls in all areas studied, such as access to leisure places, walking unaccompanied to school and cycling on roads (ibid.; cf. Armstrong and Welsman 1997).

These are, of course, only a few of the factors that have influenced children's participation in physical activities. There are many others; people's behaviour is seldom so simple. Sallis (1995) offered a neat summary of the types of factors in terms of 'personal' and 'environmental' dimensions, of which a simplified outline is presented below:

Personal Factors		Environmental Factors	
Biological	Psychological	Social	Physical
Age	Motivation	Parents	Weather
Gender	Perceived barriers	Peers	Season
Obesity	Perceived competence	Teachers/School	Access
Fitness levels	Beliefs	PE	Type of activity
Heredity	Attitudes	Culture/Media	Way activity is promoted

The role of the school, teachers and, in particular, Physical Education will be discussed later. For now, though, it is worth considering those variables that relate closely to the matters at hand in a little more detail.[5]

A number of factors related to the biological make-up of the individual have been found to influence children's participation in physical activities. Evidence identifies age and gender as particularly important variables. Both boys and girls reduce the amount of activity they do as they get older, with studies suggesting a 50–75 per cent reduction in levels of physical activity between six and 18 years of age (Rowlands 1990). However, the rate of decline is especially great in girls – about 2.5 per cent greater decline than boys between six and 17 years (Armstrong and Welsman 1997) – and this is a pattern that continues from early childhood through to adulthood (Stephens *et al.* 1985).

It is often difficult to interpret data on psychological factors: studies are often based upon discrete perspectives, making comparison and accumulation of evidence difficult; the problem becomes especially severe when the subject is a young child, since standard methodological tools like self-reporting, questionnaires and interviews might lack yield imprecise and dubious results. Nevertheless, certain patterns have begun to emerge. Young children readily accept that physical activities are important for health and fitness, but this does not necessarily lead them to take part in such activities; infants and even older children seem to have an innate sense of immortality, and long-term health benefits lack immediate appeal. More successful motivating factors seem to be fun and enjoyment (Petichoff 1992), and children's grading of activities as fun and enjoyable stem from such things as the excitement of the game, improving their skills, a sense of accomplishment, a positive perception of their own performance and the amount of exertion required (HEA 1997).

Children's perceived barriers to participation are of particular importance, as they give clues both to reasons for declining levels of activity, and to strategies for addressing this decline. Most studies focus upon adolescents, and one could hypothesise a host of obstacles raised by parents of younger children, especially in terms of concerns for independent mobility, discussed above. Offered somewhat tentatively, research suggests that perceived barriers include lack of confidence, lack of success, excessive pressure, loss of interest, expense, limited awareness of available opportunities, accessibility of activities, inappropriate provision and unsuitable weather (ibid.; Sports Council 1993).

Social factors, like parents, teachers and peers, play a strong role in influencing children's attitudes and behaviour. Adolescents are particularly guided by friends, while younger children are most influenced by parents, other family members and teachers (Sallis 1995). Toddlers have been found to be especially influenced by parental encouragement for physical activity (Klesges *et al.* 1986). Slightly older children seem to respond more directly to role modelling than verbal encouragement, so there is a strong correlation between parents' and their primary school children's physical activity levels (Freedson and Evenson 1991; Sallis *et al.* 1988). One study found that children with physically active mothers were twice as likely to be active as children of inactive mothers, and that if both parents were physically active, children were six times as likely to be active (Moore *et al.* 1991). Of course, a further, vital way in which parents help young children remain physically active is through facilitating their activity by means of transporting to clubs and financing their participation. This reliance upon parents has increased in recent years, due to their concerns about children travelling alone (Hillman 1993).

Parents' worries regarding children's safety in modern society also relate to their access to opportunities for physical activity. Hillman's (ibid.) study found a connection between restrictions placed on independent mobility and lack of participation in both organised and unorganised play and physical activity. Nevertheless, young children still do take part in out-of-doors play and sporting activities, especially if opportunities are convenient. Sallis' (1993) finding that the more places that are available in which children can play, the more they play, is particularly salutary.

How much activity do children need?

Children are not simply small adults. Indeed, they differ from adults qualitatively as well as quantitatively when it comes to exercise physiology.

(Sharp 1991, p. 70)

The claim that children are not just miniature adults has been repeated so often in post-Piagetian times that it has become something of a cliché. Nevertheless, the significance of the statement ought not be underestimated in the areas of child development and physiology, since inappropriate exercise with children can lead to frustration, discomfort and injury. Unfortunately, paediatric physiology is still a developing discipline, and the precise amount, intensity and type of physical activity that is best for the development of children's health remains uncertain (Harris and Elbourn 1997). Nevertheless, theorists have begun to offer general prescriptions.

The standard 'exercise prescription' was offered by the American College of Sports Medicine (ACSM) (1990): vigorous structured activity, for continuous periods of more than 20 minutes, at least three times a week. This prescription can make harsh medicine, and only a small proportion of the adult population achieves this level of activity; in England, for example, about 70 per cent of men and 80 per cent of women fall below appropriate levels (Activity and Health Research 1992).

There is not, as yet, a standard prescription specifically for young children. Many authorities seem to have assumed that children need to follow the same guidelines as adults (ACSM 1995; Armstrong and Biddle 1992), and it is likely that they would lead to increased levels of fitness. However, some have questioned whether physical fitness *per se* is necessary for good health in children (Corbin and Pangrazi 1992). Moreover, if adults find such an inflexible programme difficult to follow, it is extremely unlikely that young children will be able to comply; while children tend to be more active than adults, their activity rarely expresses itself in a regular, consistent way.

Recent work has offered an alternative prescription for health and

Table 4.1. Some characteristics of children's physiological response to exercise and physical activity, with implications for exercise prescription

CHILDREN'S RESPONSE TO EXERCISE AND PHYSICAL ACTIVITY	IMPLICATIONS FOR EXERCISE PRESCRIPTION
Children are wasteful of energy: they tire more easily, and use a greater amount of oxygen, relative to body size than adults	They should avoid prolonged high intensity activity
Children have a less efficient cardio-respiratory system than adults: they have a higher heart rate, their hearts pump less blood within each beat, and their lungs have to work harder to take up oxygen	They should avoid prolonged high intensity activity, in favour of work of varying intensity, with frequent rest periods
Young children have much greater reliance upon oxygen for energy than other 'anaerobic' sources (specifically glucose or glycogen)	They are well-adapted to work of moderate intensity for relatively long duration, with appropriate rest periods
Due to their reduced ability to store carbohydrates, children are unsuited to intense activity lasting between 10 seconds and one minute	They should generally avoid continuous series of powerful movements, or repeated bursts of strenuous activities
Children recover more quickly from activity than adults	They are suited to intermittent activity
Children are poor perceivers of effort in exercise	'Training' programmes for children may be inappropriate; varied tasks that emphasise fun and participation are less likely to induce harmful exercise stress

fitness, and one that seems much more appropriate for young children. This does not replace the existing guidelines, but merely supplements it. Some studies have questioned the focus upon vigorous activity, and have suggested that moderate activity can also bring about significant health gains, especially for the less fit (Blair *et al.* 1989). Other research has questioned the emphasis upon the duration and frequency of activity. While blocks of continuous exercise may be necessary for improved fitness (for example, for sports performance), total energy expenditure may be more significant for health benefits. Bouchard and his colleagues (1993) suggest that many of the health benefits of exercise are induced by the body's immediate responses during and for a while after a period of exercise, and, therefore, it may be more useful to exercise in frequent, short bouts. This turns the focus away from prolonged periods of activity towards an accumulation of activity throughout the day (Wimbush 1994).

How does this relate to the child? It has been suggested that extended periods of activity are inappropriate for many children, especially infants. Continuous, vigorous, adult-directed activity might be likely to decrease, rather than increase, motivation to participate in children (HEA 1997). Additionally, and vitally, children respond to exercise and physical activity in different ways to adults, so it is wise to offer a programme that directly acknowledges this.

The ways and extent to which children differ from adults in their response to physical activity and exercise are numerous, and beyond the remit of this chapter (see, for example, Rowland 1996; Bar-Or 1987; Armstrong and Welsman 1997). However, it is useful to outline certain key features of the differences, in order to identify developmentally appropriate guidelines for activity[6].

Adult-based guidelines for exercise fail to address adequately specific requirements and characteristics of young children. What is needed is a set of guidelines which are grounded in recent research into children's physiology, and in this respect, it is useful to consider the Children's Lifetime Physical Activity Model (CLPAM) (Corbin *et al.* 1994). Following evidence that moderate activity is beneficial in the development of children's health, and that motivational factors are important in continuing participation in physical activity, CLPAM suggests that children should be physically active at least three times a week, with an amount of activity equivalent to between 30 and 60 minutes per day of physical play and of varying intensity. This model advocates everyday children's games, lifestyle activities (such as walking or bike-riding) and basic skill learning (for example, through Physical Education lessons or simply practice with play equipment).

It is worth noting that these guidelines, as well as other research outlined above, suggest a model of children's physical activity with a great similarity to children's natural physical play. Play may well be the most natural way for young children to be active (Rippe *et al.* 1993); it could also be the most natural way for them to get fit and healthy. If this is the case, then it may substantiate the argument offered at the start of this article, that physical training is a major reason for the evolution of physical play in humans in the first place.

Promoting health, play and physical development

Play is as necessary to a child's full development of body, intellect and personality, as are food, shelter, fresh air, exercise, rest and the prevention of illness and accidents to his continued mortal existence.

(Sheridan 1997, p. 11)

This chapter has identified a number of causes for concern with regard to children's current levels of health and physical activity. It has been suggested that conditions of modern society, including media, transport patterns and physical environment, have led to a steady, consistent and measurable reduction in opportunities for physical play in young children, and that this reduction in play opportunities is a significant factor in the growing health concerns.

A positive feature of the discussion is that young children, given the chance, love to move and play. The key phrase here is 'given the chance': we, teachers, parents and the wider community, must begin to search seriously for opportunities for children to follow their natural dispositions. This need not be expensive; in fact, it need cost nothing at all. Young children require only very few elements to play: they need a place to play; they need things with which to play, of which the most flexible, exciting and effective are other children; and they need time to play.

The encouragement and facilitation of regular physical activity is best started early, building upon children's natural inquisitiveness regarding their bodies and movements at a time when they are especially open to positive influence from family, school and the community. To succeed, however, it is important to recognise that young children will not respond in the same way to health and fitness messages as adults do: threats of shortened life expectancy means little to infants living in the present, with a suspicion that they may be immortal! To succeed, any programme hoping to increase levels of physical activity and establish healthy lifestyles must be appealing, enjoyable and social (Harris and Elbourn 1997). It will also benefit from being as normal, habitual and natural as possible, if it is to carry over into the child's later life.

The role of parents in the development of active lifestyles has been discussed. Socialisation within the family unit seems to be one of the main processes through which the health behaviour of children is influenced, especially during early childhood (Sallis and Hovell 1990). Some studies have suggested that parents are a more important determinant of participation in physical activities than teachers, peers and other family members (HEA 1997).

Reliance upon parental support for participation is pivotal for children of Primary School age and younger, for whom transport to and from, and finance for, organised activities are potential barriers. Moreover, encouragement and reinforcement, and especially positive role modelling, provided by parents have been found to be very effective in establishing healthy behaviours, and this effect is particularly powerful in pre-schoolers (Klesges *et al.* 1986). By creating a social environment in which habitual physical activity and constructive use of leisure time are ever-present, parents can make a great contribution to the quality of their children's lives, both in the present and for the future.

Alongside parents, schools have a vital role to play in the development of positive health behaviour in children. The Primary School, in particular, has an important role to play, summarised by Harris and Elbourn (1997, p. 37), below:

- it has a captive audience of children for most of the year
- there are a range of relevant professionals
- there are facilities for physical activities all year round
- there is communication and often close liaison with the home
- there is an environment conducive to multi-disciplinary programmes
- young children are curious about their bodies, and are receptive to health information
- the primary school teacher oversees the whole development of the child, and can more easily integrate health information.

In recent years, a number of promotions have aimed to draw upon these virtues for the benefit of school children's health. As elsewhere, there is a general view that a whole school approach to health and physical activity is the best way to advance (Sports Council 1993), and this has been the philosophy of both the 'Health Promoting School' and the 'Active School' schemes. The former focuses upon developing effective health education in schools, against the background of a healthy environment. This involves the encouragement of a range of physical activities within and outside of the school, as well as other health factors, like a smoke-free environment and healthy eating.

The Active Schools initiative focuses more narrowly upon children's physical activity, in school and out of school. It involves the establishment of a range of policies which promote purposeful physical activities, encourage participation beyond the school, and support and reward active lifestyles (Harris 1994). Above all, active schools aim to promote physical activity and an active lifestyle as things that are fun and enjoyable, and that bring about the opportunity of success and achievement (Fox 1996).

There are numerous ways in which this aim can be achieved, and it presents a real and worthwhile challenge for teachers to generate ideas. For a start, though, it is useful to identify four broad areas that offer immediate opportunities for physical activity development and encouragement: out-of-school physical activity; informal play; organised extra-curricular activities; Physical Education lessons.

There is a limited amount of direct influence that schools can have over children's out-of-school physical activity. The amount of time their pupils spend watching television, playing computer games or other sedentary undertakings is somewhat beyond their jurisdiction. Nevertheless, discussions on such matters are clearly within the remit of Health Education or Personal and Social Education programmes, and, of course, raising awareness of opportunities for extension of skills and interests within the community is generally regarded as an appropriate and valuable school service (DNH 1995). The area of transport to and from school is one in which the school can play a more direct role, by encouraging parents and children to walk or cycle to school, providing safe and secure storage facilities for cycles, and for petitioning local authorities for cycling routes and traffic calming schemes around the school vicinity (Fox 1996).

Playtimes offer tremendous potential for physical activity. Most children enjoy moving and playing during these periods, and aside from the many benefits in terms of the development of interpersonal skills, playtime activities are self-regulated and voluntary, making them accessible to all children. Primary schools can draw upon a range of ideas for making playgrounds more activity friendly, including exciting markings, suitable equipment, a ready supply of balls, skipping ropes and the like, as well as areas where children can escape from the usual football frenzy, to follow their own activity interests in peace and safety.

Extra-curricular activities, whether after school, during lunchtime or at weekends, offer another valuable opportunity for extending children's participation. A number of agencies have raised concerns over the limited after-school sports provision in some schools, leading the

Department of National Heritage (1995) to suggest that schools ought to plan for a minimum of four hours per week. Many infant schools, in particular, come very short of that target. Nevertheless, there is a range of activities that would be appealing to young children, especially if offered at their familiar and convenient school, such as, sports specific clubs (many sports national governing bodies provide resources designed specifically for younger children), general games, clubs (for example, children might be exposed to a different game each week, or fortnight, or month, perhaps through existing schemes like TOP Play or BT TOP Sport, or through a group of teachers taking turns to offer favourite sports), keep fit clubs, dance clubs, gym clubs, the list could go on. These clubs need not only take place after school (a lunchtime dance club offers a pleasant break in the day for the teachers as well as the pupils), and need not solely be the responsibility of the school staff, as it is an important job for the school to forge links with other community groups and agencies, perhaps through offering facilities to outside sports clubs. Whatever activities are offered, it is important that a range is available, since there will always be some children for whom traditional fare is not appealing. In light of this discussion, the findings of one report on 5–18 year olds is illuminating:

> Seven out of ten of the young people indicated they would play more if there was freedom for them to play when they wanted to and there was a competition available in one of their favourite sports in which they do well.
>
> (Clough *et al.*, cited in Thorpe 1996, p. 145)

The Physical Education lesson is the most obvious arena to promote regular physical activity, and it is especially important for those children for whom school offers the only chance of regular activity. Health Related Exercise is currently a statutory element within the Physical Education Programme of study, and much has been written in recent years about its enormous potential (cf. Harris and Elbourn 1997; Armstrong and Biddle 1992; Biddle and Biddle 1989). For lack of space, it is only possible to raise a small number of ideas and proposals, but these should be indicative of further approaches.

It is important that teachers plan for maximum involvement and participation in their lessons, and that the experiences are positive for their pupils. Appropriate differentiation is necessary if all pupils are to get full enjoyment and satisfaction from their lessons. Physical Education encompasses a wide range of activities, from traditional team games, to individual events, like gymnastics, athletics and swimming, to co-operative activities like some dance forms and outdoor pursuits. Different children enjoy different activities, and the breadth of the current Physical Education curriculum is an important recognition of this fact. Many girls shy away from competitive team games, in favour of individual activities (Sports Council 1993), and some authorities have gone on to question an emphasis upon competitive games for all children. Duda (1994), for example, suggested that teachers aiming to foster greater enjoyment in physical activity ought to focus upon 'task-orientated goals', achieving personal, achievable tasks and working with other children, not just against them, rather than upon 'ego-oriented goals' to do with beating others.

Sadly, political events seem to be working against such approaches. Early statements sounded supportive of an increased profile for sport and physical activities:

> Labour's approach to sport recognises the need to focus on a foundation where young children are introduced to a broad and balanced programme of activities
>
> (Labour Party 1996, p. 6)

and

> Primary school teachers are to be given the key role of ensuring that all children experience physical activities. This is not only beneficial to children's health, it can also help equip them with social skills and the enthusiasm for lifelong sports participation.
>
> (ibid., p. 8)

Recent government announcements indicate a reversal of views. Education and Employment Secretary David Blunkett's highly publicised wish for teachers to focus even more narrowly on the basic skills of literacy and numeracy and to approach the foundation subjects with 'flexibility' (DfEE 1998) is more than political window-dressing. Moreover, the response by the Qualification and Curriculum Authority (QCA) and other quasi-autonomous agencies to these changes has been disappointing. In a paper, presumably ironically titled 'Maintaining Breadth and Balance at Key Stages 1 and 2', the QCA (1998) advocates an increased narrowing down of the Physical Education curriculum, towards competitive games and away from outdoor and adventurous activities and athletics. This consequent marginalisation of Physical Education raises great cause for concern regarding children's current activity levels and future lifestyles, especially those children who already receive limited opportunities for physical activities. Children in the United Kingdom already receive fewer hours of Physical Education than any other comparable country in Europe (Armstrong and Welsman 1997), and these reforms seem destined to place our children still further behind.

Conclusion

It is difficult to overstate the importance of physical activity and play: they are natural and necessary expressions of childhood, and need to be encouraged and facilitated by parents, teachers and policy makers. Researchers have identified a number of concerns for children's current levels of physical activity and health, and they are of such seriousness that they constitute a priority for every school and community. This chapter has begun to suggest approaches to addressing the need for increased play and activity opportunities; the reader can probably add many others. The most rewarding aspect of this area is that whilst the consequences of poor participation levels may be somewhat severe, the solutions are almost always fun. Children love to move and be active, they just need the opportunity.

Notes

1. Lack of space necessitates a rather brief and superficial outline of this argument. For a fuller presentation, see Bailey (1998).
2. There is less clarity in the issue of the relationship between physical activity and intellectual development. Certainly, it is unlikely that the 'healthy body and healthy mind' philosophy of Victorian public schools may be overstating the effects. Nevertheless, a number of studies have drawn a correlation between regular physical activity and academic performance (cf. Shephard *et al*. 1984).
3. Major risk factors include the following: lack of regular physical activity; regular smoking; excessive body fat; high blood pressure (Malina and Bouchard 1991; Armstrong and Welsman 1997).
4. The negative correlation between physical activity and television viewing can be extended to encompass computer games use.
5. This summary is based upon that of HEA (1997) and Armstrong and Welsman (1997).
6. These findings are taken and adapted from a range of sources, including Harris and Elbourn 1997; Sharp 1991, Armstrong and Welsman 1993, and Bar-Or 1987. However, the implications drawn are not necessarily those of these authors.

Issues:

1. Desirable Outcomes' refers to children moving 'confidently and imaginatively with increasing control and co-ordination and an awareness of space and others' (SCAA 1996); what should be the role of adults in this situation? Is there a risk of adult intervention in children's play becoming simply interference?

2. What can be done about the minority of children who do seem reluctant to participate in organised games and physical activities?

3. If regular physical activity is so important for young children's growth and development, is there a case for including Physical Education within the core curriculum at Key Stage 1?

References

Activity and Health Research (1992) *Allied Dunbar National Fitness Survey.* London: Sports Council/Health Education Authority.

American College of Sports Medicine (1990) 'Position Stand on the recommended quantity and quality of exercise for developing and maintaining cardiorespiratory and muscular fitness in healthy adults'. *Medicine and Science in Sport and Exercise.* 22, pp. 265–74.

American College of Sports Medicine (1995) *Guidelines for Exercise Testing and Prescription.* Baltimore: Williams and Wilkins.

Armstrong, N. (1990) 'Children's Physical Activity Patterns: The Implications for Physical Education', in *New Directions in Physical Education (Volume I).* Illinois: Human Kinetics.

Armstrong, N. and Biddle S. (1992) 'Health-Related Physical Activity in the National Curriculum', in N. Armstrong (ed.) *New Directions in Physical Education (Volume 2).* Illinois: Human Kinetics.

Armstrong, N. and Bray S. (1991) 'Physical activity patterns defined by heart rate monitoring'. *Archives of Disease in Childhood.* 66, pp. 245–47.

Armstrong, N. and Welsman J. (1997) *Young People and Physical Activity.* Oxford: Oxford University Press.

Bailey, R. C., Olson, J., Pepper, S. L., Porszasz, J., Barstow, T. T and Cooper, D. M. (1995) The level and tempo of children's physical activities: an observational study'. *Medicine and Science in Sports and Exercise.* 27, pp. 1033–41.

Bailey, R. P. (1998) 'Play and Problem-solving in a New Light'. *International Journal of Early Years Education.* 6 (3) pp. 265–75.

Bar-Or O. (1987) 'Importance of Differences between Children and Adults for Exercise Testing and Exercise Prescription', in J. S. Skinner (ed.) *Exercise Testing and Exercise Prescription for Special Cases – theoretical basis and clinical application.* Philadelphia: Lea Febiger.

Baranowski, T., Tsong Y., Hooks P., Cieslik C. and Nader P. R. (1987) 'Aerobic physical activity among third and sixth grade children'. *Journal of Developmental and Behavioural Pediatrics.* 8, pp. 203–206.

Barlow, J. J., Cosmides L. and Tooby J. (1992) *The Adapted Mind – evolutionary psychology and the generation of culture.* New York: Oxford University Press.

Biddle, S. and Biddle G. (1989) 'Health-Related Fitness for the Primary School', in A. Williams (ed.) *Issues in Physical Education in the Primary Years.* London: Falmer.

Blair, S. N., Clark, D. G., Cureton, K. J. and Powell, K. E. (1989) 'Exercise and Fitness in Childhood: implications for a lifetime of health', in C. V. Gisolfi and D. R. Lamb (eds.) *Perspectives in Exercise Science and Sports Medicine: youth, exercise and sport (Volume 2)*. Indianapolis: Benchmark.

Boreham, C. A. G., Savage, J. M., Primrose, E. D. Cran, G. W., Mahoney, C. A., Strain, J. J. and Murphy, N. M. (1992) 'Risk factor assessment in schoolchildren: The Northern Ireland 'young hears' project'. *Journal of Sports Sciences*. Conference Communications, p. 565.

Bouchard, C., Shephard R. and Stephens T. (1993) *Physical Activity, Fitness and Health: a consensus statement*. Illinois: Human Kinetics.

Central Statistical Office (1994) *Social Focus on Children*. London: HMSO.

Corbin, C. B. and Pangrazi, R. P. (1992) 'Are American children and youth fit?' *Research Quarterly for Exercise and Sport*. 63(2), pp. 96–106.

Corbin, C. B., Pangrazi, R. P. and Welk, G. J. (1994) 'Towards an understanding of appropriate physical activity levels for youth'. *Physical Activity and Fitness Research Digest Series*. 1(8), pp. 1–8.

Department of Health (1992) *Health of the Nation*. London: HMSO.

Department for National Heritage (1995) *Sport – Raising the Game*. London: HMSO.

Department for Education and Employment (1998) *News*. London: DfEE.

Dishman, R. K. (1986) 'Mental Health', in V. Seefeldt (ed.) *Physical Activity and Well Being*. Retson, VA: AAHPERD.

Duda, J. L. (1994) 'Fostering active living for children and youth: the motivational significance of goal orientations in sport', in H. A. Quinney, L. Gauvin and A. E. Wall (eds.) *Toward Active Living*. Illinois: Human Kinetics.

DuRant, R. H., Baranowski ,T., Johnson, M. and Thompson, W. O. (1994) 'The relationship among television watching, physical activity and body composition of young children. *Pediatrics*. 94, pp. 449–55.

DuRant, R. H., Baranowski, T., Rhodes ,T., Gutin, B., Thompson, W. O., Carroll, R. *et al.* (1993) 'Association among serum lipid and lipoprotein concentrations and physical activity: physical fitness and body composition in young children'. *Journal of Pediatrics*. 123, pp. 185–92.

Durnin, J. V. (1992) 'Physical activity levels past and present', in N. Norgan (ed.) *Physical Activity and Health*. Cambridge: Cambridge University Press.

Fagen, R. (1981) *Animal Play Behaviour*. New York: Oxford University Press.

Fentem, P. H., Bassey, E. J. and Turnbull, N. B. (1988) *The New Case for Exercise*. London: Sports Council/Health Education Authority.

Fox, K. (1996) 'Physical Activity Promotion and the Active School', in N. Armstrong (ed.) *New Directions in Physical Education – Change and Innovation*. London; Cassell.

Freedson, P. S and Evenson S. (1991) 'Familial Aggregation in physical activity'. *Research Quarterly for Exercise and Sport* 62, pp. 384–89.

Gruber, J. J. (1986) 'Physical Activity and Self-esteem development in children: a meta-analysis', in G. A. Stull and H. M. Eckert (eds.) *Effects of Physical Activity on Children*. Illinois: Human Kinetics.

Harris, J. (1994) 'Young People's Perceptions of Health, Fitness and exercise: Imolications for the Teaching of Health Related Exercise'. *Physical Education Review*. 17(2), pp. 143–51.

Harris, J. and Elbourn, J. (1997) *Teaching Health-Related Exercise at Key Stages 1 and 2*. Illinois: Human Kinetics.

Health Education Authority (1997) *Young People and Physical Activity – a literature review*. London: HEA.

Heartbeat Wales (1987) *Exercise for Health*. Cardiff: Heartbeat Wales.

Hillman, M. (1993) 'One false move . . . An overview of the findings and issues they raise', in M. Hillman (ed.) *Children, Transport and the Quality of Life*. London: Policy Studies Institute.

Holman, R. L., McGill, H. C., Strong J. P. and Geer J. C (1958) 'The natural history of atherosclerosis'. *Amercian Journal of Pathology*. 34, pp. 209–35.

Hutt, C. (1979) 'Play in the under-fives – form, development and function'. Unpublished manuscript.

Klesges, R. C., Mallot J. M., Boschee, P. F. and Weber, J. M. (1986) 'The effects of parental influence on children's food intake, physical activity, and relative weight'. *International Journal of Eating Disorders*. 5, pp. 335–46.

Labour Party (1996) *Labour Our Sporting Nation*. London: Labour Party.

McGill, H. C. (1984) 'Persistent problems in the pathogenesis of atherosclerosis'. *Atherosclerosis*. 4, pp. 443–51.

Malina, R. M. and Bouchard, C. (1991) *Growth, Maturation and Physical Activity*. Illinois: Human Kinetics.

Mason, V. (1995) *Young People and Sport in England, 1994*. London: Sports Council.

Moore, L. L., Lombardi, D. A., White, M. J., Campbell, J. L., Oliveria, S. A. and Ellison, R. C. (1991) 'Influence of parents' physical activity levels on activity levels of young children'. *Journal of Paediatrics*. 118, pp. 215–19.

Petichoff, L. (1992) 'Youth sport participation and withdrawal: is it simply a matter of fun?' *Paediatric Exercise Science*. 4(2).

Pinker, S. (1997) *How the Mind Works*. London: Allen Lane/Penguin.

Qualifications and Curriculum Authority (1998) *Maintaining Breadth and Balance at Key Stages 1 and 2*. Unpublished draft.

Rippe, J. M., Weissberg R. P. and Seefeldt V. (1993) 'The purpose of play: a framework for improving childhood health and psychological and physical development'. *Medicine, Exercise, Nutrition and Health*. 2, pp. 225–31.

Robinson, T. N., Hammer, L. D *et al*. (1993) 'Does television viewing increase obesity and reduce physical activity? Cross-sectional and longitudinal analysis among adolescent girls'. *Paediatrics*. 91, pp. 273–80.

Rowlands, T. W. (1990) *Exercise and Children's Health*. Illinois: Human Kinetics.

Rowlands, T. W. (1996) *Developmental Exercise Physiology*. Illinois: Human Kinetics.

Royal College of Physicians (1991) *Medical Aspects of Exercise – benefits and risks*. London: RCP.

Sallis, J. F. (1995)) 'A behavioural perspective on children's physical activity', in L. W. Y. Cheung and Richmond (eds.) *Child Health, Nutrition and Physical Activity*. Illinois: Human Kinetics.

Sallis, J. F. and Hovell, M. F. (1990) 'Determinants of exercise behaviour', in K. B. Pandolf and Holloszy (eds.) *Exercise and Sport Sciences Review (Volume*

18). Baltimore: Williams and Williams.

Sallis, J. G., Patterson, T. L., McKenzie, T. L. and Nader, P. R. (1998) 'Family variables and physical activity in pre-school children'. *Journal of Developmental and Behavioural Paediatrics*. 9, pp. 57–61.

Sallis, J. F. and Patrick, K. (1994) 'Physical activity guidelines for adolescents: a consensus statement'. *Paediatric Exercise Science*. 6, pp. 302–14.

Sharp, C. (1991) 'The Exercise Physiology of Children', in V. Grisogono (ed.) *Children and Sport – fitness, injuries and diet*. London: John Murray.

Shepherd, R. J., Volle, M., Lavallee H., La Barre, R., Jequier, J. C. and Rajic ,M. (1984) 'Required physical activity and academic grades: a controlled study', in J. Ilmarinen and I. Valimaki (eds.) *Children and Sport*. Berlin: Springer.

Sheridan, M. (1977) *From Birth to Five Years: Children's Developmental Progress (7th Edition)*. Windsor: NFER-Nelson.

Sleap, M. and Warburon, P. (1992) 'Physical Activity levels of 5–11 year old children in England determined by continuos observation'. *Research Quarterly for Exercise and Sport*. 63, pp. 238–45.

Sleap, M. and Warburton, P. (1994) 'Physical Activity levels of pre-adolescent children in England'. *British Journal of Physical Education Research Supplement*. 14, pp. 2–6.

Sports Council (1988) *Children's Exercise and Health Fact Sheet*. London: Sports Council.

Sports Council (1993) *Young People and Sport*. London: Sports Council.

Stephens,, T., Jacobs, D. R. and White, C. C. (1985) 'A descriptive epidemiology of leisure-time physical activity'. *Public Health Reports*. 100, pp. 147–58.

Thorpe, R. R. (1996) 'Physical Education: Beyond the curriculum', in N. Armstrong (ed.) *New Directions in Physical Education – Change and Innovation*. London: Cassell.

Tucker, L. A. (1986) 'The relationship of television watching to physical fitness and obesity'. *Adolescence*. 21, pp. 797–806.

Williams, T. M. and Handford, A. G. (1986) 'Television and other leisure activities', in T. M. Williams (ed.) *The Impact of Television: a natural experiment in three communities*. Orlando, Fl.: Academic Press.

Wimbush, E. (1994) 'A moderate approach to promoting physical activity: the evidence and implications'. *Health Education Journal*. 53, pp. 322–36.

5

Early intervention: the education of young children with Developmental Co-ordination Disorder (DCD)

Christopher Robertson

We think that the purpose of the child is to grow up because it does grow up. But its purpose is to play, to enjoy itself, to be a child.
(Alexander Herzen, *From the Other Shore*)

This chapter examines the educational needs of young children who experience motor difficulties (Developmental Co-ordination Disorder, or DCD) of a kind not associated with a specific or well documented neurological disorder such as cerebral palsy. Considering the needs of such children is intrinsically problematic because of this lack of specificity, and also because such a disability can be easily misunderstood or stay 'concealed' from professional educators who do not have an appropriate background knowledge.

Failure to understand such motor difficulties in young children, to provide them with no support, or inappropriate support, has long term consequences that are significantly disadvantaging across all areas of learning and social activity. These consequences may also prevent an individual from participating fully as an adult in society. Yet we know a great deal about such motor problems and can, through good quality intervention, minimise their effects.

Good quality support and provision for young children with DCD ought to be in place and be underpinned by a good working knowledge of the following themes:

- understanding developmental co-ordination disorder (DCD)
- the effects of DCD
- meeting needs: identification, assessment and intervention

- enhancing the skills of educators
- DCD and new understandings of disability.

Through a discussion of these themes, I hope that the value of early intervention will be seen as unequivocal. At the same time, I would want to caution against 'medicalising' (Oliver 1990) the needs of young children with DCD, or any other kind of special educational need for that matter. Very young children experiencing difficulties in motor development and their families are especially vulnerable to clinical understandings and constructions of disability presented to them by some professionals. To counter such perspectives on disability it is important to keep in mind that children have an intrinsic need to be *included* with their friends and peers, particularly in educational settings. It is also important, taking heed of the quotation by Alexander Herzen at the head of this chapter, that any support and intervention that children may need should be considered secondary to their higher order need to *be children*, who do childish things – have fun, play and learn. Intervention and specialist help, with the best of intentions, can all too easily override such a priori rights of childhood.

Understanding developmental co-ordination disorder

The term developmental co-ordination disorder (DCD) has gained fairly wide acceptance in recent years amongst professional groups working with children who experience motor difficulties. The term is used by *some* educational and clinical psychologists, physiotherapists, occupational therapists, speech and language therapists, and by medical practitioners such as paediatricians. At the same time, the term is perhaps less well known to many teachers, other educators and parents. The term refers to children with a range of motor difficulties that are heterogeneous (Meek and Sugden 1997), and it has had to compete with a range of other descriptors such as:

- clumsy child syndrome (or the 'clumsy child/clumsiness')
- disorder of attention, motor and perception (DAMP)
- dyspraxia, or developmental dyspraxia
- minimal cerebral dysfunction
- minimal brain damage
- perceptual motor dysfunction
- specific developmental disorder of motor function

- numerous other descriptors are also commonly used that impli-
cate, to varying degrees, language and communication difficulties.

Clearly, any parent, teacher, nursery nurse or learning support assistant running into a barrage of such terms and their associated 'symptoms' is likely to become confused at best, and shell-shocked at worst.
Some of the terms used are problematic because of their all encom-
passing approach, whilst others (e.g. 'clumsy child') convey negative
and imprecise meanings. It is not difficult to see how such terms can
create stigma and be disabling (Corbett 1996).

What does the term DCD describe? The following diagnostic features (DSM-IV 1994) devised by the influential American Psychiatric
Association are helpfully succinct:

> The essential feature of Developmental Co-ordination Disorder is a
> marked impairment in the developmental of motor co-ordination
> (Criterion A). The diagnosis is made only if this impairment signifi-
> cantly interferes with academic achievement or activities of daily liv-
> ing (Criterion B). The diagnosis is made if the co-ordination difficulties
> are not due to a general medical condition (e.g. cerebral palsy, hemi-
> plegia, or muscular dystrophy) and the criteria are not met for
> Pervasive Developmental Disorder (Criterion C). If Mental Retardation
> is present, the motor difficulties are in excess of those usually associ-
> ated with it (Criterion D). The manifestations of this disorder vary with
> age and development. For example, younger children may display
> clumsiness and delays in achieving developmental motor milestones
> (e.g. walking crawling, sitting, tying shoelaces, buttoning shirts, zip-
> ping pants). Older children may display difficulties with the motor
> aspects of assembling puzzles, building models, playing ball, and
> printing or handwriting.

> (American Psychiatric Association, DSM-IV 1994, pp. 53–54)

Of course, this American definition also uses a language that some
UK readers may find alarming ('retardation'!), but it does point to the
essentially motoric nature of DCD. The definition is prudently non-
speculative about the causes of DCD, as are leading educational
researchers in the UK (Henderson and Sugden 1992). However,
research developments in other fields have pointed to possible cau-
sation that is associated with inefficient neural pathway functioning
(Edelman 1989) and a range of factors to do with the pre-natal, peri-
natal and post-natal care of infants. Sugden and Wright perhaps cap-
ture the current state of our knowledge of DCD, noting:

There is no observable direct cause of DCD which occasionally runs in families. It may be we are simply dealing in the lower end of a normal continuum of motor skill rather than some discrete syndrome.

(Sugden and Wright 1996, p. 115)

The prevalence of DCD 'has been estimated to be as high as 6% for children in the age range of 5–11 years' (DSM-IV), whilst other estimates vary from 2–15 per cent, reflecting differences in research methods and definitions used. More boys than girls are identified as having DCD (3:1 ratio), and as Sugden and Wright suggest, sometimes it may run in families with perhaps a brother and sister being affected, or a father and son. From an educational professional's perspective the important implication is that perhaps every pre-school group and every school class is likely to include at least one child with DCD and possibly more. Or put another way, an infant school and linked nursery provision with a 'pupil roll' of 250 could easily include 15 children with DCD.

Effects of developmental co-ordination disorder

In considering the effects of DCD, it is important to examine those that are directly child focused. It is also vital to consider effects that are relational, involving parents and professional educators. Only through some understanding of the ecology of relationships and their social and educational contexts (Bronfenbrenner 1979) can we realise, or 'map', the impact of DCD and plan approaches to genuinely helpful identification, assessment and intervention.

Children

The primary effects of DCD are physical, and its associated consequences are inevitably going to impinge on other areas of development. Though one might consider these consequences to be secondary to those directly deriving from motor difficulties, it is more helpful to see them as enmeshed or 'in continuous interaction with each other' (Sugden and Henderson 1994, p. 2). The kinds of difficulties that are apparent, even in children under the age of 7, tend to be both educational and behavioural. This is well illustrated in a study of young 'dyspraxic' children undertaken by Portwood (1997), who noted that 82 per cent (sample size = 400+) of the group showed the following *signs* of difficulties between the ages of 1 and 3:

- avoidance of constructional toys (jigsaws and Lego)
- unco-ordinated, cannot hop, jump or play with a ball appro-
'priately
- high levels of excitability
- behavioural problems evident
- inability to judge heights and distances so child constantly falls
or bumps into objects
- has difficulty understanding concepts like 'in front' or 'behind'.

(Portwood 1997, p. 18)

This study used interviews with parents to ascertain possible patterns
of difficulty in children, and interestingly it also revealed a range of
problems that they identified in the first year of life, as well as those
outlined above, that were present at time of possible entry to nursery
education. It also showed that by the time children reached the age
of 5, difficulties had become greater, and clearly limited access to the
curriculum. These difficulties included: poor gross and fine motor co-
ordination, difficulties with balance, poor perceptual skills, poor
understanding of appropriate mathematical concepts, poor attention
span and short-term auditory memory, poor social skills, and particular problems with dressing.

Within a short span of time children with DCD or those with dyspraxia, to use Portwood's terminology (and here I am not suggesting
that the terms are synonymous, but 'overlapping'), begin to fall
behind their peers in a number of ways and are likely to enter a spiral of failure (Ripley *et al.* 1997) unless they are given good quality
help. This pattern failure might be characterised by three features:

1. The child finding an activity difficult – *is not motivated to do it*
2. The child tries to avoid the activity – *does not attend, does something
else, misbehaves, seeks attention*
3. The child does not practise the activity – *and therefore finds it even
harder to do it on other occasions*

(adapted from Ripley *et al.* 1997, p. 69)

This vicious cycle will certainly cause a child with DCD to fall further behind her or his peers academically; particularly when the primary school curriculum is so dominated by written work (Alexander
1992), and its premise that children have well developed specific fine-
motor skills. Academic difficulties also bring about problems of social

and emotional kinds. As Sugden and Henderson (1994) point out, learning is as affective as it is cognitive; key aspects of affective learning are: confidence, courage, motivation, optimism, response to failure and self-esteem. These aspects can be in either positive or negative interplay with learning activity, and when they are predominantly negative the spiral of failure can be quite rapid and have long-term effects.

These long term effects have been noted by Losse *et al.* (1991), Henderson *et al.* (1991) and Cermak (1985), and include significant underachievement, emotional and behavioural difficulties, poor attendance and low self-esteem. These difficulties stay with children until they leave compulsory schooling and therefore can affect educational and employment opportunities thereafter. With this in mind the importance of early intervention is vital. This is a point well made by Meek and Sugden (1997) in a study of attitude formation amongst three groups of children (age 7, 11, and 14). They show that in the primary school years children with DCD remain positive about their education, and physical education in particular. By the age of 14, however, DCD children's attitudes have become increasingly negative, making successful learning difficult and perhaps increasing the probability of their becoming disaffected.

In summary, young children with DCD are likely to lack movement skills that the majority of their peers gain automatically. This delay in development is characterised by movement that is poorly integrated, and even when skills are present children 'will have difficulty using them flexibly and automatically' as Sugden and Henderson (1994, p. 2) point out. Without appropriate intervention, the long term educational prospects for children with DCD are not good:

> *clumsy children* can be scolded by teachers, scorned by peers and be a disappointment to parents, so that secondary or social problems develop, or avoidance tactics such as playing the class fool are brought into play. *Clumsy children* are therefore very deserving of our attention.
>
> (Jowsey 1992, p. 24. My italics – for 'clumsy' read DCD)

Without wishing to stereotype the responses that DCD children receive from their peers, families or educators, it is clear that such relationships do have an impact on their progress. It is therefore worth commenting further on parental and educators perspectives on DCD (peer perspectives are important too, but space does not allow a consideration of these).

Parents

It is all too easy for professionals to make inappropriate or spurious assumptions about parents of young children with DCD. For example, a response to parents expressing concern about their child might be:

- he is always stuck indoors
- she is never taken to the park
- his mother babies him – does everything for him
- he had no pre-school experience
- she was never played with as a baby.

(Ripley *et al.* 1997, p. 9)

Such simplistic assumptions are obviously unhelpful, as Ripley notes, and they can also be damaging. Just as there are no two DCD children who are exactly alike, there are no two parents who hold precisely the same views of their DCD child. One of the only things we might purposefully assume about such parents is that they have a knowledge of living with a DCD child that is far more detailed and intense than that a professional will have, though they might not articulate this in 'professional discourse'. It may also be the case that parents of DCD children have always known that 'something was wrong' (Portwood 1996; also, the Dyspraxia Foundation information and website – see the end of this chapter). Difficulties parents encounter in this regard are likely to be due to unsympathetic and sometimes ignorant professionals rather than because they are simply going through a process of adjustment or bereavement.

Parents of DCD children may well want to know what is the matter with their daughter or son, and they may welcome a diagnosis or labelling which explains the precise nature of difficulties. This does not necessarily imply that they are 'searching for a cure', but rather that they are seeking good quality educational and therapeutic provision and support. If at times this 'seeking' is seen as unrealistic or inappropriate by professionals, it should be remembered that many parents have regularly encountered professional opinions which have not properly acknowledged their concerns, or have been simply wrong.

Perhaps because DCD has seemed hard to define in the past, or because it does not present overt difficulties to the untrained eye (Sugden and Keogh 1991) parents may have had to work in difficult circumstances with some, if not all, professionals. Educators working with the parents of young DCD children need to be aware of this and strive for non-paternalistic partnership relationships (Blamires *et al.*

1997) that recognise the strength and value of parent knowledge (Dale 1996).

Educators

In classrooms and other learning settings for children in the early years, teachers and other educators are having to face increasingly complex organisational and pedagogical demands. These demands are also being faced in a climate of incessant flux and change (Fullan 1993). The problems presented by these many demands are particularly pronounced in the area of physical education for children with special educational needs (Doll-Tepper *et al.* 1991), and it is probable that children with DCD do not have some of their priority educational and physical needs met by those designated to work with them (see David and Nurse's chapter in *Teaching Children*). Having said this, it is also the case that many educators of children in the early years do not have any significant knowledge of DCD, and therefore their skills in identification, assessment and intervention are limited. Sometimes they may be able to access 'expertise' through working with a psychologist, but it needs to be remembered that:

> Clinical and educational psychologists are experts in child development. However, their knowledge and experience rarely tends to focus upon movement and the development of motor co-ordination.
> (Ripley *et al.* 1997, p. 14)

In other words, appropriate support may not always be on hand for educators to make use of. Occupational therapists, physiotherapists and speech and language therapists tend to have a better professional training background in DCD but are not always able to provide adequate advice and intervention in educational settings. This difficulty of co-ordinating multidisciplinary early years provision was clearly identified in a report *Interdisciplinary Support for Young Children with Special Educational Needs* (HMI 1991). Nearly a decade later a Government Green Paper *Excellence for All Children: Meeting Special Educational Needs* (DfEE 1997b) indicates that there is still a shortfall in provision and the co-ordination of it is still a major problem. Training and service development needs will be discussed later in this chapter: the point to be made here is that educators themselves are not always well enough equipped to meet the needs of DCD children in early years settings, nor are they always well enough supported by other professional services (though there are notably exceptions to this general pattern).

Meeting needs: identification, assessment and intervention

The processes of identification, assessment and intervention should be interwoven. Only where this is established practice will children benefit and avoid experiencing difficulties that pervade their whole educational experience. The physical and academic benefits of early intervention are well established (Henderson and Sugden 1992), but it is also important to remember that:

> Children identified at an early stage do not suffer the trauma of social isolation and rejection from their peer group.
>
> (Portwood 1997, p. 20)

Identification and assessment

> Without a detailed assessment, an intervention programme cannot be geared to the needs of the individual child.
>
> (Sugden and Henderson 1994, p. 2)

Initial identification of a young child with DCD is often made through informal observation and a consideration of general concern about progress in the area of motor skill development. It may be that concern is expressed by an educational professional, but a parent is just as likely to be worried about their child's apparent difficulties.

Following an expression of initial concern the task of the educator is to gain more information about possible difficulties, perhaps by keeping a diary of a child's activities and difficulties over a week or two. This evidence can be linked to discussions with other co-workers and professionals, and the views of parents.

If initial concern suggests that a child does appear to have a motor difficulty and associated learning or behaviour problems, 'rummaging' around further to get a clearer picture of difficulties is needed (Wedell 1995). Though this continued observation aims to find out more about a child's problems, it should also endeavour to identify strengths that can contribute to a positive learning experience too. Structuring observations may be helpful and save time in identifying specific difficulties associated with DCD. Ripley and colleagues (1997, pp. 91–92) have developed a useful *aide memoire* (observation framework) which can help educators to note motor organisational problems, and Sugden and Henderson (1994) have devised an excellent movement skills checklist. Both of these schedules are easy to use and could be incorporated into routine classroom practice.

If initial observations provide an indication that a child does have poorly developed motor skills that are affecting educational progress then a more formal assessment may be required. Here, it is important for educators to move beyond the use of rather general baseline-assessment tools being developed for the under-fives (QCA 1998), and the rather crude summative measures of educational outcomes (SCAA 1996) for children entering compulsory education. Instead, working within a more individually focused assessment framework, the *Code of Practice on the Identification and Assessment of Special Educational Needs* (DFE 1994), will be more appropriate. Such individually focused assessment needs to be of the high quality *formative type* and take account of a child's range of needs:

> Emphasis on a narrowly cognitive view of learning, particularly when deployed in the context of assumptions of pre-determined and fixed intelligence, can lead to a pessimistic approach towards children who are failing, and to neglect of what might be the real cause of their problems, and, therefore, of their real needs.
>
> (Black 1996, p. 54)

Of course, national expectations and norms of development and progress matter, but they need to be seen as secondary to meeting individual needs effectively. The *Movement ABC Test* – part of the *ABC Assessment Battery* (Henderson and Sugden 1992) – provides a formal measurement of a child's motor performance and has been standardised against population norms. It therefore has a clear value in relation to the individual assessment of children with DCD *and* it provides comparative evidence of performance, thus enabling educators to target 'learning gaps' appropriately.

The *ABC Assessment Battery* might be a relevant 'tool' to use when a child is seen as warranting particular and formal specialist support such as a Statement of Special Educational Needs (e.g. Stage 5 of the *Code of Practice*), or expert help within the context of an Individual Education Plan (e.g. Stage 3 of the *Code of Practice*). If more formal assessment of this type is recommended, then it is also likely that multi-disciplinary input will be needed. It was noted earlier that multi-disciplinary practice is not as well developed as it should be in this country, but the benefits of it have been well documented. For example, Starr and Lacey (1996) have stressed the value of joint assessment in early years provision and suggested that:

> Although teamwork may appear to be time-consuming, joint action can prevent overlap and the duplication of expensive assessment arrangements, thus providing good value for money.

Furthermore:

> The needs of children with complex disabilities cannot be met by one person alone and a multi-professional group working collaboratively can ensure the effective use of the resources available.
>
> (Starr and Lacey, p. 60)

The benefits of such collaboration are not only to do with 'costs'. They are also linked to the pooling of expertise in the field of early child development and DCD, and this is of course, what parents value most. Finally, good collaborative assessment avoids the pitfalls of unidimensional approaches which tend to focus only on one area of difficulty, to the detriment of the 'whole' child.

Intervention

> Without a well formulated intervention programme, a detailed assessment is of only limited value.
>
> (Sugden and Henderson 1994, p. 2)

A strong feature of Henderson and Sugden's *Movement Assessment Battery* is the way in which it connects identification and assessment directly to teaching and evaluation. At the level of intervention it is grounded in principles that stress the importance of planning and considering stages of learning that children go through. These principles are similar to those identified as important by Haring *et al.* (1978) and Wedell (1995). My own summary of these principles, and their application to the needs of young children with DCD is as follows:

1. Educators need to *understand* the nature of a child's motor difficulties and to plan learning activities containing tasks that enable these difficulties to be addressed;

2. Educators need to recognise that DCD children will *acquire* appropriate skills if they are taught them. At this stage teaching methods might include: demonstrating, modelling and physical prompting, preferably in ordinary learning contexts. The aim here is for the establishment of *accuracy* in movement. Some children with DCD might also need to 'unlearn' certain responses they make, and here sensitive teaching will be required to avoid discouraging her or him;

3. Once a child with DCD can accurately produce desired movements the emphasis should be on using these more *fluently*. This means that a skill needs to be mastered (automated), and this is achieved through practise. Again, practising is best done in ordinary learn-

ing contexts, and perhaps supported in the home setting – especially during holiday periods when learning can be forgotten! Fluency also has a cognitive dimension, and being able undertake a movement quickly, to 'remember it'. To facilitate this, surprise and spontaneous practise can be helpful;

4. Once the learning of motor skills has been maintained over a period of time, *generalising* the use of these is important. This may involve encouraging the DCD child to use skills in a range of contexts and settings (e.g. classroom, playground, park or at home). It will also involve the use of different teaching and learning materials. It is only at this stage of learning that the child will be able to use skills *flexibly* and to *problem-solve* in the face of new challenges.

Obviously, there is not always a clear delineation between these stages of learning, but the important thing is for educators to always bear in mind that notion that learning is progressive and not simply at one level. If this idea can be internalised, and become part of a teacher's mindset, used in conjunction with DCD formal tools of assessment and intervention, then young children with motor difficulties will be helped to make good progress.

Good intervention for DCD children does require knowledge and expertise of a specialist kind that is more substantial than the 'general good practice' guidance of the kind that proliferates in education (e.g. the British Association of Advisers and Lecturers in Physical Education SEN guidance 1996). However, this is not of the kind that I would see as 'high specialism', associated more with working in clinical and experimental contexts. Rather, it is knowledge and expertise layered onto good quality pedagogy of a generic kind. Bloom (1985) has argued that ordinary teachers can be much better at helping children than specialist ones, especially with regard to initial learning – pointing out that enthusiasm and making learning fun are more important facets of teaching than those which focus strongly upon techniques and skills. Both Meek and Sugden (1997) and Wall *et al.* (1985) have also pointed out how important the affective aspect of learning is for children, and how important it is to develop their confidence. Whether or not good teaching, which positively addresses children's confidence, can be seen in terms of pedagogic skills which can be learnt, as Kounin (1970) has suggested, is a matter of contentious debate (Barrow 1984). The interesting point to note in the context of this chapter is that the skills of good early years educators are likely to be particularly beneficial in teaching children with DCD.

To summarise, intervention for DCD children in educational settings should be based on an appropriate use of well designed approaches to motor learning. The *ABC Movement Assessment Battery* is one example of such an approach. Madeleine Portwood's (1996) intervention programme used in County Durham is another and, interestingly, shows how much can be achieved by regular, short (20 minutes) planned inputs to children's learning. For such approaches to be most beneficia,l however, they need to be embedded in good early years teaching that is child centred, confidence building, enriching and motivating. The following might be regarded as axioms for intervention, drawing together some of the ideas presented in this section:

- a teacher's, or other educator's, attitude to formal and informal physical education activity is important. A positive and sympathetic attitude to the involvement of a DCD child in such activity will have a major positive impact on that child's approach to participation. This impact will also have positive effects across the spectrum of learning activity;

- breaking the learning of skills into manageable 'chunks' or steps is likely to prove helpful to the DCD child (as long as these are intrinsically meaningful) and to boost confidence;

- a structured approach to the planning of teaching is important. This should involve a recognition that any discrete physical skill is related to stages of learning – *acquisition, fluency and maintenance, generalising* – and that the DCD child will need to progress through these;

- children with DCD should be able to participate in a wide range of physical learning activities. Individual activities well matched to a child's ability are likely to be particularly valuable, but attention also needs to be given to paired and group learning. In these situations the individual will have much to learn from and with other children, and much to share too. However, teaching must be sensitive to the DCD child's possible concern about failing, and appropriate support needs to be put in place. This support should provide a framework for further successful learning, and not be dependency creating;

- if certain tasks and activities are clearly too difficult for a DCD child, these should be replaced with those that have educational equivalence, but are appropriate for the individual. The dictum here is 'remove barriers to learning';

- wherever possible, educators should be trying to identify areas of motor learning where the DCD child finds enjoyment. These areas of learning provide the environment for confidence building and success.

These axioms, and the aforementioned consideration of approaches to intervention have a value for all young children, so their integration into early years educational provision could be seen as a natural one. This need not imply that all learners must do everything together, but as Halliday notes in relation to physical education there:

> must be a balance between enabling pupils to have two sets of opportunities. The first set of opportunities lies in giving access to the [physical education curriculum] the child shares alongside their peers. The second is in maintaining options for inclusion in specialist opportunities just as other pupils with particular needs are given access to non-routine events.
>
> (Halliday 1993, p. 210)

Enhancing the skills of educators

Educators of children with DCD need to have an appropriate training. It may be unrealistic to expect all educators working with a DCD child to be highly trained, but there is good reason to expect that trainee teachers, nursery nurses and learning support assistants should have a working knowledge of DCD and its educational implications. These professionals should have routine and regular access to other professionals who have more highly developed skills in the identification and assessment of children with DCD, and who can help plan intervention that is effective. Various types of schools and other kinds early years provision need to be supported (Lacey and Lomas 1993) by a network of expertise that operates across education and health service boundaries. This has been clearly acknowledged by the Government in its Green Paper *Excellence for All Children* (DfEE 1997b). Building on its commitment to improving early years education generally (the White Paper *Excellence in Schools* 1997a), the Green Paper states:

> An integrated approach by child health professionals, social services and education staff is needed right from the start, making full use of the children's services planning process.
>
> (*Excellence for All Children*, p. 13, para. 6)

Such an integrated approach will only be effective if it incorporates a coherent training perspective. What current and foreseeable *specific* training initiatives could or should benefit educators of DCD children? Here are some examples for consideration:

1. Provision within initial teacher education (ITE) courses needs to be made. An example of how this can be done within the physical education strand of such a course is available from the author (see Note at the end of this chapter). This approach to training provides student teachers with a working knowledge of DCD related identification, assessment and intervention procedures and these can be 'practised' during teaching placements. This approach could also be adapted for use on courses for nursery nurses and learning support assistants.

2. Trainee educational psychologists also need to have specific training in the area of DCD. This training too, should focus on the three facets of identification, assessment and intervention. The Green Paper (p. 68) explicitly states that it anticipates educational psychologists being involved more closely in classroom intervention in the future. If they are to be effective in this role, they will need to increase their knowledge of DCD. Where this does occur, the benefits for educators will be great, because psychologists will also be able to contribute to training close to learning contexts.

3. The Teacher Training Agency (1998), on behalf of the Government, is committed to improving standards throughout the teaching profession, and to enhancing the continuing professional development needs of special educational needs (SEN) specialist teachers. It will in 1999 be outlining new training standards which will relate to a number of specific kinds of SEN, and it seems feasible that, within standards relating to physical disability, the needs of DCD children will be addressed. Any such development is to be welcomed, given that SEN training has either diminished or become very fragmentary in recent years (Special Educational Needs Training Consortium 1996). In inclusive educational settings it may be appropriate for a designated member of staff to take on a specific DCD responsibility. This person need not be (in schools) a special educational needs co-ordinator (SENCO); these teachers are already overburdened with work, so broadening the base of staff expertise would be very valuable.

4. As well as having to address specific DCD related knowledge, skills and understanding, all kinds of training identified here also need to consider issues of multi-disciplinary practice (e.g. joint training initiatives) and collaborative working approaches. In all kinds of early years educational settings today, a variety of staff find themselves working alongside one another to support children with difficulties. The presence of 'more adults' does not however, always benefit children (Thomas 1992, 1998). Professionals need to explore ways of

working effectively with each other, to ensure that children are supported well. Some good training material is available (Balshaw 1991; Fox 1998) but its use is not commonplace or placed within a coherent national framework.

The types of training initiatives discussed so far are relatively formal. With the development of information and communication technology (ICT) however, a new kind of more informal and open learning is 'happening'. Educators are using electronic mail (EMail) to share ideas, seek advice and knowledge (Wedell *et al.* 1997). Through this communication medium too, we are beginning to see professionals and parents engage in discussions – with barriers to partnership becoming 'virtual' rather than real. The worldwide web is also providing many people with access to knowledge of SEN generally, and DCD specifically. For example, at the end of this chapter the website address of the Dyspraxia Foundation (UK) is listed. This site contains a wealth of information about DCD related matters, is accessible to a vast audience and has links to global sources of more information about DCD. The existence of such powerful information in accessible forms is challenging old fashioned notions of who owns so-called 'professional knowledge', with many parents learning about DCD issues before educators do. Of course, not everyone has access to ICT, but its potential in the area of training and knowledge sharing is immense.

Developmental co-ordination disorder and new understanding of disability

To conclude this chapter it is useful to consider the needs of young children with DCD and their families in the wider context of our developing understanding of disability. It is self-evident that services to meet the needs of DCD children need improving and to become available on an equitable basis. Professional educators have a central role in teaching children, but in service development too. These professionals though, have significant training needs that have to date been met in an *ad hoc* and unsatisfactory way. Recent political and educational policy statements made by the Government suggest that there is a commitment and a will to making necessary improvements for DCD children, their parents and the professionals who work with them. We must wait and see if the detail of policy implementation matches the picture painted in 'broad brush strokes' of White and Green Papers.

However, improvements of the kind mentioned here need to be

seen in the light of deep seated understandings of DCD and other disabilities that permeate much professional practice and thinking. Barton (1993) has questioned whether the curriculum that all children are entitled to access in schools is premised on an enabling view of disability. He suggests that important issues still need to be critically engaged with if disabled children and young people are really going to be able to participate in education on an equal basis with their able bodied peers. In relation to physical education in particular, he suggests that the following factors need to be considered carefully:

- that physical education is the creation of and for able-bodied people;
- it gives priority to certain types of human movement;
- individual success is viewed as a means of personal status and financial well-being. It is depicted as a way to the 'good life'.
- A whole consumer industry has been generated around such activities. Sport has become a commodity to be sold in the market-place.

(Barton 1993, p. 49)

One may wish to challenge some aspects of Barton's analysis, but the central message that it signals is important:

> The motivation to participate is encouraged through the articulations of idealized notions of 'normality'.

(ibid., p. 49)

The fact that education operates a 'normalising' gaze over its participants exerts significant pressure on children with DCD and their families. Whilst it is vital (and the central theme of this chapter) that young children with DCD are helped to overcome their difficulties and to fulfil their potential, they should not *in any way* be made to feel that they must conform to a normative view of what it is to be a child. Unfortunately, just this kind of normative perspective has dominated education and health service practice for many years and conveyed, overtly and subliminally, messages about the imperative of *curative* and *therapeutic* intervention (Oliver 1996, pp. 95–109).

A positive way forward in thinking about these issues, and the needs of children with SEN, including those with DCD is to conceptualise needs in a new way. Norwich (1996) suggested the following typology:

individual needs – arising form characteristics different from all others

exceptional needs – arising from characteristics shared by some, e.g. DCD, visual impairment, high musical ability

common needs – arising from characteristics shared by all

(adapted from Norwich 1996, p. 103)

Though this typology does not contain a political dimension of the kind Barton's concerns address, it provides a helpful way of conceptualising new ways of thinking about children's needs and providing for these in an inclusive educational climate. It acknowledges for example, that a DCD child will warrant specific support (a need shared with other DCD children), will have unique needs as a young person (individual) and needs that are the same as her or his peers (common needs). If we can begin to view needs in this way, we implicitly take account of difference and value it, yet recognise specialist help to be the imperative that has been argued for in this chapter.

Note

Christopher Robertson, with Richard Bailey, has developed a course which addresses DCD and related motor difficulties within a physical education course. This course enhances knowledge of the National Curriculum and focuses particularly upon Gymnastics, Games and Dance. Further details are available from the author at: The Faculty of Education, Canterbury Christ Church University College.

Issues

1. Think of a child you have observed whom you suspect has developmental co-ordination disorder. On reflection, what were the child's i) individual needs; ii) exceptional needs; iii) common needs? How were the different needs addressed?

2. At 10 months old, Ben's mum began to feel a little worried about his development. He did not seem to have progressed anywhere near as quickly as his older sister. During his years in nursery school, Ben's difficulties became more apparent – he found balancing hard and often bumped into other children. He also did not find it easy to play with either large or small toys. A physiotherapist attended each week and ran an 'exercise session' involving Ben, a lively, talkative little boy and his friends. She also gave advice to staff and to Ben's parents.

Both the staff and Ben's parents were advised to encourage him to 'slow down' and to 'think through' his actions, but also to positively encourage him. Compile a list of activities that would be fun for Ben *and* help him to make progress in the development of his motor skills.

References

Alexander, R. (1992) *Policy and Practice in Primary Education*. London: Routledge.

Balshaw, M. (1991) *Help in the Classroom*. London: David Fulton.

Barrow, R. (1984) *Giving Teaching Back to Teachers: A Critical Introduction to Curriculum Theory*. Brighton. Wheatsheaf Books.

Barton, L. (1993) 'Disability, empowerment and physical education', in Evans, J. (ed.) *Equality, Education and Physical Education*. London: Falmer Press.

Black, P. (1996) 'Formative assessment and the improvement of learning', *British Journal of Special Education*, 23, 2, 51–56.

Blamires, M., Robertson, C. And Blamires, J. (1997) *Parent–Teacher Partnership: Practical Approaches to Meet Special Educational Needs*. London: David Fulton.

Bloom, B. (1985) *Developing Talent in Young People*. New York: Ballantine Books.

British Association of Advisers and Lecturers in Physical Education (1996) *Physical Education for Pupils with Special Educational Needs in Mainstream Education*. BAALPE, Dudley: Dudley LEA Publications.

Bronfenbrenner, U. (1979) *The Ecology of Human Development: Experiments by Nature and Design*. Cambridge MA: Harvard University Press.

Cermak, S. (1985) 'Developmental dyspraxia', in Roy, R. (ed.) *Neuropsychological Studies of Apraxia and Related Disorders*. Amsterdam: North Holland.

Corbett, J. (1996) *Bad-Mouthing: The Language of Special Needs*. London: Falmer Press.

Dale, N. (1996) *Working with Families of Children with Special Educational Needs: Partnership and Practice*. London: Routledge.

Department for Education (1994) *Code of Practice on the Identification and Assessment of Special Educational Needs*. London: Department for Education.

Department for Education and Employment (1997a) *Excellence in Schools* (White Paper). London: The Stationery Office Ltd.

Department for Education and Employment (1997b) *Excellence for all Children: Meeting Special Educational Needs* (Green Paper). London: The Stationery Office Ltd.

Doll-Tepper, G., von Selzam, H. and Linnert C. (1991) Teach the Teachers – Including Individuals with Disabilities in Physical Education. Presentation at the AIESEP World Congress, Atlanta, Georgia.

DSM-IV (1994) *Diagnostic and Statistical Manual of Mental Disorders* (fourth edition) Washington DC: American Psychiatric Association.

Edelman, G. (1989) *Neural Darwinism: The Theory of Neuronal Group Selection.* Oxford: Oxford University Press.

Fox, G. (1998) *Handbook for Learning Support Assistants: Working in Partnership with Teachers.* London: David Fulton.

Fullan, M. (1993) *Change Forces: Probing the Depths of Educational Reform.* London: Falmer Press.

Halliday, P. (1993) 'Physical education within special educational provision – equality and entitlement', in Evans, J. (ed.) *Equality, Education and Physical Education.* London: Falmer Press.

Haring, N., Lovitt, C., Eaton, M. and Hansen, C. (1978) *The Fourth R: Research in the Classroom.* Columbus, OH: Charles Merrill.

Henderson, S., Knight, E., Losse, A. and Jongmans, M. (1991) 'The clumsy child – are we doing enough?', *British Journal of Physical Education Research Supplement*, 9, 2–7.

Henderson, S. And Sugden, D. (1992) *Movement Assessment Battery for Children.* Sidcup, Kent: The Psychological Corporation.

Herzen, A. (1956) *From the Other Shore*, tr. M. Budberg. London: Weidenfeld and Nicolson.

Her Majesty's Inspectorate (1991) *Interdisciplinary Support for Young Children with Special Educational Needs.* London: DES.

Jowsey, S. (1992) *Can I Play Too? Education for Physically Disabled Children in Mainstream School.* London: David Fulton.

Kounin, J. (1970) *Discipline and Group Management in Classrooms.* New York: Holt, Rinehart and Winston.

Lacey, P. And Lomas, J. (1993) *Support Services and the Curriculum: A Practical Guide to Collaboration.* London: David Fulton.

Losse, A., Henderson, S., Elliman, D., Hall, D., Knight, E. and Jongmans, M. (1991) 'Clumsiness in children – do they grow out of it? A 10-year follow up study', *Developmental Medicine and Child Neurology*, 33, 55–68.

Meek, G. And Sugden, D. (1997) 'Attitude formation towards physical activity in children with Development Co-ordination Disorder', *European Journal of Special Needs Education*, 12, 2, 157–70.

Norwich, B. (1996) 'Special needs education or education for all: connective specialisation and ideological impurity', *British Journal of Special Education*, 23, 3, 100–104.

Oliver, M. (1990) *The Politics of Disablement.* Basingstoke: Macmillan Press.

Oliver, M. (1996) *Understanding Disability: From Theory to Practice.* Basingstoke: Macmillan Press.

Portwood, M. (1996) *Developmental Dyspraxia: A Practical Manual for Parents and Professionals.* Durham: Durham County Council.

Portwood, M. (1997) 'Step by step', *Special Children*, 104, 18–20.

Qualifications and Curriculum Authority (1998) *The Baseline Assessment Information Pack: Preparation for Statutory Baseline Assessment.* London: QCA Publications.

Ripley, K., Daines, B. and Barrett, J. (1997) *Dyspraxia: A Guide for Teachers and Parents.* London: David Fulton.

School Curriculum and Assessment Authority (1996) *Nursery Education Desirable Outcomes for Children's Learning on Entering Compulsory Education*. London: DFEE/SCAA.

Special Educational Needs Training Consortium (1996) *Professional Development to Meet Special Educational Needs: Report to the Department for Education and Employment*, SENTC, Flash Ley Resource Centre: Staffordshire County Council.

Starr, A. and Lacey, P. (1996) 'Multidisciplinary assessment: a case study', *British Journal of Special Education*, 23, 2, 57–61.

Sugden, D. and Keogh, J. (1991) *Problems in Movement Skill Development*. Columbia: University of South Carolina.

Sugden, D. and Henderson, S. (1994) 'Help with movement', *Special Children*, 75, 13, 1–8.

Sugden, D. and Wright, H. (1996) 'Curricular entitlement and implementation for all children', in Armstrong, N. (ed.) *New Directions in Physical Education: Change and Innovation*. London: Cassell.

Teacher Training Agency (1998) *National Standards for Qualified Teacher Status, Subject Leaders, Special Educational Needs Co-ordinators, Headteachers*. London: TTA.

Thomas, G. (1992) *Effective Classroom Teamwork: Support or Intrusion*. London: Routledge.

Thomas, G., Walker, D. and Webb, J. (1998) *The Making of the Inclusive School*. London: Routledge.

Wall, A., McClements, J., Bouffard, M., Findlay, H. and Taylor, M. (1985) 'A knowledge-based approach to motor development: implications for the physically awkward', *Adapted Physical Activity Quarterly*, 2, 21–42.

Wedell, K. (1995) *Putting the Code of Practice into Practice: Meeting Special Educational Needs in the School and Classroom*. London: Institute of Education, University of London.

Wedell, K., Stevens, C., Waller, T. and Matheson, L. (1997) 'SENCOs sharing questions and solutions: How to make a more convenient phone call', *British Journal of special Education*, 24, 4, 167–70.

Further information and useful resources for parents and professionals

Books

The following two books contain valuable practical advice and are accessible to a range of readers:

Portwood, M. (1996) *Developmental Dyspraxia: A Practical Manual for Parents and Professionals*. Durham: Durham County Council.

Ripley, K., Daines, B. and Barrett, J. (1997) *Dyspraxia: A Guide for Teachers and Parents*. London: David Fulton.

The next text is an excellent generic guide to working with young children who have special educational needs, including those with DCD. A recommended read for professional working in early years provision:

Dare, A. and O'Donovan, M. (1997) *Good Practice in Caring for Young Children with Special Educational Needs*. Cheltenham: Stanley Thornes.

Formal assessment

The following assessment pack is recommended for professionals carrying out formal assessments of children with DCD. It also contains excellent advice about effective intervention and provides examples of teaching activities:

Henderson, S. and Sugden, D. (1992) *Movement Assessment Battery for Children*. Sidcup, Kent: The Psychological Corporation.

Advice, information and support

The Dyspraxia Foundation provides an excellent service for parents and professionals on all matter pertaining to DCD. The foundation can be contacted at:

Dyspraxia Foundation
8 West Alley
Hitchin
Herts SG5 1EG
Tel: 01462 454986

The foundation also operates an excellent website:

http://www.emmbrook.demon.co.uk/dysprax/homepage.htm

The site contains a wealth of helpful information, including some that is accessible to children. It also includes links to other websites concerned with dyspraxia and DCD across the world.

Educators wanting to access information concerning special educational needs discussion groups can find out about a range of developments by contacting the National Council for Educational Technology (NCET). Its WWW information site is:

http://www.ncet.org.uk/senco

Getting help with motor skills

Physiotherapists and occupational therapists can offer specific advice on developing motor skills in young children with DCD. Such children may also benefit from swimming and 'fun' motor learning activities, using structured methods. The following organisations can provide advice, training and details of local activity groups:

Halliwick Association of Swimming Therapy
(Training and Publications)
42 Goodhew Close
Yapton
West Sussex BN18 OJA

Two excellent books on the Halliwick swimming method are:

Association of Swimming Therapy (1981) *Swimming for the Disabled.* Wakefield: EP Publishing.

Reid Campion, M. (1985) *Hydrotherapy in Paediatrics.* London: William Heinemann Medical Books Limited.

For a 'fun approach' to motor learning contact:

Tumble Tots (UK)
Blue Bird Park
Bromsgrove Road, Hunnington
Halesowen, West Midlands
B62 OTT

The Tumble Tots organisation has a national network of activity groups for children under 7. These groups are run by trained staff and they aim, through structured activities, to develop motor skills in young children, including those with motor difficulties.

Both the Halliwick and Tumble Tots approaches are beneficial to *all* young children and can therefore be seen as educationally and socially inclusive.

6

Pressure, stress and children's behaviour at school

John Cornwall

Do we put up with too much stress and pressure as part of our everyday lives, in schools, at home and in the adult world of work? Is stress a necessary part of our lives and, if so, how much is necessary? Why is stress generally regarded as an adult thing? Is it, and should it, be a part of children's lives? What effect does stress in schools and classrooms have on children's learning and future achievements? Where is the dividing line between acceptable challenge and overwhelming pressure? Is academic attainment a true indicator of future success or happiness? What effect does academic pressure have on children's long term health? Going to school can be enlightening or damaging for children and young people and there are whole batteries of questions associated with stress, pressure, children's health, development and learning. This chapter explores some aspects of stress and its management in learning environments, such as nurseries, schools and colleges. It cannot answer all of the many difficult questions but examines some ideas that might promote a more human and humane approach to schooling, teaching and learning.

The physical and mental consequences of overwhelming pressure or stress are well documented (e.g. Gray 1987; Stroh 1971; Smith and Cooper 1996; Cartwright and Cooper 1997; Fontana 1989). The negative effects of stress (Yerkes-Dodson Law – see Figure 6.1) on exam performance (Yerkes 1921), on teaching effectiveness (Dunham 1983), on working performance (Cartwright and Cooper 1997) or sporting achievement (Hardy 1988; Bakker *et al.* 1990) are also well known. The athlete who has 'peaked' in performance or the professional who has 'burnt out' are becoming common parlance. Research and discourse over the past seventy years clearly indicates the important effects of anxiety, stress and pressure on attention, learning, psychological health, academic performance and self-actualisation (e.g. Yerkes 1921;

Maslow 1968; Stroh 1971; Gray 1987). There are clear relationships between stress and motivation (Maslow 1954) and between stress and significant life events and lifestyles (Fontana 1989; Bailey 1994). Similarly, the role of attribution and locus of control in coping with success and failure links with life events. For example, the degree to which a child or young person blames or congratulates themselves for failures or successes will have a great impact on their learning (Rotter 1954; Lawrence 1987) and potential for achievement. They will also be affected by a range of cognitive factors (see later) and possibly subject to learned helplessness (Seligman 1975; Bandura 1989) through demoralising experiences. A child's self-esteem and self concept (Lawrence 1987; Fontana 1989) are also involved in positive or negative responses to stress. It is now also accepted that stress affects the activity of our immune systems. Short term stress can downgrade or upgrade our immune system activity but chronic or intense stress can impair the immune system and its functioning (Evans *et al.* 1997), causing both short and long term health problems. As well as a physical 'emergency reaction', causing biochemical changes in the body, there are long term biological changes brought forth by prolonged stress (Gray 1987). These are what can cause significant short and long term health problems.

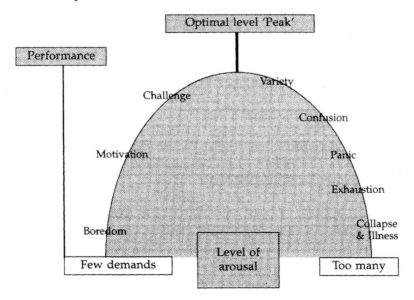

Figure 6.1. An illustration of the Yerkes-Dodson Law.

Great skill is needed to set up realistic challenges for the child but ones that don't become stressful and counter productive. Teacher's expectations (e.g. Rosenthal and Jacobson's classic research 1968) and an individual's personal response to rewards and punishments or to those who inflict them will affect the balance of stress or stimulation. Teacher's decisions and realistic or informed appraisal of a situation are absolutely crucial. Over arousal, through excessive stimulation or challenge, can lead to stress and stress induced behaviour as well as to a significant decrease in performance (see Figure 6.1). These are complex and sensitive areas that are not considered in the current debate about 'standards' or in the current rush to make the teacher a mechanical deliverer of curriculum. It is possible that the 'politicisation' of education is responsible for the increasing stresses upon pupils. Only sometimes is this made worse by individuals' behaviour in classrooms or by classroom practices.

Previous work on stress, childhood and behaviour

Hitherto most of the work on stress, with some notable exceptions (e.g. Leach 1992; Varma 1977; Wolff 1981), relates to adult stress. There has been a fair degree of research and valuable discussion about teacher stress that clearly links their stress to both their working conditions on a grand scale (Dunham 1983; Cole and Walker 1989; Mills 1995) and personal disposition or personality types. Children share these working conditions and also have specific and additional pressures of their own to contend with. There is good reason for continuing to examine the causes and consequences of stress as a result of the school environment. Disaffection and disruption may have much to do with a negative reaction to the 'structural functionalist' view of pupils as being trained and selected to fit their 'place' in society (Meighan 1981). Working with pupils defined as having emotional and behavioural difficulties, like other special educational needs, is a complex and interactive process. In education, particularly with respect to pupils with emotional and behavioural difficulties, thinking has moved away from the assumption that problems are associated within an individual and more recognition has been given to the effects of the social environment upon the learning, attitudes and behaviour (Bandura 1977). This change of thinking emphasises the value for teachers of establishing a conceptual framework in which to consider different explanations for emotional and behavioural difficulties (Smith and Cooper 1996). The construct of 'stress' may provide such a framework, or at least part of one, not just for pupils with special needs, but for all pupils.

There is still an assumption abroad that stress is an adult 'thing' and does not really apply to children. After all, what have they got to be stressed about? What responsibilities do they carry? Their decisions are less important because they are young. Their fears and anxieties are not as potent as adult fears and anxieties because we can protect them from 'reality'. They are part of a cultural myth of happy, endless childhood, reinforced by stereotypes of children in TV adverts and superficial literature or media presentation.

> It is also important to recognise that our perceptions of childhood undergo constant change and are in many ways ambivalent and contradictory. For many adults, childhood is imbued with a rather romanticised notion of innocence – a period free from responsibility or conflict and dominated by fantasy, play and opportunity. Yet for many children of all cultures and classes the dominating feature of childhood is powerlessness and lack of control over what happens to them.
>
> (Lansdown 1994)

Childhood is far from 'the carefree time for loving, laughing and learning' (Leach 1992). It is certainly not like that for most children all of the time. If we reflect back to childhood, all of us have probably experienced extreme pressures and stress, albeit short term in most cases. For a significant number of children, stress has become a way of life or else a permanent feature of their lives that could limit their capacity for growth and learning. Some children will have constitutional difficulties that can turn the normal pressures of school life into extremely stressful situations. Other children are the victims of conditions brought about by adults through their inability to cope with their own lives, to moderate their own behaviour or to understand a child's viewpoint. These assumptions about model childhood are very much linked with a readiness to dismiss young people's behaviour as 'naughty' or 'bad'. These behaviours could be regarded as symptoms of stress (see Figure 6.2) and as a normal, emotional or even rational response to impossible circumstances.

Our world is changing rapidly and one of the tensions for pupils and teachers resides in an outdated view of education and teaching in a rapidly changing world. These tensions affect a large proportion of pupils in the education system, not just those with 'special' difficulties defined in medico-educational terms. Figure 6.2 illustrates some of the causes, including constitutional disorders that could result in stress and its accompanying emotional and behavioural difficulties. It would be foolish to ignore the weight of research evidence that links stress and academic performance, health risks or

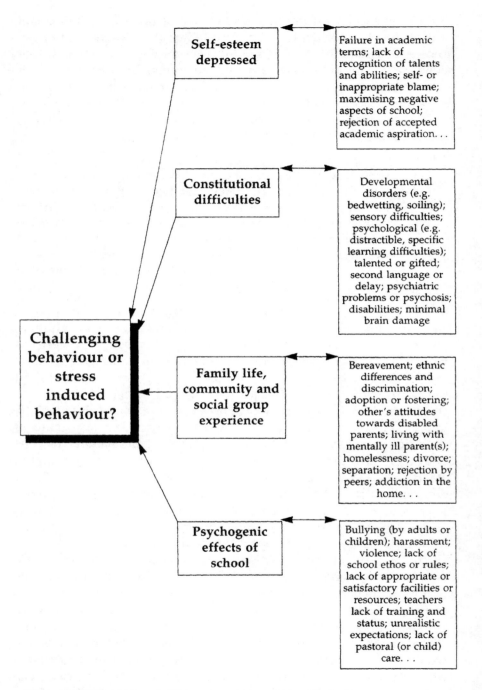

Figure 6.2. Illustrating possible sources of stress induced behaviour.

challenging behaviour in schools. Understanding the factors and issues of stress in children can help us to support a child's full development whilst at school and understand some of the behaviour that is labelled 'naughty', 'uncooperative', 'dysfunctional' or 'bad'.

Conscious reactions to excessive pressure are intended to maintain self-esteem and stability of personality in the face of insane and unreasonable demands. Unconscious reactions to stress and unrealisable demands are more complex, involving sensory, motor or visceral responses or even the whole immune system. They can have far reaching consequences leading to ill health and even death. What are the characteristics of the education system that affect the health and well-being of children? Hard line attitudes involving too much reliance on discipline and behavioural management are beginning to re-emerge. Fixed rewards and sanctions (although hopefully more rewards than sanctions!) do not deal with the causes of challenging behaviour. There is an obvious link between stress and its emergence in challenging behaviour. There are also many children who are quietly suffering and trying to succeed in a school system that does not acknowledge individual or emotional needs. The psychogenic effect of schools (McGuiness 1994) is a nettle that remains to be fully grasped (see Figure 6.2).

Political drums, personal battles.

Is the rise in the number of school exclusions (Parsons 1996) since the inception of the 1988 Education Act just a coincidence? The ethos of a school can make learning and school life an enjoyable and celebrated experience or make it full of nasty surprises and a constant battle to escape disapproval. For some children, school is an adventure; for other children school is a nightmare. In the current hard political education milieu, curriculum content and measures of school effectiveness are narrowing with consequent squeezing out of a broader, more liberal view of education (Raven 1997; Kelly 1990; Lindsay 1997). It is becoming increasingly difficult to preserve a humane view of children's learning, or to practise teaching methods, that recognise the inherent uniqueness of each child and the way they make sense of the world around them. Teachers are under pressure to produce results and drive up so-called standards in large classes, overcrowded rooms, noisy and often stressful working environments. Schools that have formerly been concerned with the wider outcomes of education are now concentrating exclusively on exam performance (Raven 1997). The effect of this is to deny pupils who possess any of the wide

variety of hugely important talents which do not show up on traditional examinations, and more recent standardised tests, the opportunity to develop or to get recognition for these talents.

> What we are witnessing is a world-wide reinforcement of a move
> towards widespread acceptance (of the kind most desired by fascists)
> of the right of others to dictate what one will do and what one will
> learn, of the right of others to issue demeaning and degrading orders
> and expect compliance, and of the right of authority to test one, assess
> one's 'integrity' according to their standards, and allocate one's life
> chances on the basis of criteria they have established.
>
> (Raven 1997, p. 4)

Each of us will respond to challenges and difficulties in our lives in
distinct ways and with varying degrees of emotional involvement.
One person's stimulation or pressure is another person's stress and
anxiety.

> Psychological stress is a relationship between the environment and the
> person.
>
> (Lazarus and Folkman 1984)

Stress can be short or long term and can challenge an individual beyond
their own perceived capacity to deal with life circumstances. An individual begins to feel overwhelmed and unable to control events around
them or are increasingly driven by them. A person can also put themselves under stress through their own demands or expectations of themselves. These expectations are usually a result of a number of factors
including conditioning and upbringing in youth and early years. These
drives and expectations may have started in trying to please teachers
in the nursery, and later in school. A child may well be very sensitive
to the expectations of others but have little ability to assert their own
needs and exert control over their circumstances. How do they protect
themselves from overwhelming pressure to succeed?

Although some children experience permanent stresses due to constitutional disorders or emotional difficulties it can be argued that
adult sensitivity to stress is important in all aspects of schooling and
for all pupils.

> Indeed it can be argued that stress is most likely to be evident during
> periods of most rapid change. And since childhood is the period dur-
> ing which we develop most rapidly, then a strong case can be made
> for stress being especially prevalent in children.
>
> (Varma 1973)

Behavioural difficulties, conduct disorders and **challenging behaviour** are apparently on the increase in our schools. Are these obvious and apparent symptoms of stress? Could it be that education provision is just not equipped to deal with the rapid changes taking place in our society as a whole and little to do with a collapse of moral standards? This places children under greater and greater stress over a period of years as the gap between what they need and what they get in schools becomes wider and wider. Could it also be that our expectations of both behaviour and academic standards in school have changed immeasurably over the past thirty years or so? Is the gap between what pupils can attain and what is expected of them widening to the extent that a significant proportion of pupils are voting with their feet and pulling out? Or, is the gap between the kind of behaviour and free expression that young people see around them on TV, in films, in their communities and the conformity that is expected in schools irreconcilable in young minds? Another possibility has to do with the ethos of schooling. Schools have been very hierarchical and authoritarian structures since the 1800s. Are they changing? Is education itself in a state of flux and about to re-define itself? If so, there will be stress on teachers and pupils that have to do with the way the system is changing.

Recognition of stress in children and young people

An individual's defence or coping mechanisms are intended to maintain the stability or integrity of the personality. If these defence or coping mechanisms are counter-productive they can end in creating further problems. Hence the medical consequences. Medical models require considerable interpretation and extension to make them useful in educational and social terms. In this instance, I hope that the reader will make the links between behaviour described as 'challenging' and yet emanating from a child or young person's stress and coping responses.

- **Repression** occurs when a child puts experiences that cannot be dealt with away into the unconscious mind in such a way as to become inaccessible to further conscious thinking. This can be shock reaction to traumatic and stressful events or it can be simple lapses of memory.
- **Regression** can occur when a child is under stress and reverts to behaviour reminiscent of an earlier stage of development (e.g. bedwetting or thumb sucking).

- **Denial** allows the individual to falsify or change experience to reduce emotional discomfort (e.g. stealing and vigorously denying it). Often, the more forceful the reality proffered, the more vigorous become the denials.

- **Displacement** allows an individual to shift anxieties or negative, perhaps aggressive, feelings from one person to another. For example, instead of expressing the feelings to brother or father, a child may 'take it out' on a class mate.

- In some cases, pent up stress and anxiety can take the form of **reaction formation** where, simply put, unwelcome feelings or anxieties are turned into their opposite (e.g. over attention, solicitude, being too 'goody goody').

- **Projection** is different from displacement in that, instead of simply 'taking out their feelings' on somebody else, a person will go further and actually perceive the other person as being hostile, aggressive or indifferent. One's own unacceptable impulses are attributed to someone else, hence escalation in aggressive situations where each is attributing the hostility to the other!

There are various ways in which children and adults may choose an escape route when under stress. Escape routes can be useful but can also be counter-productive in many situations. Children and adults can experience **isolation of feelings** where they become detached from their own everyday experiences but remain attached to other's actions or experiences. A child may mess himself or hit another child but be revolted or angry when another child does the same thing. **Flight into fantasy, ritualistic behaviour** and **intellectualisation** or **rationalisation** can all become defence mechanisms to ward off anxiety and repress unwelcome feelings. We must be careful here because there is a thin dividing line between taking the path of unhelpful defence mechanism and what is called **sublimation** (Wolff 1992) where a child or young person allows full creative use of the primitive impulses induced by stress and turns them into positive social action. This often leads to diminution of guilt and is rewarded, raising self-esteem and confidence. It is easy to see how the two pathways are very near each other but can have totally different effects on an individual. One child or young person's sublimation can become another's nightmare and desperation. It has been shown that unqualified positive regard from teachers and adults, where children are concerned goes a long way to enhancing self-esteem and reducing stress (Charlton and Hunt 1993).

Assessing whether a child or young person is under stress is not a simple matter and requires observation and objectivity as well as considerable insight, empathy and intuition. There are no set patterns of behaviour that can be classified purely as stress. Nor are there obvious or easily identified sources of stress. Sometimes, the apparently obvious may be misleading, such as a child living in relative poverty. There may well be stresses but these may be offset by a loving and caring family or parent or sibling. Sometimes a child who appears to be extremely talented may be exerting sustained stress upon themselves by having taken on board other people's expectations too much. Each child or young person will respond differently to stress. We may be looking for extreme changes in life circumstances or sudden changes involving uncharacteristic behaviour. It is likely that a child who has been under stress for a prolonged period of time will have developed various defence mechanisms. Many of these may well be identified as unacceptable behaviour in the school or classroom. It is helpful to identify the behaviour and then look beyond into some of the underlying causes of that behaviour.

Cognitive effects

- attention and concentration decrease. Powers of observation diminish;
- distractibility increases and the thread of what is said or happening is lost;
- memory span reduces and even familiar material cannot be recalled;
- response speed decreases and pupil may try to make up for this by guessing or making snap decisions;
- error rate increases. For example, when a child has a specific learning difficulty – they will tire more easily and errors will increase;
- powers of organisation and planning deteriorate – conditions or requirements cannot be accurately assessed or positive moves planned;
- reality testing becomes less efficient and critical powers reduced. Child can become more detached from what is happening and become irrational (even if only temporary).

Emotional effects

- Physical and psychological tensions increase – muscles become tense, simple movements can become difficult, teeth clench, emotional outbursts may increase and so on . . . ;

- can manifest in physical pains or maladies (e.g. headache, tummy ache, existing aches are magnified . . .) through inhibited emotions;
- some personality changes can occur (easy going child may become irritable, caring child indifferent . . .) and existing personality traits can become amplified (e.g. over-sensitive, over anxious . . .);
- a child may sink into depression and apathy. Feeling that nothing matters and there is nothing worth doing. They are powerless to influence anything in their surroundings. These are generalised negative thoughts and deactivated emotions;
- self-esteem lowers as feelings of worthlessness and incompetence increase.

General behavioural effects

- Speech problems may appear or increase (e.g. stuttering, stammering or hesitancy);
- interest and enthusiasms (i.e. personal enthusiasms) may decrease or disappear in a general feeling of inability to affect anything positively;
- absenteeism and avoidance increases (e.g. more often finding ways of avoiding tasks or activities);
- energy levels may be low or fluctuate rapidly;
- sleep patterns may be disrupted and disturbed;
- general feeling that nobody likes me or cares about what I do;
- excessive tendency to blame (outwardly others – or inwardly self);
- unpredictability or uncharacteristic behaviour may develop through out of control emotions.

(Constructed by the author with extracts from Wolff 1989, Gray 1987, Fontana 1989 and Evison 1988)

Children are in the early stages of development of their language and their ability to express themselves verbally. Establishing friendships is also something of a hit and miss process until children have learned a fair degree of tolerance and begun to be able to visualise from another's viewpoint. We can apply this knowledge to, for example, a counsellor's viewpoint about the characteristics of people who are likely to be under stress.

Over stressed people '... tend to be the persons who find that they cannot state ... that they are unhappy with particular issues and therefore tend to be the persons who internalise their resentment about their physical environment, their workload.'

People '... who have not developed friendship or other systems ... to express difficulties ... receive help'.

(Ridgeway 1988)

A humane response to stress?

In the same way that the symptoms of stress can be divided into cognitive, emotional and general (including physical), so we could do this with stress management strategies. Some of these, children might do naturally or for themselves, or with some encouragement. Some may need to be demonstrated and learned in order to generate stress management type behaviour. An effective and affective social skills programme will contain many of these elements.

Cognitive methods

- active recognition and description of negative emotions and moods whenever they occur (helping the child to describe their feelings – not internalise them);
- verbal feedback about the pupil's own (perhaps rigid) responses and blocks to questions, to other pupils or to tasks. Helping children to reframe and redefine their experiences;
- noting small successes in work or in other activities. Sometimes actively finding these;
- recognise, describe and encourage pupil to recognise their own natural methods of diffusing or disrupting stressful situations (e.g. telling a joke, laughing. giggling, changing the subject, asking for help ...);
- helping pupil to recognise when their own attention or concentration is reducing through stress or pressure. Encourage and allow them to switch attention (most children do this naturally enough!) briefly and productively;
- take care about 'loading on' pressure in academic situations. It can very quickly become counterproductive. A relaxed mind will work better;
- children need skills to help them plan in both the

short and the long term. When under stress, it is helpful to be able to plan the next step or to see what the longer term results might be;

Emotional strategies

- celebrating mastery experiences. Encouraging and working from strengths is a good technique for building up a child's personal resource kit to apply to the next difficult or challenging situation;
- positive attention switching means helping a child or young person to switch their attention. Feelings tend to follow the focus of attention – think of something pleasant and feelings will often follow;
- interrupting 'out of control' feelings (aggression, panic) and giving support. Showing how to get support when these feelings begin to emerge;
- supportive relationships minimise and mitigate stress whether they are natural or specifically set up;
- good relationships between teachers, parents or carers can reduce a child's anxieties and stress.

General behavioural or physical strategies

- natural physical movements interrupt and disrupt stressful situations – yawning, stretching limbs and body, shaking hands or feet, laughing . . . ;
- inhibited feelings leading to anger and hatred need 'safety' to let go outside of normal situations. Children often do this in soft play areas, ball pools or bouncy castles;
- children (particularly very young children) derive great security from predictable routines – regular events that cannot be anticipated will heighten stress levels.

(Adapted and extended from material by Fontana 1994, Evison 1988 and Leach 1992)

Considering stress as one way of looking at the behaviour of children and young people brings forward the importance of relationships in their widest sense and including home and the community. Teaching and learning is not just about curriculum content but about the process of acquiring and using knowledge, skills and understanding.

Successful teaching is not just about measuring attainment against arbitrary and pseudo-developmental standards but about establishing a relationship between the teacher, the learner and his or her environment. As is often the case, discussion is long on the causes and assessing these but shorter on remedies. Many of the remedies lie in the hands of those that have power in the education system. Teachers have power over pupils in the classroom but there are many more people who wield power to change the system outside the classroom. Politicians, education managers (including Headteachers), education research and the purveyors of good practice (e.g. Ofsted Inspectors, school consultants) have great power over the quality of pupils' lives. The current political educational milieu can be stress producing. For example:

- an over emphasis on 'didactic' teaching methods where there is potential for a 'power through knowledge' relationship;

- emphasis on pure content without the skills and the possibility of using or generalising this knowledge content effectively outside school;

- a surfeit of fairly arbitrary and demanding external 'standards';

- a general lack of understanding about, or unwillingness to accept, the 'affective' nature of learning;

- limiting and ageing physical environments, overcrowded and noisy classrooms;

- too much content squeezed into too little time;

- little consideration for the 'interactive' nature of learning and effective teaching;

- insufficient appreciation of the impact of social mores in the classroom and insufficient means to change schools to respond to broader changes in society.

Children and young people who express their stress reactions in outward and 'challenging' ways are those most likely to get away from the stress in the short term but whose lives may be socially damaged in the long term, for instance, by being excluded. Those who cannot express the effects of stress through outward behaviour may not be such a problem in the short term but may end up suffering from illnesses, both physical and mental, in the longer term. A child or young person may well succeed academically but questions have to be asked. What is the cost of academic success and conformity to a very competitive system? At what point should teachers modify the pressures exerted by the education system on children and young people in order to preserve their health and well-being in the long term? At what point is it worth losing health and well-being for academic attainment and the illusory promise of success later in life?

In the 1980s Mr Justice Coleman said that employers should be not be excluded from responsibility for the risk of psychiatric damage to their employees through the scope of their 'duty of care' (Lazarus and Folkman 1984). At the turn of the century, shouldn't legislators and managers be held responsible, as part of their 'duty of care', for the psychiatric well-being of pupils and students? As well as an overview of the global causes of stress in children at school, there is a need for insight and empathy from professionals because stress is not something that is easily classified with obvious and 'standard' symptoms or responses. It is as unique as the individuals who experience it and it can show itself in many ways.

Competent and inspirational teachers know the infinite variety of personalities, perspectives and circumstances of their pupils and the massive impact of cultural and social influences that pervade the classroom. We still attempt to measure individual needs as deficiencies against fixed, and often discriminatory labels. The concept of stress as something that is imposed upon individuals by the organisation of schooling and the political systems that drive it is not far fetched or radical. If there is anything to be learnt from the literature and research on 'stress' and stress management, it is that it often generates challenging behaviours and disaffection, resulting in exclusion or rejection of schooling and education. On the positive side, proper recognition of the whole learning process as interaction and as a human activity can lead to many benefits. Amongst these benefits are accelerated learning; proper application of emotional intelligence and later adjustment; appreciation of multiple intelligences and individual talent or 'giftedness'; a feeling of valued education in a caring society; a reduction of difficult or challenging behaviour and consequent exclusion or marginalisation. A significant number of these benefits to statutory schooling seem to be eluding us at the moment.

Issues

1. Do we put up with too much stress and pressure as part of our everyday lives, in schools, at home and in the adult world of work? Is stress a necessary part of our lives and, if so, how much is necessary?

2. Why is stress generally regarded as an adult thing? Is it, and should it be, a part of children's lives? What effect does stress in schools and classrooms have on children's learning and future achievements?

3. Where is the dividing line between acceptable challenge and overwhelming pressure? Is academic attainment a true indicator of future success or happiness? What effect does academic pressure have on children's long term health?

Sources and references

Bailey, R. (1994) *LISA: Lifestyle Information and Stress Analysis.* London: Warwick IC Systems. Centre of Advanced Learning.

Bakker, F. C., Whiting, H. T. A. and van der Brug, H. (1990) *Sport Psychology: Concepts and Applications.* London: John Wiley & Sons.

Bandura, A. (1989) Perceived self-efficacy in the exercise of personal agency. *The Psychologist.* Vol. 2, p. 411–24.

Bandura, A. (1977) *Social Learning Theory.* Englewood Cliffs USA: Prentice Hall.

Cartwright, S. and Cooper, C. L. (1997) *Managing Workplace Stress.* London: Sage Publications.

Charlton, T. and Hunt, L. (1993) Towards pupil's self-image enhancement: The EASI teaching programme. *Support for Learning,* No. 8. August.

Cole, M. and Walker, S. (1989) *Teaching and Stress.* Milton Keynes: Open University Press.

Dunham, J. (1983) Occupational Stress. In A. Paisley (ed.) *The Effective Teacher.* London: Ward Lock.

Evans, P., Clow, A. and Hucklebridge, F. (1997) Stress and the immune system. *The Psychologist.* Vol. 10, No. 7, July.

Evison, R. (1988) Effective Stress Management = Management of Inappropriate Negative Emotions. *The Occupational Psychologist.* British Psychological Society. No. 6. December.

Fontana, D. (1989) *Managing Stress.* London: The British Psychological Society and Routledge.

Gray, A. G. (1987) *The psychology of fear and stress* (2nd ed.). Cambridge: Cambridge University Press.

Hardy, L. (1988) The Inverted-U Hypothesis: a catastrophe for sport psychology. Paper presented at the British Psychological Society Annual Conference, Leeds. April.

Kelly, A. V. (1990) *The National Curriculum: A Critical Review.* London: Paul Chapman.

Lansdown, G. (1994) Children's Rights. In B. Mayall (ed.) *Children's Childhoods: Observed and Experienced.* London: Falmer Press.

Lawrence, D. (1987) *Self-Esteem in the Classroom.* London: Paul Chapman.

Lazarus, R. and Folkman, S. (1984) Psychological stress is a relationship between the environment and the person. In *Stress, Appraisal and Coping.* New York: Springer.

Leach, P. (1992) Young Children Under Stress (Section1). *Starting Points 13: Practical Guidance for Early Years Workers.* London: NEYN.

Lindsay, G. (1997) Open Dialogue: Peer Review (of Raven, J.). *BPS Education Section Review.* Vol. 21, No. 2, p. 19.

Maslow, A. H. (1954) *Motivation and Personality* (2nd ed.). New York: Harper and Row.

Maslow, A. H. (1968) *Towards a Psychology of Being.* New York: Van Nostrand

McGuiness, J. (1994) *Teachers, Pupils and Behaviour: A Managerial Approach.*

Meighan, R. (1981) *A Sociology of Educating.* London: Holt, Rhinehart & Winston.

Mills, S. (1995) *Stress Management for the Individual Teacher: Self study modules for teachers and lecturers.* Lancaster: Framework Press Educational Publishers.

Parsons, C. (1996) Permanent Exclusions from School: A Case Where Society is Failing Its Children. *Support for Learning.* 11 Vol. 3, pp. 109–12.

Raven, J. (1997) Education, Educational Research, Ethics and the BPS. The British Psychological Society. *Education Section Review.* Vol. 21, No. 2, p. 3.

Ridgeway, C. (1988) Stress: A counsellor's viewpoint. *The Occupational Psychologist.* British Psychological Society. No. 6, December.

Rosenthal, R. and Jacobson, L. (1968) *Pygmalion in the Classroom: Teacher's Expectations and Pupil's Intellectual Development.* New York: Holt, Rhinehart & Winston.

Rotter, J. B. (1954) *Social Learning and Clinical Psychology.* Englewood Cliffs, NJ: Prentice-Hall.

Seligman, M. E. P. (1975) *Helplessness: On Depression, Development and Death.* San Francisco: W. H. Freeman.

Smith, C. J. and Cooper, P. (1996) Emotional and Behavioural Difficulties: Theory, Practice and School Effectiveness. *Emotional and Behavioural Difficulties.* Vol. 1, No. 1, p. 3, Spring.

Stroh, C. M. (1971) *Vigilance: the Problem of Sustained Attention.* Oxford: Pergamon Press.

Varma, V. P. (ed.) (1973) *Stresses in Children.* London: University of London Press Ltd.

Wolff, S. (1992) *Children Under Stress.* (2nd ed.) Harmondsworth: Penguin Books Ltd.

Yerkes, R. M. (ed.) (1921) Psychological examining in the United States army. *Memoirs of the National Academy of Science,* 15.

7

Co-constructing reality: the child's understanding of the world

Mike Radford

There are two key factors that I wish to explore in this chapter. The first is the essentially social nature of the child's developing understanding of reality and the second is the role of the child as an active and, initially at least, an equal participant in this social process. Although social processes in most descriptions are important to the child's developing understanding of the world, the process of development itself is often seen as subject to conditions that lead us to a relatively individualistic point of view in relation to experience and understanding. Language development, for example, is seen in some descriptions, in terms of an innate language acquisition device, a pre-programme within the individual that enables her to respond to linguistic stimulus in a given way. More generally it might be argued that, despite various critical analyses, cognitive development is still seen as dominated by various stages of growth that are inherent to the psychology of the learner. In this context the learner is seen as reactive to experiences, experiences 'triggering' certain kinds of language activity or to be 'processed' within a particular inner framework that is the internal 'property' of the individual.

I would like to argue that experience is not an individual event but a social one. It is shared in a social context and the development of understanding on the part of the learner is a feature of this socially shared process. Furthermore the individual is an active agent in this sharing process, negotiating and creatively interacting with her social group in the co-construction of a shared view of reality.

In these days of the National Curriculum and the proposal that teachers adopt more directive and instructional techniques in their pedagogy, this analysis might be seen, at least superficially, as out of keeping with the times. The problem is that whatever kind of curriculum and teaching approaches are being required, learning theory has a logic of its own. It will describe how young people learn regardless of the patterns of their schooling. Schooling, it may be argued, has more to do with acculturation and training than with the developing sophistication with which young people come to make sense of their experiences and understand their environment. Within the curriculum there are clearly growth points for the development of such understanding but it is questionable as to how far what is formally learned in school is relevant to the needs of the individual in relation to the reality in which she finds herself. This is not to say that a great deal of useful learning doesn't go on in schools and some schools are very good at creating the right environment for this to happen. Either way, however, one might argue that learning will happen despite the school experience of the learner and that perhaps where the learning environment in school is fertile this is as much due to informal factors as to the curriculum and stated intentions of the teachers.

In order to explore this learning process it may be useful to go back to the basic principle of the nature of experience in relation to the reality that gives rise to it. This relationship is not straightforward and gives rise to confusions which, in her developing understanding, the infant seeks to unravel. Mention was made in the introductory paragraph to the 'individual' orientated theories of language development and stages of developmental growth and I would like to deal with these in more detail.

The chapter consists of three parts, the first dealing with theories that tend to the idea of learning as a process of individual construction, the second with learning as a socially shared process, and the third looking at the relationship between experience and that which is experienced.

Individual construction

There are a number of possible structural bases for the infant child to make sense of experience and reality. The first is that of the possibility of a pre-packaged set of wirings, a 'program' to use the I.T. metaphor, that enables the child to process data in particular ways. This program might, at its simplest, take the form of basic needs and interests of a biological and social nature that pre-dispose the infant to make distinctions in the context of various experiences. There is, however, much evidence and analysis to suggest that this pre-packaging consists of more than this and reaches further into the early stages of experiential processing. The infant, it is claimed, is preprogrammed to participate in particular patterns of social exchange (Trevarthen 1975). These exchanges show, in an embryonic form, the give and take structures that are necessary to the sophisticated collaborations that make both language and social life in general possible. Noam Chomsky (1976) and, more recently, Stephen Pinker (1994) take this position further, arguing that not only are we born with the social disposition to collaborate with others but that we are actually given the linguistic tools, the 'language acquisition device', that enables this collaboration to take on a level of sophistication denied to our socially orientated evolutionary cousins in the animal world. Social engagement and language are thus seen as central factors in the way in which the infant child comes to make sense of the world around her.

In contrast, though in some ways complementary to these views, is the understanding that sees the growth of the infant understanding as an essentially constructive process. Under this view the infant child constructs an internal framework within which experience is organised and reported to others. This view derives from the work of Jean Piaget (1971) and more recently the radical constructivist, Ernst von Glasersfeld (1995). In Piaget's view the developing intelligence is subject to certain principles derived from a biological perspective. Development is seen as a two way process. On the one hand the individual interprets experience in terms of his/her internally constructed framework, what Piaget terms assimilation, and on the other, he/she is continuously making minor alterations to the framework in order to meet those experiences that will simply not fit in: accommodation. The developing understanding of the child proceeds on the basis of a balance between assimilation and accommodation, in other words these two processes exist in equilibrium. At certain stages of intellectual development this equilibrium is upset and the child experiences a radical reconstruction of his/her internally constructed framework, and when this happens the child moves to a new stage of equilibrium. There are three broad stages of equilibrium, the sensori motor, the stage of concrete operations and the stage of formal operations. Overlaying this relatively simply model, Piaget offered two further concepts that characterise the growth of understanding as it proceeds through these stages. The first is that of decentration, the progressively developing ability of the child to realise that her perception of reality is not the only one, and that to achieve a more objective understanding of reality she must learn to align her own perceptions of reality with those reported by others. The second concept is that of reversibility. Piaget sees this process as lying at the basis of all logical thinking, that is the ability to reverse a process 'in one's own mind' as it were. In mathematical terms this is characterised by the ability to realise that having multiplied 6 by 4 and come to 24 we can then divide 24 by 4 and get back to 6 – the operation can be reversed.

Piaget wrote prolifically, following through the implications of basic explanations for the development of human understanding, and offered many incidents of evidence to support his model. Some might argue that Piaget was in reality interpreting or, to use his term, assimilating this experiential data to his model rather than seeking to challenge the model itself. In more recent years his findings have been subject to critical scrutiny (Grieve and Hughes 1990; Donaldson 1986) but the general model is brilliant in its conception and has proved a fertile ground for succeeding developments. One such post-Piagetian development is that of radical constructivism, a leading proponent of which is Ernst von Glasersfeld (op. cit.). Glasersfeld persists with the Piagetan belief that understanding is essentially informed through the process of the construction of interior models of the world which the young learner is constantly testing against experience, a kind of internal scientific procedure of hypothesis and experimentation. The learning process is one of trying to establish successful models, i.e. ones that accord with the realities offered by experience, and successful teaching will take place when the teacher is able to access the learner's models and support her in this process of development. Again we have a process of the social alignment of internal individual models.

Thus we have two broad viewpoints, the first emphasising the innate conditions to human beings that ensure that we are essentially social beings with the facility to use language and the second offering an understanding of the development of human understanding in terms of proactive construction on the part of the individual contained within a context of environmental/experiential limitations and governed broadly by principles that are biological in origin. Both sets of understandings fall into a European tradition of emphasising the origins of understanding in terms of innate or biologically derived conditions.

The tendency in the above accounts, in trying to explain the development of human understanding, is to look at the conditions for what happens rather than try to explain what is happening itself. It may be that we feel that if we have explained the conditions for an event that we have somehow explained the event itself. Furthermore these conditions are seen very much in terms of the development of the individual. The key question that these theories address is, 'what are the conditions pertaining to the individual that enables her to come to share in the experiences and understandings that we, as mature intelligences, see as the appropriate goals of children's development?' Because there is this tendency to see child development as a response to adult understandings, as a way to move towards those understandings, the infant is cast in an essentially reactive role. Thus human understanding is seen as individually constructed within the context of basic biological or cognitive pre-conditions and reactive to the fully formed adult perceptions and understandings towards which it is moving. This is not to say that the child does not actively impose explanations on events within the context of the conditions described. Amusement is often generated by stories of young children generating basic misconceptions as a result of their partial understanding of experience and reality. Among 'child centred' proponents of early education there may even be an element of celebration with respect to the generative capacity of the infant to construct these misconceptions. In the longer term, however, they are seen as errors that characterise the semi-formed stage of individual development.

There is an alternative approach to our attempts to explain the development of human understanding which seeks to examine the intrinsic logic of human constructions both infant and adult. From an analysis of such constructions the view may be derived of learning as a socially shared process. Rather than seeing the individual as making her own constructions and seeking to align them with the constructions of others or of teachers trying to access the constructions of individual learners in order to lead them to more suitable alternatives, learning is to be seen as a process of co-construction. It is a process of trying to establish common understandings in the context of shared experiences. The social learning environment is not the struggle of a group of individuals to make common sense of their own particular ways of experiencing the world, but of seeking to construct a social understanding of one experience in which they are all sharing.

Construction in the social context

Trevarthen (op. cit.) in research with infants of only a few weeks of age, identified a sharing, democratic nature to the early interactions between parent and child. The infant actively seeks out face to face contact with the parent, responding positively to expressions of feeling and engagement in terms of sound and gesture. Silent and impassive faces resulted in distress on the part of the infant. The sounds and gestures of the parent figure, that seem to be a psychological need on the part of the infant, are imitated and in turn she initiates responses to these. There develops a pattern of exchanges that are a delight to both parent and child and that take on the rhythm of later linguistic exchanges. As these exchanges continue, certain patterns may emerge that appear to have some meaning for parent and child, particular sounds and gestures that relate to the daily routines in the experience of the parent and the infant child. Thus we have an embyronic language emerging. The interactional 'vocabulary' and 'syntax' of this 'language' are shared, a 'co' construction based on common experiences and a need for social engagement. It may be necessary to clarify this notion of 'common experiences'. It is certainly not the case that the parent is experiencing the same experiences as the infant but that the experience of hunger or physical discomfort is a common one, an experience that we share. If you say you are hungry, I know what you mean because I too occasionally feel hungry. The feeling of hunger is a common experience identified with various physical states, gestures and expressions. If I had never shared in the experience of hunger (or anything like hunger) there is no way that I could understand the state that you describe, unless that is we could find some common factor in another experience. In associating certain events with particular gestures and sounds the infant child comes to share in the common experience of hunger.

It may be suggested that this model of the social construction of language based on common understandings and needs is distinctive to a particular social, cultural context and that if we observe other cultural groups we may find different patterns of social engagement and learning. While it may be true that the patterns of the parent/child relationship vary across different cultural groups, the principle of the social construction of language and the accompanying structures of understanding, are not. Stephen Pinker (op. cit.) has gathered descriptions from various sources of how different social groups, in some instances very youthful ones, generate their own languages in the context of common experiences and a need to engage in social exchange. Pinker's intention is to make the point that the tendency to develop complex linguistic forms is innate. He gives the example (ibid. p. 33) of a group of children who, at their language learning stage, were only exposed to a pidgin English of simple phrases, instructions, etc., but had, between themselves, developed complicated structures that enabled them to engage in mental operations that were not available had they remained with the simple structures initially given to them. This may be evidence of an innate linguistic constructional device but it is also evidence of social agreements in the context of shared experience, of social construction, since the language is a social event. These young people must, to some extent, have negotiated the vocabulary and syntactical constructions to meet the needs of their common experiences.

Experience and reality

The title of this chapter refers to the construction of reality in the process of the child's developing understanding of the world. The argument so far has been to try to move the perspective that we take on this process away from the individualistic accounts where the child tries to make sense of experience on the basis of various cognitive acquisitiion devices, be they specifically linguistic or otherwise, and then seeks to align her individual constructions with those of others, towards the view that the whole process is a social one right from the start. This argument is based on the view that experiences and the means by which they are articulated are not the property of individuals but rather are social events. There are not many experiences of hunger, but one experience that we all share and identify through various public forms from the personal and intimate communications between parent and infant child through to the sophisticated statements of poets or politicians. We identify the feelings that we have in the context of this public language and we do not know what we are feeling until we have this public language which enables us to organise the experiences to which that language gives articulation.

Supposing I had a quite unique feeling that I labelled 'x', a feeling that nobody else, as far as I could ascertain, had ever experienced. I might keep a diary in which every time I felt 'x' I recorded it. The problem that I would face is how do I know that the feeling I am recording as 'x' now is the same one as I felt earlier? The answer is that without any external point of reference I wouldn't know. The external reference point is the language with which I use to describe it. I might not tell anybody about my feeling and to that extent I might keep it private – however, it is not logically private. It is dependent upon a public frame of reference by which I can identify and locate it within the context of all other experiences. The philosophical credentials for this argument can be found in Wittgenstein writing on the possibility of a (logically) private language (Wittgenstein 1953, paras 243–75), and by Nelson Goodman (1987, ch. 1).

A final point that needs to be made in relation to experience and reality is that of the relationship between that which is experienced and the experience itself. This seems to be a perfectly natural distinction to make and yet it has given rise to a number of confusions, not least in terms of the use of the notion of construction in relation to reality. If there is an object of experience, separate to that experience but giving rise to it, how can my experience or understanding of that object be a construction? The world of objects is not constructed by my experience but exists separate from it. Experience does not construct reality, rather reality gives rise to experience.

It is difficult to know what to say of this 'reality' that is the basis of the child's understanding. All that we know of reality is that it is experienced under certain conditions and the conditions will determine to some extent the understanding that we have of it. The range of colours and sounds that we can identify is bounded by the sensory apparatus with which we are endowed. Other creatures are able to identify sounds and colours that are beyond our perceptual facility, thus the reality that we experience is filtered by the sensory organs that are part of our physical being. Having said that, the child does not construct the range of colours or sounds that she is able to identify (this may lead us into various philosophical and conceptual problems as to whether there is any sound at all if there are no ears to interpret the vibrations that cause us to hear them) although she does have to construct the cognitive framework within which such colours and sounds will be articulated. At the heart of this construction lies the common experience and the social framework within which it is objectified.

It is not necessary to get embroiled in debate regarding the ultimate nature of any 'mind independent' reality that forms the basis for human understanding and objective knowledge. What we can say is that there is a commonality in human experience and that for the purposes of talking of reality we are in effect talking of that common experience. If this is the case then reality consists of far more than any external source, objects in themselves that give rise to experience, but in the reality of experience itself. Experience is not just of objects but of feelings and interpretations. There is no neutral reality but only an experienced one. It is a reality of feelings, perceptions, interpretations and it is objective by virtue of the fact that it is a shared reality in the consciousness of human beings.

Conclusion

The argument in this chapter is an attempt to relocate the point of focus for our understanding of the child's developing understanding of the world away from the idea that each individual is a unique centre of consciousness attempting to make sense of her experiences via a variety of innate dispositions or in reaction to particular events to that of the person as a member of a cognitive community that shares experiences and the means of communicating them. Human consciousness is a complex and organically developing phenomenon in which we all share and of which we all struggle to make sense. An analogy might be made with medical understanding of the organism. A study of the developing physiological system gives us insights into the nature and control of various conditions. A study of how the body reacts to certain events in its early stages of growth is important to our understanding of how it functions later in life. Similarly it might be argued with the development of understanding. In order to understand the reality of consciousness, we look to the way in which human beings share experience within and across ethnic, cultural and gender contexts and also across the range of the lifespan from infancy to old age. It is unfortunate that as teachers we are generally too bound up with the processes of training and acculturation that is the purpose of schooling. We are more concerned with the question of how to get the learner to make the right response, rather than why she made the 'wrong' one. It has been said that in mathematics, for example, learners do not get the answers wrong, but fail to answer the question that is being set. The job of the teacher is to find out the question that they are answering. The problem is that we do not have time to analyse learners' responses in such depth. We seek to impose procedures and conceptualisations in order to meet the requirements of the curriculum and assessments that are in turn imposed upon us.

Children will develop a sophisticated understanding of the reality of their conscious lives and it may be that the schooling environment is as good as any in order for them to accomplish this. It is an intensely social and experientially rich environment and offers the opportunity for a subtext to the range of activities that constitute school life. This subtext consists of the ways in which shared experiences are explored between peers and teachers and how the language and the other communicational forms, the gestures and routines, give articulation to these experiences. Perhaps the final point to make is that if this relocation of the focus that we take on the nature of the child's developing understanding of reality is accepted, then it is a matter of importance that teachers are aware of the real nature of the learning that is going on in the classroom and do not get overly preoccupied with the formal processes of schooling.

Issues

1. How do children 'construct' reality? What are the main constructional principles?
2. Why can't children have their own logically private constructions?
3. Can these constructions be objective and if so how?

References

Chomsky, N. (1976) *Reflections on Language*. London: Temple Smith.

Donaldson, M. (1986) *Children's Minds*. London: Fontana.

Glasersfeld, E. von (1995) *Radical Constructivism: A Way of Knowing and Learning*. London: Falmer.

Grieve, R. and Hughes, M. (1990) *Understanding Children*. Blackwell: Oxford.

Goodman, N. (1988) *Reconceptions in Arts and Philosophy*. London: Routledge.

Lewin, R. (1975) *Child Alive: New Insights into the Development of Young Children*. London: Temple Smith.

Piaget, J. (1971) *Biology and Knowledge*. Edinburgh: Edinburgh University Press.

Pinker, S. (1994) *The Language Instinct*. London: Penguin.

Trevarthen, C. (in Lewin, R. 1975).

Wittgenstein, L. (1953) *Philosophical Investigations*. London: Routledge.

8

Using interpretive procedures

Keith Sharpe

The question then arises whether ... the process of interpretation in which children engage differ from those of adults.
It may be that much of the time they do not differ greatly.
(Margaret Donaldson 1978, p. 69)

Do young children construct 'human sense' in the same way as adults? Donaldson's (1990) groundbreaking work on children's thinking has provided solid evidence to challenge the Piagetian thesis that the child's mode of cognitive functioning is qualitatively different from the adult mode. The perspective on child development she has put forward offers a resolution of the serious theoretical paradox that emerged in the 1960s as both Piaget and Chomsky became widely influential. On the one hand Piaget argued that the child was extremely restricted intellectually even to the point of not being able to imagine what an object would look like seen from the other side, and on the other Chomsky posited the ability of very young children to deduce for themselves the highly complex grammatical rules of the language spoken in the surrounding community. Clearly the same child could not be both so limited and so astonishingly capable simultaneously. Donaldson's synthesis proposed that children have

a capacity for making sense of certain types of situation involving direct and immediate human interaction

(Donaldson 1978, p. 59)

which in their respective ways both Piaget and Chomsky had neglected. By setting some of Piaget's well-known experiments in contexts which made 'human sense' to children it was shown that they could do things he had suggested were impossible for them. In particular young children in more 'subject-friendly' experimental situations did display the ability to 'decentre' and understand how things appear from the viewpoint of others, an ability which is of course crucial in managing scenes of human interaction through which socially shared meanings are constructed. Similarly Chomsky's contention that children have 'a language acquisition device' needs to be understood, Donaldson argues, in relation to children's general ability to interpret patterns of human interaction. Rather than having a specific aptitude for language learning, children learn language because they have this general interpretive competence. The work of Wells (1981, 1987,) has offered further impressive research evidence for the thesis that children are 'meaning makers' from an early age.

How do adults construct 'human sense'?

At the same time as this change was taking place in conceptions of children's thought there were comparable developments occurring in many other branches of social science. From the 1970s onwards social theories emphasising the human capacity to interpret gained wide acceptance. Ingelby (1986) has suggested that taken together these perspectives which include symbolic interactionism, phenomenology, ethnomethodology, analytic philosophy and some forms of marxism and structuralism can be seen as constituting a new paradigm which he calls 'social constructionism'. In specifically advocating the usefulness of this paradigm for the study of education Pollard (1988, p. 3) points out that, although there exist important theoretical, philosophical and methodological differences between these perspectives:

> They all share the conviction that human action is best understood as being meaningful and as a product of social contexts and social interaction.

Over recent decades a large number of research studies produced by sociologists and psychologists working within these perspectives have shed light on the processes of human interaction through which socially constructed meanings are created and negotiated. Crucial in all analysis of human interaction is the role of language in constituting and sustaining social practices. This general view proposes that through language members of society actually 'constitute' social reality, and in particular they construct social identities, relationships between these social identities and systems of socially plausible knowledge and belief (see, for example, Fairclough 1995).

Discourse theorists such as Fairclough concern themselves with how any 'text' (i.e. incident of language use, spoken or written) makes its own small contribution to shaping these social and cultural structures. For the group of analysts who identify themselves as 'ethnomethodologists', however, the central question is how human interaction actually occurs at all. They have attempted to identify the basic underlying social mechanisms which make interaction possible. In the ethnomethodological literature certain 'interpretive procedures' (Cicourel 1975) have been described which, it is argued, make up the interpretive competence possessed by adult members of society and which underpin their ability to engage in meaningful social interaction. The description of these adult interpretive procedures provides a useful framework with which to assess Donaldson's suggestion quoted above, since if it can be shown that children draw on these interpretive procedures in managing their interactions with others this would afford some evidence that child and adult processes of interpretation 'do not differ greatly'.

Ethnomethodological writers do not share a unanimous consensus on terminology nor on the exact number of interpretive procedures (henceforth referred to as I.P.s) at least partly because these are seen as all interrelated. There is agreement, however, on the nature of I.P.s as 'deep structure' procedures which adult members of a society ordinarily rely on but do not normally think about, just as they do not normally analyse their 'deep structure' (grammatical/syntactic) knowledge of language to produce linguistically acceptable utterances. It is through the taken-for-granted use of I.P.s that individuals become and remain recognisably competent members of society who are able to produce and understand socially acceptable behaviour and talk.

The following account of five basic I.P.s has been compiled for the purpose of this research exercise from the work of eight authoritative writers (Cicourel 1975, Douglas 1971, Garfinkel 1967, Heritage 1984, Leiter 1980, Livingstone 1987, Schutz 1966 and Turner 1975). In this chapter these I.P.s are referred to as 1) The reciprocity of perspectives assumption 2) The etcetera procedure 3) The presumption of normal forms 4) The adhocing procedure 5) Documentary interpretation.

What interpretive procedures do adults employ to construct 'human sense'?

The reciprocity of perspectives assumption

This assumption instructs participants in a social setting to take for granted the interchangability of their standpoints. In any scene of interaction between two members of the society A assumes that B perceives the scene in the same way as he does and also assumes that B assumes it also. In addition there is an accompanying assumption that both can 'for all practical purposes' and 'until further notice' disregard any differences in their personal ways of assigning meaning and judging relevance. In short, the competent member assumes that any other member would see the scene as he does, assumes everyone else assumes this also, and assumes that they assume he assumes it.

The etcetera procedure: managing indexical expression

An utterance or behavioural display cannot be understood outside of a context within which it is intelligible and rational. The etcetera procedure enjoins members to 'fill in' an appropriate context from their stock of common-sense knowledge so as to provide for the required intelligibility. It exhorts members to search for a relevant set of 'background expectancies' which will guarantee the sense of what is being said and done. Even where the meaning of events is not immediately obvious members adopt a 'let it pass' stance, firmly trusting that 'all will become clear' eventually. The existence of this crucial I.P. was spectacularly demonstrated in Garfinkel's famous counselling experiment (Garfinkel 1967) where students attributed definite meanings to specifically meaningless counsellor replies that had been randomly decided beforehand. The students used each reply as an index of a larger context of meaning and an intention to construct the sense of it. All linguistic and behavioural expressions are irremediably indexical in this sense. There is, as Garfinkel points out, no such thing as a context-in-general.

The presumption of normal forms

The stock of knowledge members use as a resource in recovering intelligibility in everyday encounters consists of a set of structured typifications (Schutz 1966) which inform them about what things are like. The typifications are presumed to be obvious, normal and natural, they are 'what everyone knows' and 'what everyone knows everyone else knows'. Members presume that the social stock of knowledge will cover all eventualities. Any event, any action, any utterance will always be taken to be an instance of a 'normal' category that is 'known-in-common'. Since all forms are treated as normal forms the member simply has to 'see' the form for what it 'really is', i.e. which typification it is 'really' an instance of. The ordinary member invariably expects that other members will generate recognisable utterances and behaviour in which he will be able to see what they 'had in mind' and so grasp their intentions in the shape of their 'in-order-to' and 'because-of' motives.

The adhocing procedure: managing the fit between instance and category

Recognising that some happening is an instance of a known-in-common category is, however, not a matter of ordinary looking. Particular features are attended to the course of constructing an account which simultaneously glosses and constitutes the phenomenon in such a way that its status as an example of a normal form is rendered 'obvious', or 'visibly-rational-and-reportable'. Whether elaborate written records are being filed in a formal coding system (Garfinkel 1967), or crimes being detected (Sudnow 1965), or school pupils being streamed by ability (Cicourel and Kitsuse 1963), the adhocing procedure is an inescapable practice in societal members' claim to recognise that something is an example of the thing they take it to be.

Documentary interpretation: managing the reflexivity of accounts

While the meaning of utterances or actions depends on the context in which they are perceived and analysed, that same context which supplies this indexical meaning is itself seen for what it is through the very same discrete utterances/actions it is used to interpret. Thus in any interaction participants are continually engaged in 'documentary interpretation', that is, searching for an underlying pattern to provide a contextual base for the interpretation of indexical particulars which once identified in this way can then be treated as 'documenting' the pattern. What has happened and what is happening is therefore forever open to reinterpretation; members have a 'retrospective-prospective' sense of occurrence in which what is or what was 'really going on here all along' can be continually revised. Things, as it were, can neverendingly be 'seen in a different light'. Meaning is never fixed because there is no necessary context for any given act of speech or behaviour. The grasp of meaning is an 'ongoing managed accomplishment' of members perceiving a reflexive interdependence between observed act and presumed context.

Do young children use interpretive procedures in the same way as adults?

A research exercise: four scenes from a nursery

The research exercise described here has attempted to shed some light on the question: do young children in nursery school use these interpretive procedures in the same way as adults to make sense of human situations and engage in orderly social interaction? The nursery class studied formed part of a small urban primary school housed in a Victorian building alongside a main road in a major city in the South of England. The nursery room was large and had been divided into different areas by the teacher, Mrs Peters, using items of furniture to mark boundaries. Two nursery nurses assisted the teacher. Fifteen or so children between the ages of three and five, from mixed but pre-dominantly working class backgrounds, attended the nursery each morning and a different group of fifteen attended in the afternoon. The same programme of activities was undertaken each day by both groups. The children were given considerable choice amongst the activities set up each day, some formal and specifically educational, others more loosely structured, but at some points during the session the children would be called together and treated a whole class, e.g. for listening to a story or singing.

My role as an observer was legitimated by my position as a college tutor liaising with the school for a variety of purposes including the supervision of teaching practice students. This commitment entailed making approximately weekly visits over a three month period. Although generally a non-participant observer in terms of avoiding any kind of organisational responsibility I inevitably became involved in some activities as the children were used to having adult visitors in the room and approached them freely. Cassette tapes were used to record utterances and conversations. Fieldwork notes were kept of non-verbal exchanges and other incidents. The research conclusions were presented to and discussed with both the class teacher and the children as a specific validation technique.

Throughout the research period it was abundantly clear that these very young children are constantly involved in using the five inter-pretive procedures described above to make sense of their experience in the nursery. Even very small scenes of interaction reveal how much 'interpretive work' they are putting in. Sacks (1975) has demonstrated how much meaning inheres in very short utterances. He takes several pages of closely argued text to unravel the full depth of meaning in the single sentence 'The baby cried, the moma picked it up'.

The analysis proposed below of a remark made by a four year old boy suggests that he too is capable of managing all the intricacies of perception and understanding which make an apparently simple utterance sensible, rational and intelligible in a context of human social interaction.

Scene 1

An indignant child is looking at several books scattered in disarray on the floor. He calls out to the teacher:

'Look what they did, Mrs Peters!'

It would be difficult to find a clearer demonstration of the assumption of reciprocal perspectives than this urgent injunction. Implicit in the child's plea is the presumption that if Mrs Peters 'looks' she will 'see' what the child 'sees' and will assign it the same meaning. Additionally, native English speakers would 'hear' (and his tone of voice reinforced this) in this statement what 'they did' is something irregular that stands out as worthy of note since there would be no point in drawing attention to ordinary mundane normal features. In 'noticing' that the display before his eyes is irregular, i.e. not 'normal', this youngster is also evidently drawing on the presumption of normal forms. He is identifying an instance defined as deviant in relation to these forms in the social context of the nursery. He is, in Becker's (1963) terminology, 'blowing the whistle' on others perceived as having infringed rules. His recognition of the infringement is equally a tribute to his ability to manage the adhocing procedure. He has codified the behavioural display he has observed and drawn on 'evidence' of the books lying on the floor to substantiate and give warranty to his claim that rule violation has occurred. The indexicality of the outburst is plainly apparent in the dependence of the utterance for its rational character on an unstated set of background expectancies to do with how children should behave in the nursery, what books are for and how they should normally be treated, who Mrs Peters is and what her role is, and so forth. By the same token the utterance is reflexive because, in the process of being recognised by speaker and hearer for what it is, it simultaneously documents as real the socially defined context of the nursery from which it derives its meaning.

Mrs Peters was preoccupied with other children and over the hubbub of the room did not hear what was said. This precipitated in the speaker a change in his definition of the situation. Faced with no response he abandoned his outrage and quietly replaced the books on the shelf. One perhaps unsurprising difference between adult and infants use of I.P.s is that meanings assigned by children have a much more tentative character. Assumed contextual backgrounds are allowed to evaporate and re-emerge in seemingly kaleidoscopic fashion. The young child has still to learn that adults treat 'reality' as 'fixed' and therefore are extremely loath to alter their recognition of meaningful context. Young children do not have the experience to make firm decisions about ontological certainties and have a much more playful and frivolous approach to defining reality. It is important to stress, however, that even though adults may therefore find infant notions bizarre and exotic they are arrived at through the use of the same basic I.P.s. The following piece of romancing by Sarah illustrates how I.P.s can be used to produce sensible 'nonsense'.

Scene 2

The teacher is reading a story to the children about a boy who took down a star from the sky and befriended it. Part way through Sarah feels inspired to invent her own story on the spot.

Sarah:	I carried a star home once . . . and it was crying.
Teacher:	Did you Sarah? Really? How did you reach it out of the sky?
Sarah:	I climb, I climbed up my ladder.
Teacher:	A ladder? It's a very big ladder? You reached a star of the sky? What did you do with it?
Sarah:	I hided it underneath my bed.
Teacher:	You hid it underneath your bed?
Sarah:	And John took it out.
Teacher:	And John took it out? What did John do with it?
Sarah:	He broke it to pieces.
Teacher:	That wasn't very nice, was it?

Throughout her narrative Sarah was consciously intent on sharing her story with the teacher and her fellow pupils. She took it for granted that they would hear what she was saying as what she intended to say. Nobody mentioned a ladder and it did not figure in the story yet drawing on her knowledge of normal forms and understanding of the indexical question of how the star was reached she gave an explanation that was recognised as natural and reasonable in the circumstances. Again making use of 'what everyone knows', i.e. that a good place to hide precious/embarrassing/unusual/special things is under the bed, she gave an acceptable account of what followed in which clarity of meaning is in no way impeded by the inappropriate use of the regular past tense. She correctly interprets the teacher's interrogative repetition of her statement as a 'request for more', as meaning 'and what happened next?' John is her brother, which was well-known in the nursery, so it was unnecessary to offer further elaboration of his role, and 'of course' everyone knows that brothers are wont to be destructive so that John is easily 'ad hoced' into that familiar category in order to round off the story.

Inherent in the concept of reflexivity is the proposition that accounts do not describe events but actually constitute events as describable occurrences in a world known-in-common. And herein may lie the explanation for the common adult view that young children tend to confuse fantasy and reality. If reality is socially defined and ongoingly negotiated in structured scenes of interaction by members using I.P.s the reality/fantasy distinction is clearly far from self-evident, and indeed something that is itself a feature of that socially defined world. In the history of mankind all manner of fantasmagorical and ethereal entities have been accorded the status of reality in different societies at different times. Children told stories about fairies in one society will be expected to grow up with a serious concern to keep on the right side of them for fear of what they might otherwise do, and in another to treat them as a harmless piece of make-believe. The problem for the young child is that in using interpretative procedures to discover what the world is like by learning what its constituent/descriptive socially defined categories are, he/she has little basis in remembered experience for rejecting the ontological claims of any of them. In short, the entire world coming alive in the infant mind through social interaction is, to use Weber's term, 'enchanted'.

It would seem therefore unreasonable to regard infant fantasising as evidence of an entirely different modus operandi of intellectual and social functioning. It is likely that children use the same interpretative procedures in the same way to the same effect as adults. Their knowledge is quantitatively not qualitatively different. At their own level they can be seen to do what adults do, including knowing that imaginary objects and real objects are different and need to be responded to differently in everyday life.

Scene 3
Sitting in the 'home corner' I am offered a cup of tea. There is no tea in the cup but we 'pretend'. I take a 'sip' and declare that it is not sweet enough. Instantly the cup and saucer are removed and a spoonful of invisible sugar is heaped in and stirred. It returns and I begin to drink. I am now offered a plateful of delicious looking but plastic jam tarts. I reach out and take one. I put it to my mouth. My host is horrified:

'Oh no you mustn't! It's only pretend!'

My actions had been read as signifying the intention to eat this inedible thing. This gave grounds for believing that we no longer 'saw things the same way'. Within the parameters of his own experience and understanding this boy had a firm grasp of the difference between reality and fantasy.

Furthermore, it is clearly a matter of some consequence to these young children that important events in their lives are acknowledged by others as sensible, rational and real, and not dismissed as arbitrary invention, as the following conversation makes clear.

Scene 4

The children are sitting together on the mat with the teacher. Joanne has brought in an unopened Christmas card. The teacher asks whether she is going to open it. Before an answer can be given Wayne calls out:

Wayne:	Everybody gives me a Christmas card.
Teacher:	Everybody gives you . . . ?
Wayne:	My milkman gives me a Christmas card.
Teacher:	Who gave you a Christmas card?
Wayne:	I think, I think my milkman's going to give me Christmas card today . . . 'cos he always says hello to me.
Teacher:	He always says hello to you?
Wayne:	Yeah, my milkman.
Teacher:	Oh, his milkman!
Wayne:	He always says hello to me.
Teacher:	He always says hello to you, does he?
Wayne:	Yeah, he always sees my cat, and while he, like . . . at the door, when I get my milk in . . . the cat likes him.

Wayne relies heavily on his familiarity with normal form typifications and on the adhocing procedure to fit his particular claim to have had experience of 'what everyone knows' into them. Reconstructing the intentions behind his utterances reveals a planful reasoned sequence.

People 'normally' get Christmas cards at this time of year, but he gets an 'unusually' large number. Everybody gives him Christmas cards, even the milkman. At the same time as reference to the milkman substantiates the claim to a surprisingly wide circle of Yuletide generosity around him it also creates a difficulty in being a departure from normal form. He knows he cannot expect his listeners just to 'fill in' unproblematically from the social stock of knowledge as they would be able to do if the donor had for example been a relative who might be expected to behave in this way. Yet it is essential to his account of himself as the worthy recipient of such extensive goodwill that the milkman be 'ad hoced' into the category of believable Christmas card giver. He must provide further particulars which change the context within which his milkman is 'seen' otherwise what he has said is liable to be rejected as false/ridiculous/silly/incomprehensible etc.

The first strategy is the statement that the milkman says 'hello' to him. He thereby implies that there is a special friendliness towards him on the part of the milkman which might betoken the kind of relationship in which Christmas card giving is possible. This, however, does not entirely explain away all the queries listeners might have since it is not obvious why the milkman should always say 'hello' to this boy. Even if it were an ultra friendly milkman who habitually said 'hello' to all and sundry common sense suggests he would be unlikely to dispense Christmas cards on the same basis. What is needed is some exclusive connection, and this comes in the form of the boy's cat liking the man who brings the milk. In the hearer's imagination are conjured up touching homely scenes of smiling boy picking up bottle of milk, furry feline rubbing up against legs and purring, jovial milkman with an avuncular word or two before returning to the milkcart with the empties. All can readily understand that over time a particular warmth might develop which could warrant the card sending. In this way the rationality and plausibility of the account have been deliberately and artfully accomplished by the skilful use of the five I.P.s analysed above.

Conclusions

What the analysis of these four scenes suggests is that children, like all human beings, act rationally within the parameters of their own definition of the situation they believe themselves to be in. In this respect the evidence put forward here would seem to accord with Donaldson's hypothesis that children use the same processes of interpretation as do adults. It implies that children's capacity for understanding is grounded in the same set of interpretive procedures and is therefore not in essence qualitatively different.

The validity of the argument being advanced here depends on the analysis proposed rather than the quantity or representative character of the evidence. The five interpretive procedures taken from the ethnomethodological literature appear to offer a helpful analytic framework with which to examine 'interpretive competence' and the method employed has been to apply this framework to a small number of utterances and exchanges in the social context of a nursery. Whether correct conclusions have been reached about the children's use of interpretative procedures is a function of how effectively the analytic framework has been applied. However, if the analysis is correct in the case of these four small incidents there are nonetheless some broader implications; there was nothing exceptional about these four children, these four events or this nursery. If this is what these children were doing, it is likely that it is what most children are involved in doing most of the time. More research on children's use of these interpretive procedures in other social contexts would help to clarify the question further.

Issues

1. How useful do you consider the concept of 'interpretive procedure' to be? Does it help us to understand the process of 'making human sense'? Do you think there are other 'interpretive procedures' not discussed in this chapter?

2. Is it really true that adults and children use interpretive procedures and make 'human sense' in the same way?

3. What can parents and teachers do to promote the more effective use of interpretive procedures in young children?

References

Becker, H. S. (1963) *Outsiders*. London: Macmillan.

Cicourel, A. V. and Kitsuse, J. (1963) *The Educational Decision Makers*. New York: Bobbs Merrill.

Cicourel, A. V. (1975) *Cognitive Sociology*. Harmondsworth: Penguin.

Coupland, N. and Nussbaum, J. (eds.) (1993) *Discourse and Lifespan Identity*. London: Sage.

Douglas, J. (1971) *Understanding Everyday Life*. London: R.K.P.

Donaldson, M. (1978) *Children's Minds*. London: Croom Helm.

Fairclough, N. (1994) *Critical Discourse Analysis*. London: Longman.

Fairclough, N. (1995) *Media Discourse*. London: Edward Arnold.

Garfinkel, H. (1967) *Studies in Ethnomethodology*. New York: Prentice Hall.

Heritage, J. (1984) *Garfinkel and Ethnomethodology*. Oxford: Polity Press.

Ingleby, D. (1986) 'Development in Social Context', in M. Richards and P. Light (eds.) *Children of Social Worlds*. Cambridge: Polity Press.

Leiter, K. (1980) *A Primer on Ethnomethodology*. London: Oxford University Press.

Livingstone, E. (1987) *Making Sense of Ethnomethodology*. London: Routledge.

Pollard, A. (1988) *Children and their Primary Schools – a New Perspective*. Hove: Falmer Press.

Sacks, H. (1975) On the Analysability of Stories by Children. in Turner op. cit.

Schutz, A. (1966) *Collected Papers*. The Hague: Martinus Nijhoff.

Sudnow, D. (1965) 'Normal Crimes', *Social Problems*, 12, pp. 255–76.

Turner, R. (1975) *Ethnomethodology*. Harmondsworth: Penguin.

Wells, G. (1981) *Learning Through Interaction*. Cambridge: Cambridge University Press.

Wells, G. (1987) *The Meaning Makers*. Cambridge: Cambridge University Press.

9

Young children are natural scientists

Judith Roden

Close observation of young children at play suggests that they find out about the world in the same way as scientists explore new phenomena and test new ideas. Young children may not be able to verbalise new ideas forming in their heads, but they may still apply similar processes to the scientists'. During this exploration, all the senses are used to observe and draw conclusions about objects and events through simple, if crude, scientific investigations.

The scientific process is evident almost from the moment of birth. Newborn babies seek out their mother's breast and soon know how best to gain attention from the older, more powerful, experienced humans in their close, somewhat restricted environment. Initially this could be said to be merely a response to a stimulus, but the process is more sophisticated than the learning pattern explained by behaviourists such as Pavlov.

Scientists find out about the world primarily through observation, asking questions, forming hypotheses, setting up testable situations to answer their questions, making more observations, looking again, drawing conclusions, asking more questions and setting up even more investigations to test their new or modified hypotheses. What is discovered depends not only on previous understanding, but also on how systematically the process is applied. Early exploration, and hence what is discovered, is frequently characterised by trial and error. So, too, is early learning by infants as the following example demonstrates.

An observed child, given a musical recorder, instinctively placed the recorder in its mouth and sucked the end of the instrument. Next, the child discovered that if one end of the recorder was blown, instead of sucked, a sound could be made. Immediately the recorder was turned 180° and an attempt was made to blow through the opposite end of the recorder to answer the unverbalised question 'I wonder what happens if I turn the recorder around and blow'. The words were not spoken, but the question was asked. Later, through further observation, the child would discover the function of the air holes and learn rudimentary ideas about how to make 'music' with the instrument.

Much can be learned by systematically applying the process of the scientist. The more persistent the child, the more can be learned. The length of time spent by very young children on an item of interest can often be surprising. Even very young children can be rapturously engaged in a new, or re-discovered, item for 30–45 minutes or longer, without interruption. Note the example of a child, no older than twelve months, observed on a poolside surrounded by a large family and visitors on a 'busy' afternoon. Given a set of square tower building blocks, totally oblivious to other people loudly enjoying themselves, he ordered the pieces, selected the largest block and placed it on the ground. Totally unaided and unnoticed by his family, each smaller block was selected in turn, inserted on top of each larger piece until the tower was built. Next, the tower was knocked down, the pieces reordered and the sequence was repeated systematically three times more before the toys were taken away and the family moved off.

The child was familiar with the toy, knew which pieces fitted where and in which order, but he continued to test the order, rather as a scientist tests and re-tests in order to try to falsify a hypothesis. Whilst doing so he would be gaining understanding of the properties of the shapes, the materials, the laws of gravity and many other ideas about building towers.

Life for the young scientist gets off to a good start! The world, however, is fraught with difficulties and can be like an obstacle course set up to dissuade the young child from learning in a scientific manner. The world is not always what it seems. Without encouragement, a child may soon lose the ability to think 'scientifically' and fail to develop scientific skills. The real world can be unfriendly towards the developing scientist. The child is on a voyage of discovery, but often finds confusion. The modern word is dominated by the products of scientific and technological advancement achieved by the application of science to problems of the world, yet hampered by a world largely populated by people who could be called 'scientific illiterates'. Despite modern-day life depending on science and technology more than ever before, the 'real' world is dominated by the latter who, it is generally accepted, value science and scientists less than the arts and more perceived creative facets of life. Consequently, the 'real' world of the child frequently conspires against the development of sound scientific understanding. As Bradley (1996) says:

> Children are learning all day long, as they go about their business, their daily experiences contribute to their ideas and to the interpretations and explanations which they make about the world around them.
>
> (Bradley 1996, p. 3)

but that world may reinforce ideas that are not helpful to the budding scientist.

Nevertheless, Bradley (1996, p. 4) suggests that children have an innate understanding of science acquired by physically using scientific principles in their play, long before they come face to face with them in their formal education. Science friendly educational toys can teach much about the basic concepts in science. Sometimes such toys along with potentially worthwhile and valuable experiences are consigned to, and remain in, the toy box, or alternatively children are given many items to explore simultaneously! In such circumstances the 'toys' frequently become mixed up, constituent parts separated, making 'educational' play described by Sylva *et al*. (1986) difficult because of the chaos of the nursery toy box which may appear to be a kaleidoscope of colours and small pieces bearing little or no resemblance or relationship to each other.

The mixed up experiences of science in the real world continue. Young children are avid watchers of TV which permeates and punctuates much of the waking day. The quality of educational or semi-educational programmes is undeniably very good or excellent, but left to their own devices children select cartoons, or watch and re-watch familiar favourite videos. Fictional programmes may, at best, do little to further scientific learning, but at worst 'popular' children's programmes may introduce false ideas about scientific concepts, resulting in confusion. Few children may receive a scientific explanation for those things that can be explained or a challenge to those found confusing and consequently fail to optimise upon their good start in life.

Unsurprisingly perhaps, conclusions drawn from children's scientific exploration rarely concur closely with the scientist's view of the world. Extensive research has revealed that children's ideas are often very different from currently 'accepted' scientific ideas (Driver *et al*. 1985 and 1994; Northern Ireland Council for Educational Development. 1986; CLIS 1987 and SPACE (various authors and dates). Osborne *et al*. (1985) say the differential arises because children's views of the world are human centred and anchored in every day experience, whereas scientists are concerned with abstract reasoning. Russell and Harlen (1990, p. 97) suggest it is because of children's limited experiences, which means that they lack supportive evidence to make accurate interpretations about happenings in their lives.

Within the constructivist theory of children's learning, well documented and strongly held by many science educators, children's ideas do not develop from scratch. Harlen and Jelly (1989, p. 39) explain this simply by saying that children learn by linking new ideas with existing ones and changing them when necessary as more evidence comes available. Piaget described this process as assimilation – i.e. dealing with new situations and problems and accommodating them through the process of mental change (Althouse 1988, p. 4), therefore the level of children's understanding depends on their ability to be flexible in their thinking.

Like many contructivists, Johnson (1996) believes that children will only progress in science and develop scientific ideas through investigation, experimentation and interaction with informed adults. She analysed children's ideas and placed them into three useful categories:

1. factual knowledge;
2. fictional knowledge or myth;
3. inferred knowledge.

Factual knowledge is seen to be acquired through first hand experience and secondary sources such as books. Fictional knowledge can also be acquired through such secondary sources as the media and stories. Inferred knowledge results from the interaction of children's practical experiences with the existing ideas they hold. Taking this into account it is easy to see why many children have difficulty differentiating between fact and fiction and consequently develop ideas which are 'non scientific' since the categories will not be discrete in the child's mind and ideas from the real and imaginary worlds may interact with and 'infect' each other.

Scientists and children alike draw upon their present understanding to aid them in exploration and drawing conclusions. Existing scientific ideas inform observation, the questions asked and therefore what investigations follow. Children and scientists obviously differ in the sophistication of the use of the process and the knowledge base. It is worthwhile considering these differences in certain ideas and process skills in relation to young children. A glimpse of the world from the child's perspective can be very revealing. The following sec-

tions examine examples of children's thinking in science in relation
to aspects of the scientific process.

Observation

> Observation is the process through which we come to take notice, to
> became conscious of things and happenings.
>
> (Harlen 1985, p. 21)

Observation is an important aspect of the scientific process and crucial to children's learning about the world. The whole of science
depends upon scientists making accurate observation of aspects of the
real world. Scientists look for similarities and differences about natural and man-made phenomena. They look for patterns within their
results of investigations which help them to draw valid and reliable
conclusions. There is an obvious link between observation and the
development of concepts. Developing skills of observation, it is recognised, enable children to seek consciously for information which will
extend their ideas. Ollerenshaw and Richie (1997) regard observation
as the starting point for science. So it could be argued, observation
could be the starting point for young children's science. Young children observe the world around them and use their observations to
try to make sense of what they see. Observation in science involves,
where appropriate, the use of all the senses. Young children are frequently asked to touch an object and to describe how it feels.
'Observation tasks enable children to look at objects or events in a scientific way' (Gott and Duggan 1995, p. 55). Children need to look
closely and see things not noticed before. Observation helps to build
up ideas of similarity and difference and can form the basis for pattern finding and further investigation using other materials. Pattern
seeking is viewed as the process through which children acquire scientific knowledge and understanding and come to appreciate important scientific relationships (DES 1989). Observation is of vital
importance to children's learning because it enables children to focus,
question and develop broader understanding of scientific concepts.

Young children's observations are frequently crude and may lead
to conflicting ideas about the same item. This was illustrated by an
observation of four year old children with limited vocabulary playing in the sand. When encouraged to talk about the texture of sand
some said the sand was hard, some said it was soft. One said it
depended on the way it was handled, if left to filter through the fingers it felt soft, but if rubbed between the fingers it was rough. The

same children found difficulty in describing the colour of sand. Some said it was brown or yellow and disagreed with the view that sand was made up of lots of different colours.

On the other hand children's observations can be more sophisticated. On another occasion, following the observation of a pineapple, one child looked intently at the pattern of shapes on the skin. He said, 'They fit together like the Clixi we play with when it rains. I could make one of those fruits using it, couldn't I?' Next wet playtime he was found playing with Clixi. When asked, he said 'I am makin' one of them fruits we looked at. Do you like it?' Through close inspection and observation he had made an association between the pattern on the pineapple and its tessellation and the way that Clixi fits together and tessellates. The fruit activity had made an impact upon him and led to his further exploration through free play activities.

Applying children's own observations from experience will broaden both expertise in the scientific process and their knowledge and understanding of the world. Observation can also provide the catalyst for informed debate promoting much discussion even amongst very young children. Children learn to obtain information from an object by consciously looking in detail at its features. Developing observational skills enables children to look more closely for clues that will extend their ideas and promote understanding. Developing the skills of observation enables children to see details which might otherwise have been missed.

Children's drawings

Willig (1990, p. 5) reminds us that 'the ideas of young children are often most clearly and widely expressed in drawing and painting'. Children's drawings at a young age are often far in advance of their language skills. Drawing helps develop understanding and focuses children's attention on features that they may have missed, but young children appear not to see things as adults do. Osborne *et al.* (1985) say that children will tend to focus on very small, specific, things whereas scientists are concerned with looking for general explanations and laws. Harlen (1985a) says:

> Most children ... do not produce drawings which truly represent objects in front of them. Instead their drawings are influenced by prior conceptions about the object ... they become engrossed in their drawing or painting and stop observing the details of the objects they are representing.
>
> (Harlen 1985, p. 103).

Johnson (1996), on the other hand, asserts that children often find the world too large and complicated to take in, so they simplify what they see. Therefore the drawings are not really what they see, but their way of representing the world.

It is common practice for researchers to draw conclusions about children's ideas from looking at and analysing children's drawings. Pictorial representations highlight the additional scientific ideas children hold based on their observations. Bradley (1996, p. 60) considers that 'observational drawings can provide us with information about their ideas of scale and space, and how they see the various parts of an object fitting together to form a whole.'

Evidence from children's drawings, however, suggests that children *do* see some aspects of observed objects in great depths, but then factors other than the observation appear to take over so that the representations of the observation do not truly represent what was observed. This should not lead to the conclusion that young children do not observe very small details in an object, but rather they may not illustrate them accurately in a drawing. The following example illustrates this notion. Marcus, a six year old child, was asked first to look at and then carefully to draw an old wind-up toy. His attention was captured by the cogs he saw, consequently he packed his drawing with cogs, far more numerous and complicated than those he was actually observing. The drawing of the outside case was accurate and the screws which held the toy together were beautifully drawn, but he totally disregarded the spindles and springs which he found less interesting.

Sometimes children's representations of phenomena appear strange to adults. For example, one group of reception age children asked to draw a shadow following observation drew the outline of a shadow on a piece of paper, but as soon as the children were asked to shade their shadows they put clothes on them!

Bradley (1996, p. 51) believes that 'Each child sees and interprets differently' and Wenham (1995, p. 7) suggests that 'observation is a very disciplined activity'. Different children do appear to see the same object in different ways based on their prior knowledge and experience, as the following example suggests. Stuart and Anna, two reception age children, were observing candles with which they were both familiar. Stuart said 'Candles are small and are used when there is no electricity in the house'. Anna, whose mother owned a shop where candles are manufactured, explained in detail what the candles were made of and how they were made. Later drawings showed marked differences. Anna's picture was carefully and meticulously drawn including the decorations at the bottom of the Christmas candle. She included the markings made by the melted wax running down the candle and shaded the flames in various hues. Stuart included all the individual parts of the candle, but his drawing was not as accurate. The proportions of the candle parts were not as accurate and the tones of colour were not so clear. Stuart's drawing was characterised by global rather than detailed observation – attention to what is expected rather than what is already there.

When talking about children's observations it is important to raise three important points:

1. Not every child will observe the same thing;
2. Accurate observation is a skill that has to be learned.
3. Many children have a problem recording what they see. Often they cannot resist the temptation to embellish their drawings with their own interpretations.

Infant or pre-school children's drawings are sometimes considered to demonstrate 'low level' observational skills, but it could be argued that young children provide a different rather than a low level response. However, it may well be 'low-level' judged against a continuum of skill development, but nevertheless be highly sophisticated in its own right.

> Low level development of this skill is characterized by global rather than detailed observation, attention to what is expected rather than what is actually there and a greater attention to differences than similarities.
>
> (Harlen and Jelly 1989, p. 40).

It may well be, though, that young children's attention to gross features is frequently a response to 'the rush' and the lack of time in the infant classroom rather than to lack of observational skills. It is sometimes suggested that children can identify differences rather than similarities, and frequently, in their drawings, pick out and represent general features, like shape, rather than the more complicated aspects of what could be seen. It has been noted that children see things differently from older people, that is that young children differ from adults in what they see as significant, but lack of specific resources in the classroom may not help children to realistically represent what they are observing.

Some children produce very detailed drawings, but yet their work still demonstrates contamination with 'other ideas' as the next example illustrates. Anita, a six-year old child, produced very detailed drawings of flowers. The ones observed were pink, but some of her drawn flowers were coloured blue. She justified this by suggesting that she wanted to distinguish between the leaves and the stem and wanted to portray the brightness of the flower compared with other objects around it. Her ideas of the flowers were focused on the brightness of their colours. She coloured the stems red. She did know that the stem was green, but she had a rational reason for colouring them red.

One further factor affecting the quality of the representation of an observation could be that the child may not consider him/herself a good drawer and may be reluctant to put pencil to paper. Sometimes children may select gross features rather than more detailed ones because they do not have the time to draw everything or may focus more specifically on one aspect of an object. Alternatively this could merely be due to laziness, wanting to finish the task and get on to the next, or even the child's perception of what teacher wants – drawing not 'real work'. The examples given do not support the notion of 'low level' observational skill, but one that is clearly different from what an adult 'wants' or expects.

Experience suggests that for some children what they say as they observe an object might be a better indicator of what was observed whereas a drawing might suggest limited observation skills. Sometimes children are unwilling to draw and worried about their drawings being incorrect and frustrated at not being able to draw what they saw. Such children can frequently communicate their ideas though talk.

Harlen (1985a) claims that children often do observational drawings with firm preconceptions, so that they ignore contrasting evidence. Observation is said to be conceptionally driven, so that they draw what they see as significant. Chamberlain (1990) supports this view, providing an example of a child who was unwilling to draw a tadpole having only three legs. However, it is difficult to tell whether children's drawings really show evidence of the children's pre-conceived ideas or whether, as Johnson (1996), suggests they represents children's attempts to simplify the world.

Johnson (1996) also identified a creative aspect to observation. She believes that when children observe, they link in previous observations which may explain why their ideas are contaminated as they link in ideas drawn from other sources such as storybooks which are highly influential in a child's life. This is characterised by, for example, children colouring objects in less than real life colours which may not be surprising given that in many nurseries, pre-school playgroups and reception classes creativity, especially in drawing and painting, is encouraged. Bright primary colours are provided for painting and adults praise the brightly coloured paintings of young children.

Children's observational drawings are often striking because of features added to their drawing not present in the observed object. That is children sometimes draw what they 'know' and not what they see, sometimes reflecting stereotypical views of objects often represented in children's books such as perfectly round apples with two symmetrical leaves, or a house with four windows, a door and a chimney with smoke billowing.

Johnson (1996) believes that this creative aspect of children's observations should be encouraged as it is important that adults do not impose their own beliefs on children's observation and therefore undermine their drawings and lessen their confidence. She believes that the observation is not lessened by their creative additions, but rather indicates their wider powers of observations and their ability to relate to and form associations with previous observation or experiences. She suggests that as children get older they only observe those things which they think we value and they rarely include imaginative ideas or observation. On the other hand though, Sherrington (1993) warns that:

> It is important that teachers demand that children observe objects and phenomena through 'scientific spectacles'. Without this, observation in science is in danger of becoming a language, maths or art activity.
>
> (Sherrington 1993, p. 55)

Even in the early years' classroom, there seems to be antagonism between the development of creativity and accuracy in scientific observation. From the point of view of the developing young scientist it is important that the child knows from his helper or teacher what is expected. There should be room in the early years' curriculum for the development of both aspects since both are important for development of a creative approach which is also important in science as will be explored later in the chapter.

Prediction and hypothesis

> A prediction is a statement about what might happen in the future, or what will be found to happen that has not so far been found, that is based upon some hypothesis or previous knowledge.
>
> (Sherrington 1993, p. 47)

Many children are able to put forward a prediction, which in the case of a very young child may well be only a guess. Sherrington (1993) says that a prediction is quite different from a guess which, as a guess, cannot be justified in terms of a hypothesis or evidence. Prediction allows children to relate and apply their current understanding and previous experience of events to a new situation.

With encouragement children will put forward predictions, or respond to the question 'What do you think will happen if . . . ?', with confidence unless they are afraid they will be wrong. Getting the 'correct' answer is very important for success in the early years classroom so this could be quite a hurdle for the young scientist to negotiate. So often adults and teachers require 'the right, predetermined answer'. In science this is usually not the case because adults are trying firstly to improve children's ability to make predictions based on evidence, and secondly to refine their predicting skills.

The main difference between a prediction and a hypothesis is that a hypothesis contains an explanation. The Northern Ireland Council for Educational Development (1986) points out that hypotheses do not need to be correct explanations, just sensible ones. Older, more experienced children relate previous experiences and their own ideas to put forward reasons to support their predictions. The prediction then becomes a hypothesis.

Even very young children will offer an explanation if asked to justify their prediction, but their explanations sometimes bear little resemblance to reality. Children frequently suggest that colour explains why, for example, a ball bounces higher than another. Kyle, a bright five year old, after finding that a yogurt pot floated when placed in an upright position and sank if she turned it upside down, reasoned that 'It was all white inside'.

Children think logically, but to adults their responses may seem far from logical. Children are usually quite capable of providing a justification for their beliefs as the following example shows. Six year old children were investigating which materials absorb or reflect sound. A book and a sponge were used. When asked to predict which material will reflect sound better, several children suggested a sponge. Conventional experience would suggest that the sponge absorbs sound whilst the book reflects it. When asked for an explanation for their prediction, they said 'Because the sponge has got holes in it'. They had concluded that holes let sound through. A logical response was formed, based upon the child's experience. Adults, drawing on their greater experience, know that sound is muffled by soft materials. Experience informs decisions, so the children needed to test their ideas by practical experience. This is why practical exploration is so important for the developing scientist as the following scenario demonstrates.

Two six year old children were investigating floating and sinking. Holly said 'light things float, heavy things sink and when they get heavier again they float like boats'. Through exploration Holly began to develop what looked like a simple prediction: 'All plastic things float'. She then began to collect objects and test whether she was correct – she was quite structured and methodical in her approach.

Initially Holly predicted that all plastic things would float. Later when she discovered a cracked pot she said 'Because the pot is cracked the water will get into the pot and push it down'. Without realizing it she was relating the concept of floating and sinking to the action of forces. A sophisticated explanation for a six year old! When asked to predict whether an apple would float Holly said that apples float 'because I've seen them at a party'. She said 'If the apple floats so will the orange because they are fruits'. Other children had a much less sophisticated or logical approach. Jamie correctly predicted that a lolly stick would float and then predicted that a shell would float 'because it was found in the sea'. The shell was small and it was likely that he associated small things with light things – thus it will float. Once Jamie had tested the shell to see if it would float he would not believe the outcome that it would not and said that although it would not float in the water tub it would float in the sea 'because the sea is bigger'. Not all children's predictions, then, can be tested, and ideas challenged, by practical work at home or in the classroom! It is possible that Jamie was not being stubborn, but really thought that a bigger mass of water would be able to hold the shell on the surface of the water. On the other hand, sometimes sea shells can float on water if they are positioned carefully. This idea may seem silly to adults, but it is not difficult to believe that small children could associate 'big' with 'heavy' and 'stronger'. As the shell sinking challenged his idea about light things floating, he might have decided to hold on to his ideas and justified them in another way.

> To apply concepts or knowledge from one situation to another the child has to recognize some similarity between these two situations or events. The clues may be fruitful and lead to suggested explanations . . .
>
> (Harlen 1985b, p. 32)

Linking one experience to another frequently leads to 'incorrect' ideas. When making a prediction in a floating activity one child said 'The

stone will sink because that other time when we did that thing . . .'
(making reference to a previous experiment to see what items fell to
the floor the quickest) 'it fell fastest because it was heavy . . . so it will
go to the bottom of the water'. She was reminded of the feather they
had used in the previous experience and asked if she thought that
would sink. She said it would float 'because it's light and went down
"swish swash to the ground slowly" '. She thought that heavy objects
would sink and that light objects would float and was clearly relating her previous knowledge to the situation. When asked to justify
her idea about feathers, the child said 'Ducks float and they have
feathers!'

Sometimes children's predictions, like their drawings, are contaminated by irrelevancies. Children working together bring different
skills and previous experiences to a new situation. These can often
lead to further learning of a different nature for all participants. Whilst
testing boats children were first asked to predict what would happen.
One child said, 'It will float cause it's made of yoghurt pots and water
falls off it, look' (as he placed his boat into the water and showed the
droplets rolling off the boat). He then went on to say that 'my boat's
like that at home, but it goes down when I put lots of animals in it.
Then all the people have to get out and swim because they might get
drowned.' The child correctly predicted that his boat would float and
he seemed to be making use of his knowledge of waterproofing which
he had gained through a discussion a few days previously. He was
also relating it to previous knowledge of how his toy boat behaved
in the bath at home as well as demonstrating an understanding of
consequence. He understood that if a boat was to sink then people
would need to swim to the surface (of the water) to avoid drowning,
but this knowledge was concealed by other known information seen
as relevant to the child.

Children's questions and investigation

Tiny Niels, beaming, bare and beautiful, crawled on the wet sand of
the beach. He moved where the sea reaches out to the land, where the
ocean barely touches the continent, where the exhausted waves drag
themselves up the incline and withdraw and sink into the sand.
Whenever this happened in slow and steady rhythm there appeared,
all around Niels, tiny holes in the sand which bubbled and boiled with
escaping air. These little marvels drew his attention, and with immense
concentration he poked his finger in hole after hole, until a fresh wave
wiped them all out and created new ones . . . the bubbling holes invited

Niels: 'Come here, look at us, feel and poke' ... he could not yet talk ... not a word was exchanged, but the boy himself was the question, a living query: What is this? What does it do? How does it feel?

(Elstgeest 1985, p. 9)

Questions and investigations are inextricably linked as are other aspects of the scientific process. Isaacs (1958) studied children aged 3-5 years old. He identified children's questions as one of the factors that links both how the scientist and the young child finds out about the world. He said children were like scientists in their:

natural curiosity ... finding out about things ... asking questions ... what they are ... where they come from ... what they are made of ... how they work ... by exploring and finding out for themselves ... their particular interest in grounds and reasons and above all explanations as expressed in their persistent 'why' questions.

(Isaacs 1958, p. 1)

Very young children all pass through a sometimes irritating phase when they ask 'Why' of everything and everybody. 'Why' questions are fundamental to the development of understanding and should be encouraged, but additionally it is important for children to develop their ability to ask other kinds of questions too. Scientists do not only ask 'why' questions, but also ask investigative questions or those questions which lead to investigation. When practised, investigative questions will promote new explorations and allow investigations. Children's questions, however, are frequently not what they seem. Questions can be categorised and many attempts have been made to do so. Young children sometimes do not ask questions in a recognisable form. Frequently questions are expressed as comments or observations. The most important questions for the young scientist to develop are those that can lead to their own enquiry, further observation or investigation. Harlen points out that:

Raising a variety of questions, including poorly expressed and vague ones, is important to children's learning, for questioning is the means by which a child can fill in some links between one experience and another and can make his own sense of the world.

(Harlen 1985b, p. 33)

Johnson reminds us that 'the questions children raise are likely to indicate gaps in their experience or misconceptions they hold' (Johnson 1996, p. 33). The following example demonstrates this process well. A group of children looked at a group of rather unattractive, to them, unfamiliar fruit which allowed them the opportunity to observe using all their senses. This led to them asking questions and making hypotheses. One child said, 'What are they called? They would smell funny and taste funny wouldn't they? Do they smell horrid?' The fruit was cut in half and some of the smells of the fruit were found quite pleasant. The child particularly liked the smell of the passion fruit saying, 'mmm, nice, you could eat that'. Initially she had concluded that because the fruit was unattractive on the outside that it must taste and smell unpleasant. Other children assumed that the brightly coloured fruit must smell the nicest. The children's questions led to further exploration and investigation of the fruit which allowed them to build upon their knowledge and make more informed judgements.

The fruit activity highlighted the great variation of the children's knowledge. Some children were unable to name even the most common of fruit whilst others could name the different parts of a fruit. One child while looking at the inside of an apple said spontaneously, 'They're pips and grow into other apples. If you plant them you get apple trees with more apples and do you know what, they have pips too!' This provided much information about the child's level of understanding. Care needs to be taken when dealing with children's questions because they frequently ask questions to:

- obtain information;
- understand something that puzzles them or;
- to entice the adults into doing their thinking for them.

(Harlen *et al.* 1990)

Sometimes, children ask questions that adults find impossible to answer. This is not necessarily because the adult lacks sufficient scientific understanding to answer the question, but because often there is no acceptable scientific answer. Scientists are frequently perceived to know everything, but this is not always the case.

Adults often find difficulty in explaining ideas to children because of difficulty in selecting language that children can understand. This is an additional difficulty in relation to science in that the true scientific language is very precise and in attempting to search for appropriate language the meaning or idea is frequently distorted. Children's language is sometimes more useful to the child than the teacher's explanation. Children can learn much from working together, asking questions of each other. Collaborative work is beneficial because they can share their ideas and answer their own questions in their own terms. For example, one child asked another child why he thought the water would go through the cardboard to which he replied it was 'a bit like paper, only fatter'. They understood each other. 'Correct' scientific language may not be used amongst the children immediately, but the role of the adult, over time, is to modify and develop language and vocabulary, to enable children to use more precise and scientific vocabulary correctly and with confidence.

Sutton (1992) suggests that children's answers and questions may not be what the teacher is specifically seeking, but no good educator can afford to ignore them because they can hold the key to the next stage in learning and provide a starting point for investigation:

> Investigations are about using and developing concepts, skills and processes in a way which will assist children in finding the solution to a problem or question or in following an idea.
>
> (Feasey 1993, p. 58)

Investigations allow scientists and children to explore their ideas about the world. McMurdo (1989, p. 220) explains that science progresses when one idea is proved false and is replaced by another idea. Scientists and children therefore repeat investigations to try to disprove their theories even if children's explorations may be unsophisticated. 'To a casual observer a child's exploration might look unstructured; an ad hoc series of actions. However, children invariably have a particular idea which they try out in a deliberate manner' (Harlen 1993b, p. 56).

Investigations provide the link between previous experiences and new experiences. They extend ideas so that what was not previously understood can now be understood because it fits into the new found evidence. Harlen describes this as being created by development and change in ideas as investigations offer a platform for the use of knowledge and understanding.

Investigations play an enormous role in the development of the young scientist. They are fundamental to the learning process. Babies and very young children build up their ideas, firstly by carrying out simple, unsophisticated investigations, frequently termed explorations, and as they get older their investigations become more sophisticated, more structured and systematic. Children need to build up a bank of experiences. Their science investigations provide a vehicle for linking what is already understood to inform the application of scientific concepts.

One aspect of investigation in need of development as children get older is the idea of the fair test. This asks children to apply the principles of controlling variables to the design of a fair test. Johnson (1996) rightly points out that when considering fair testing children must identify key variables, they must know what they are changing (the independent variable), and what happens as a result, in this case the effect on the distance travelled (the dependent variable). Young children, however, do not instinctively know these terms nor can they be expected to be able to control variables without experience, but this does not mean they do not have an idea about the fair test.

'Fair testing' sometimes has a different meaning to children and the scientist. The concept of fairness is important to young children. Investigating the best surface for a car to travel the furthest, two able six year olds, like many other children of similar age, believed that fair testing, largely based upon their previous knowledge, was only the need for each child to have a turn at pushing the car. This understanding comes from their general social development where they have learned that to be fair to others they must take turns.

The following description of six year olds investigating wind powered boats illustrates how children's ideas of what they are doing sometimes differ from the adult perspective. A group of children had been given different designs of boat to construct. All children in each group had built a boat and, as the testing time grew near, there was great excitement and much discussion about whose boat would be the best. Every child within each group tested their boats and decided which one would represent the group in the later class race. Some children had wanted to change the design of the boat, but since they had all been built in the same way it was explained that they all had to be the same to make it fair. The children were asked to give reasons for their choice of boat. Various reasons were given. They depended mainly on observational skills – 'It went faster', or 'It won'.

Finally the class race began. Benjamin and Matthew were testing their boats. Benjamin was very good at blowing and Matthew tried to adopt his style. Benjamin's boat won. Asked why they thought his boat had won, answers included, 'The sail made it go faster', 'He blewed it better', 'It went sideways', 'He got on top of it', but to illustrate already formed ideas Iain said, 'Benjamin's boat went best 'cos he's me mate'. Iain had previously demonstrated understanding of the ideas being tested, but in the end his allegiance to his friend and not to the results of the test won the day. He did not consider the evidence in front of him. He needed to be encouraged to do so. Sometimes children do not really understand what to look for. Willig (1990) points out that children need their attention directed 'towards significant features of an object and away from the peripheral in order to encourage most relevant and disciplined observation and interpretation.'

Nevertheless, children can grasp the idea of a fair test from quite a young age as long as it is set in context. Children often point out unfairness, but in this case in a scientific context the children pointed out exactly why it was unfair and how this related to the investigation.

Drawing conclusions

Children arrive at conclusions irrespective of whether they are asked to verbalise these. Their conclusions are reflected in the ideas they express. Harlen (1985b, pp. 55–73), exploring children's ideas, tells us that children jump to conclusions all too readily on limited evidence. Children often arrive at a conclusion and are often content to agree with each other rather than testing to find out whether they are right or not.

Children in a year one class, exploring flotation, all predicted that a sponge would float, because of its lightness, but Elli said the sponge would sink because 'It always does in the bath'. When the sponge floated all the children thought that Elli's prediction had been wrong, but they had to adjust their ideas as the investigation progressed. They watched as the sponge was squeezed, the air bubbles coming from it as the air was replaced with water, making it heavier and sinking. The children spent some time watching the sponge float, then they filled it with water several times in order to make it sink. This conflicted with their original ideas, caused them to doubt their existing ideas and to reflect on their new experience.

Children's conclusions can also be informed by their own creative imagining, possibly from television. A six year old child in a year two class when asked how a sound was made in a guitar said 'Gravity'. She said that it was the circle in the guitar that made the sound. When asked if cutting a circle in paper would sound the same she said 'No'. She was convinced that sound was trapped inside the guitar. She said 'It's inside all the time'. When asked what made it come out she thought for a while and then said that it came out because there was no gravity inside the circle, so the sound floated up. She obviously has some familiarity with the idea of gravity and weightlessness, but had incorrectly applied these ideas to a 'new' situation.

In another example where children are asked to give suggestions to explain phenomena that might be an example of an occurrence that could not be seen (Knaggs 1989, p. 27), Reception children were discussing plants and how they grow. When asked when he thought that plants grew, Donald said 'At night'. When asked whether plants needed the sun to grow if they grow at night, both Joseph and Andy said 'No' and were asked why they thought this. Donald said, 'it's always sunny in the desert and there aren't no plants there, only sand'. When asked if there really weren't any plants growing in the desert he said 'only spiky ones'. He did not know the names of any of these spiky plants. When asked how these plants survived he said 'They hold water, and this helps them to grow at night'. Again the idea of plants growing at night came up so he was asked what happens at night. 'We know that plants grow,' he said, 'but we don't see it, so they must grow at night while we are asleep.'

Obviously not totally true, but Donald was particularly unwilling to accept the fact that plants also grow during the day. He also contradicted himself by saying that no plants grow in the desert and then said that cactuses did. As Bradley (1996, p. 52) explains, children use 'contradictory reasoning to explain an phenomenon and easily change from one explanation to another'. They do this because their experiences to date have led them to believe that is how things work in practice. A child's interpretation of life is dependent on and governed by past experiences. When faced with something unknown they look inward for something that can be linked to this unknown factor. The child tries to understand a new phenomenon by extending from what they do know now to what they can hypothesise. Donald had an idea that plants grow only at night and it made sense to him therefore he was unwilling to change his existing idea. Harlen says that 'children may ignore contradictory evidence in interpreting findings and hold on to their initial ideas even when these do not fit the evidence' (1993, p. 39).

'Children's daily experiences contribute to their ideas and to the interpretations and explanations which they make about the world around them' (Bradley 1996, p. 3). Children pick up their knowledge from a variety of sources such as parents, televisions, books; they take these ideas and then form them into their own scientific thinking.

Children need to be encouraged to formulate their ideas and justification for them and adults must be careful not to discourage children's ideas. It is far more effective, in the long term, to allow children to explore their ideas for themselves so that they can come to their own conclusions about the world. When children reach their own conclusions they are practising the scientific process, therefore engaging in thinking and solving problems and eventually attaining well developed understanding of scientific concepts. Sometimes, as we have seen earlier, children's ideas seem bizarre, but these ideas are symptomatic of their exploration of their own ideas and their developing thought processes. In this way children acquire a whole host of concepts before starting school which are formed on the basis of experience. Harlen and Jelly report on children's existing ideas and say that they are:

> a mixture of partially formed scientific ideas, probably already changed by experience and ideas we might call everyday, rather than scientific as they do little to aid understanding.
>
> (Harlen and Jelly 1989, p. 39)

These existing ideas need to be explored before a more scientific understanding can be reached. Part of the development of understanding relates to scientific language.

Use of language

Everyday language is littered by non-scientific usage of 'scientific' words. Attempting to simplify explanations to young child by the use of words of similar meaning in 'real' life causes problems of understanding for the young scientist. Usage of words in dictionaries and crosswords usually fail to provide adequate information about the differences between common words which belong in both worlds. Referring to a dictionary definition to aid understanding of 'scientific' terms can often cause even more confusion.

Sometimes children are unable to explain fully the conclusions that they arrive at because they are limited by their own vocabulary as well as their own understanding of particular words and ideas, and yet it is important for children to express themselves accurately as:

> concept formation is a genuine process of assimilation based on experience with phenomena and the ability to organize thoughts through language.
>
> (Bentley and Watts 1994, p. 46)

When an adult is looking for a scientific response from a child, lack of appropriate vocabulary can pose problems. Words like 'roll' and 'bounce' sometimes hold different meanings for children and adults. As children get older they need to adopt correct use of scientific terminology. It is important that they use vocabulary within its accepted scientific meaning (Vickery 1993, p. 26). Osborne *et al.* (1985) state that children will apply language with which they are familiar whereas scientists have strict and precise definitions and language. Sometimes a huge gulf exists between everyday and scientific meanings of words.

Children's comments might seem trivial, but logical reasoning might be evident if the reasons why children used the words were explored. Sherrington says 'it is very important to listen to children's ideas in order to understand how and what to teach them'. She points out that:

> language has a crucial part to play in children's learning of science, in turn science offers a context for children to develop and improve their skills in using language.
>
> (Sherrington 1993, p. 196)

She goes on to stress, however, that children should start from everyday language. Scientific vocabulary should be built upon gradually when the child is ready. It is, however, also imperative for children to be introduced to scientific vocabulary, using correct explanations from a very young age, if children are fully to benefit from their interactions with adults and the world. Misunderstandings of 'scientific symbols' i.e. words are common in everyday life and in everyday children's ideas. Words are not only misused in everyday language, but misunderstandings are perpetuated through everyday misuse of scientific language. A number of examples can seek to illustrate this notion. The word 'animal' is problematic. Generally the word 'animal' to most people relates to large creatures, usually mammals such as dogs and cats. Creatures such as insects and spiders are not usually thought to be animals. To the scientist, however, in simple terms, 'animal' is a much more over-arching term which describes living things that are not plants. The everyday notion of animals is further aggravated by ignorance amongst many adults, many of whom describe all 'creepy crawlies' as insects, when in fact, insects, spiders, slugs, snails, crabs and others all belong to further sub-groups of animals. During an infant assembly where a headteacher was trying to instil the need for children not to fight in the playground she said 'We are not animals, we must not behave like animals'. The headteacher was full of good intentions by this statement, but she inadvertently reinforced the misunderstanding that humans are not animals, what probably was a highly influential piece of learning for young children. Scientists too do not help in this respect. The term 'minibeast' was introduced in the 1970s within the Schools Council Science 5-13 project. Unfortunately, the term introduced to avoid misunderstanding may well have reinforced the idea that 'minibeasts' are not animals. Similar problems exist in relation to words such as energy, force, and power which in everyday use are used synonymously. In science each has its own particular, precise definition. Force is a word which poses more problems for the young scientist. A group of young children were asked 'What is a force and how are they used?' – a common question in the infant classroom since the introduction of the Science National Curriculum in 1989. Children asked about forces could not suggest any ideas except 'Police force'. Sherrington (1993) explains that this is 'because of their more limited experience they may not have an idea available to them which really fits and they use what seems most reasonable to them.'

It is often thought that children's ideas are not 'scientific'; however, children's ideas may often be masked by a lack of access to appropriate language. Take, for example, Nick predicting what would happen to water placed in the freezer: 'I think the ice cube in the fridge will grow'. The ability to grow is one of seven things distinguishing living from non-living things. Of course Nick meant expand, but the word did not exist in his vocabulary.

Interpretation of what children mean by their use of particular vocabulary is frequently fraught with difficulty for adults helping children to develop their scientific ideas. Sometimes the common misuse of English confuses children as the following example illustrates. Asked to classify six objects as man-made or natural, Sheryl, working with Chloe, examined a sponge shaped like a strawberry. She ticked 'man-made' on the sheet recording their ideas. Chloe said 'Sponges aren't made, you know, they grow, in the sea, because I saw them on a telly programme and they pick them and sell them in the shops. We've got one from the chemist.' Sheryl said, 'Have you? We've got one too, I've got one that looks like a pineapple.' Chloe replied, 'They don't look like pineapples when they grow in the sea, or like strawberries and my one doesn't look like that, it's sort of yellow. It's nice, this one's nice too. They probably get them from the sea and sell some of them like mine and make the rest look like these ones.' Then shrugs her shoulders. Sheryl concluded that 'If they make them look like this then they must be man-made'. They drew on Chloe's information from a TV programme and discussed their ideas with good use of vocabulary. Each listened to what the other had to say and related it to their own experience of sponges. They did not ask specific questions of each other, but each child stated what she already knew and the other responded. Had the children more experience of questioning, they might have extended their discussion.

Although Chloe was unsure of how sponges come to look like fruit, she decides on a sensible hypothesis based upon the information and experience she has. Sheryl listens and makes her own decision using the information she thinks is relevant. A further example from the same children emphasises the difficulties children have in sorting through the mine-field of the use of everyday language.

Sheryl's reasoning proceeded along similar lines when asked to find objects and to categorise them using their own criteria. Sheryl chose a biscuit and placed it in the man-made category. Her reasoning was thus: 'Someone had to use the margarine and sugar and, I think you might need eggs, yes you do because I've made them and I can remember my mum let me crack it, so someone had to make them, but it doesn't have to be a man.' She laughs.

Sheryl had used sound reasoning skills to work out that ingredients change when put together and can be made into other things. She may not have been as sure as this without drawing on her previous experience of making biscuits. Through her own experience of cooking, she was developing scientific understanding. Sheryl had decided that 'man-made' did not necessarily refer to a man, but to a person, although when she laughed, she may have been looking for confirmation that her decision was correct. A less able child, or a child without relevant previous experiences of the term, might have found it confusing and therefore been prevented from making informed choices.

Children also need to be guided towards the appropriate use of scientific terms from a young age. There is a great need for adults to become aware of the problems of misuse of language. However, it is important not to introduce vocabulary too early to the exclusion of the child's own language as there is a danger in trying to seek for the use of 'proper' scientific terms inappropriately.

Conclusion

Throughout this chapter the nature of children's science has been explored and some perhaps surprising ideas about the nature of the young child-as-scientist have been revealed. Throughout the chapter there have been examples of children approaching scientific ideas and activities in a scientific manner. What is clear is that not only do children inherently think in a scientific manner from a young age, they frequently do so creatively. It is a common misconception that science is a convergent rather than a divergent activity, that it is uncreative and narrow rather than creative, diverse and dynamic. In reality science can be very creative, but there is often an antagonism between traditional and creative science. Whilst there are scientists who work within existing paradigms, filling in the depth of knowledge about things that are already known, Kuhn (1996) explains how 'scientific revolutions' take place because of those scientists more creative in their thinking. Scientists such as Copernicus, Kepler and Galileo all looked anew at the existing view in science and provided alternative theories about the known world which challenged the scientific community in a manner which was frequently unpopular. They did not merely accept what was believed at the time, they observed anomalies and looked for alternative explanations. Courage was needed to put forward alternative ideas – ideas which made others think about what is already known and re-look at the evidence. This is very important in the development of science over time. There is a need for people to work within existing paradigms, but progress comes largely from those creative people who can look beyond existing paradigms to a new order, people with new insights. Such people make life uncomfortable for the majority of the scientific community. So it is with children.

Issues

1. How can the natural 'scientific trends' in young children be developed in the classroom?
2. How can the natural antagonism between the development of creativity and accuracy in scientific observation be minimised?
3. At what age should specific scientific vocabulary be introduced to young children?
4. To what extent should teachers and other adults 'correct' wrongly used scientific vocabulary?
5. How can adults ensure that children are introduced to 'correct' scientific vocabulary?
6. Children will inevitably misuse scientific vocabulary in their everyday lives. How should adults approach this problem?

References

Althouse, R. (1988) *Investigating Science with Young Children.* London: Arnold.
Bentley, D. and Watts, M. (1994) *Primary Science and Technology.* Buckingham: Open University Press.
Bradley, L. (1996) *Children Learning Science.* Oxford: Nash Pollock.
Chamberlain V (1990) Developing observational skills in the classroom. *Primary Science Review*, 12.
CLIS (1987) *Children's Learning in Science Project.* Leeds: Centre for Studies in Science and Mathematics Education.
DES (1989) *Aspects of Primary Education: The Teaching and Learning of Science*

HMI and Inspection Review. London: HMSO.

DFE (1995) *The National Curriculum*. London: HMSO.

Driver, R., Guesne, E. and Tiberghien, A. (1985) *Children's Ideas in Science*. Milton Keynes: Open University Press.

Driver R., Squires, A., Rushworth, P., Robinson V. (1994) *Making Sense of Secondary Science*. London: Routledge.

Elstgeest J. (1985) Encounter, Interaction, Dialogue, in Harlen, W. (1985a).

Feasey, R. (1993) Scientific Investigation, in R. Sherrington (ed.) *Primary Science Teacher's Handbook*. London: ASE.

Gott, R. and Duggan, S. (1995) *Investigative Work in the Science Curriculum*. Buckingham: Open University Press.

Harlen W. (1993a) Chapter in Sherrington (1993). ASE.

Harlen W. (1993b) *Teaching and Learning Primary Science* (2nd ed.). London: Paul Chapman.

Harlen W. (1987) Finding out about children's scientific ideas. *Primary Science Review*, SR 3.

Harlen W. and Jelly, S. (1989) *Developing Science in the Primary Classroom*. Edinburgh: Oliver and Boyd.

Harlen W., Macro. C., Schilling M., Malvern, D. and Reed, K. (1990) *Progress in Primary Science*. London: Routledge.

Harlen, W. (1985a) *Primary Science: Taking the Plunge*. Oxford: Heinemann.

Harlen, W. (1985b) *Teaching and Learning Primary science (1st ed.)*. London: Paul Chapman.

Harlen, W. (1993) *Teaching and Learning Primary science (2nd ed.)*. London: Paul Chapman.

Issacs N. (1958) *Early Scientific Trends in Children*. London: National Froebel Foundation.

Johnson, J. (1996) *Early Explorations in Science*. Milton Keynes: Open University Press.

Knaggs, J. (1989) *Primary Science Review*, 9, Spring. What do children think about growth?

Kuhn, T. S. (1996) *The Structure of Scienctific Revolutions 3rd ed*. Chicago: University of Chicago Press.

McMurdo, M. (1989) Some Thoughts on the Philosophy of Primary Science. *Primary Science Review*, Spring 1989.

Northern Ireland Council for Educational Development (1986) *Guidelines for Primary Schools*. York: Longman.

Ollerenshaw, C. and Richie, R. (1997) *Primary Science: Making it Work (second ed.)*. London: David Fulton Publishers.

Osborne, R., Freyberg P. and Bell, B. (1985) *Learning in Science the Implications of Children's Science*. Auckland: Heinneman.

Russell, T. and Harlen, W. (1990) *Assessing Science in the Primary Classroom: Practical Tasks*. London: Paul Chapman.

Russell, T. and Watt, D. (1991) *Primary SPACE Research Report – Growth*. Liverpool: Liverpool University Press.

Russell, T., Longden, D. and McGuigan, L. (1991) *Primary SPACE Research*

Report – Materials. Liverpool: Liverpool University Press.

Sherrington, R. (1993) *Primary Science Teacher's Handbook*. London: Simon and Schuster Education.

Sutton, C. (1992) *Words, Science and Learning*. Buckingham: Open University Press.

Sylva, K., Roy, C. and Painter, M. (1986) *Childwatching at playgroup and nursery school*. Oxford: Blackwell.

Vickery D. (1993) Developing scientific ideas – a common sense approach. *Primary science review* 26 Feb.

Wenham, M. (1995) *Understanding Primary Science*. London: Paul Chapman.

Willig, C. J. (1990) *Children's Concepts and the Primary Curriculum*. London: Paul Chapman.

10

Bilingual children in a monolingual society

Martine Jago

The results of early national assessment tests, underpinned by existing research in the field, have demonstrated the crucial nature of a child's home language in early concept development. Adequate and appropriate provision for bilingual pupils in play groups, nurseries and primary schools can have beneficial effects not only for children learning English as an additional language, but also for their monolingual peers. Interactions with different languages and cultures can enhance a child's sensitivity to the mother tongue and its structure, and an awareness of the nature of communication, a notion that it is constructed, and reconstructed, by people to serve their needs. This chapter will explore some of the limits set on pupils in the early years of primary education by traditional English attitudes towards modern foreign languages, as well as the wider issue of learning opportunities afforded young children by their families, schools, communities and the society in which they are participants: what do our children learn from the informal curricula of home, school and other services?

All babies learn a means of communicating with other human beings in order to fulfil their basic needs. Some are able to acquire two or more languages at a very young age. A major consideration for teachers working with bilinguals is the celebration of the skills and knowledge that each child brings to school, the development of self-esteem and pride in ethnicity by strengthening relationships between home and community. What assumptions are made about the requirements of bilingual children in school? Are their skills deemed by care givers and early years educators to be a specific learning difficulty or a valuable teaching resource?

The term 'bilingualism' is not easily defined, since it refers to a continuum of linguistic ability, ranging from the receptive bilingual who understands a second language without necessarily being able to speak or write it, to the rare ambilingual child who operates in two languages on a daily basis as fluently as native speakers of either language. Individual children make progress in the acquisition of a second language in different ways and at differing speeds. The process is not necessarily linear, but may be described as a series of phases such as beginner, developing, intermediate and fluent according to the degree of fluency and the level of involvement. How are bilingual children best supported?

The bilingual child might be that young person in the playground somewhat confused as to the status of the language that must be left at the nursery gates, who will be immersed, at a critical stage in conceptual development, into an environment which does not recognise all languages within the learning process. This child is in fact equipped with skills that can enhance the curriculum for other bilingual and monolingual pupils. The interaction between home and school should engender a creative, positive, learning experience for both adults and children. What is the effect of family and teacher expectations on the child entering the education system?

Research: bilingualism and thought processes

In the twentieth century, research has focused on the expectation of the positive consequences of bilingualism. Studies seem to indicate that not only can conceptual skills in the mother tongue provide a firm foundation for the development of second language skills, but that bilingualism can have beneficial effects on intellectual performance. Salient features arising in the assessment of young children with two or more languages have included divergent thinking, analytic orientation and field independence.

'Divergent thinking' is a creative skill which is assessed by asking the child to produce answers to an open ended question, and is measured by the absolute number of responses, as well as their flexibility, originality and degree of elaboration. A variety of concepts and emotions attached to each word or phrase creates a link between culture and language, and allows a wider context of thought with more than one perception of reality.

'Analytic orientation' refers to metalinguistic skills or the awareness of language forms and properties, and points to the possibility that bilinguals can be more responsive to cues and display greater sensitivity to feedback than their monolingual peers. The issue becomes one of interpersonal and social skills, rather than simply cognition.

'Field independence' describes a method of storing, memorising and using information, and indicates the degree to which an individual can overcome embedded contexts. A bilingual sees the parts as well as the whole picture more readily than a monolingual. Ostensibly a perceptual skill, field independence can point to cognitive clarity and analytical functioning such as problem solving.

Cummins (1976) offers three hypotheses to explain a link between bilingualism and divergent thinking, an analytical orientation towards languages, Piagetian conceptual development, communicative sensitivity and field independence. He believes most bilinguals possess: (1) range of experience (two languages and two cultures), (2) switching mechanism (flexibility of thought and perspectives), (3) objectification (comparison of meanings and grammatical form).

Alladina (1995) suggests that teachers and scientists have tended to link bilingualism with 'language interference', which refers to the confusion suffered by a child operating in two languages. A more appropriate term is 'language transference', where knowledge about the grammar and rules of one language is applied to the acquisition of a second or third language.

Lyon (1996) describes some of the unresolved theoretical issues in childhood bilingualism, and compares three models of bilingual language acquisition: the gradual differentiation model, the separate development model and the sequential model. The first two refer to degrees of language mixing and syntactic fusion before differentiation, whereas the third also considers context and the developmental dimension. She believes the links between cognition, metalingual awareness and bilingualism require further research.

The limitations of research

In a discussion of bilingualism and cognitive functioning, Baker (1988) critically examines the limitations and implications of recent studies. He cites numerous examples of research where the chosen participants are not a representative sample, but tend to belong to the rather idiosyncratic group of balanced bilinguals, and suggests that projects must control adequately for differences between categories. Subjects need to be matched according to age, gender, ethnicity and socio-economic background. The sample size needs to be appropriate so that attempts at generalisation and replication are valid. Baker recommends clarification regarding the temporary or cumulative benefits of bilingualism as an issue for development, and suggests that ideological assumptions by positivist authors in the past have tended to affect both the results and the interpretations of previous research.

Influences on policy and practice: official reports and the National Curriculum

The Bullock Report (1975) was the first to acknowledge that to lose one's first language is to lose one's culture and identity: 'No child should be expected to cast off the language and culture of the home as she crosses the school threshold, and the curriculum should reflect that part of his life' (Bullock 1975, p. 286). The Committee recommended changes in objectives, curricula and methodology in language education.

During the following decade, schools and education authorities were expected to establish language policies that would recognise and support a variety of mother tongues. Bilingual children were to be considered an advantage in the classroom. The Cox Report (1988) reiterated this viewpoint, suggesting that 'these children would make greater progress in English if their mother tongue skills were encouraged and valued' (Cox 1988, p. xx).

The Kingman Report (1988) discussed the significance of language awareness in the English curriculum and advocated:

> It should be the duty of all teachers to instil in their pupils a civilised respect for other languages ... based on the recognition that all languages are able to express complex emotions and ideas.'
>
> (Kingman 1988, p. 43)

Since the Education Reform Act of 1988, the National Curriculum guidelines have recognised that pupils with limited experience of English should be assessed in their mother tongue, yet, until now, the documentation has offered little in terms of practical advice for the teacher involved with bilingual children. Recommendations appear not only to have been simplistic, but also to have ignored key issues in the debate.

Two recent publications from the School Curriculum and Assessment Authority have addressed the theme of bilingualism from the perspective of teaching and learning English as an additional language. The first, a report of the 1996 SCAA international conference, takes 'a fresh look at the problems and issues surrounding the education of pupils who are in the process of learning English on entry to school' (SCAA 1996a, p. 2). The second, with a foreword by Sir Ron Dearing, offers a framework for policy with suggestions for using National Curriculum programmes of study and resources to meet identified needs (SCAA 1996b).

Teaching bilingual children

The role of the support teacher for English as an additional language has evolved in recent decades in response to changing ideologies, specific school contexts and local educational needs.

Bourne (1989) offers four definitions of a support teacher, based on her survey of local authority provision for bilingual learners: remedial, specialist, catalyst and good teacher. Current policy recommends collaborative teaching where English language support takes place in the mainstream education.

Whilst proficient bilinguals bring special talents to a classroom, the teacher is far more likely to encounter children who are in the process of learning a second or third language rather than balanced bilinguals. This factor has logistical implications for lesson planning and classroom management. To place bilingual children in a withdrawal situation would not appear to be the most appropriate method of teaching English or communication skills. If no support staff are available for collaborative work, the class teacher needs access to essential information from the family and community in order to provide a quality experience for the child.

Where bilingual children are unable to meet the demands of the National Curriculum, and are apparently underachieving, certain questions need to be raised regarding teacher expectation, staff perceptions of bilingualism as well as the provision of adequate and appropriate support. 'Assessment is affected by teacher expectations and children's confidence and so where both are realistically high teachers will be presenting children with the best possible opportunity to do well' (Browne 1996, p. 166).

Schools do not exist as insular institutions, but are influenced by, and a resource for, the wider community. A language policy that supports linguistic diversity will, by implication, promote language awareness as an enriching experience for all children.

> An acceptable early years curriculum for bilinguals extends their thinking, self esteem, language, literacy, creativity, problem solving, social skills and understanding of the world. What more could we want for young monolinguals?
>
> (Whitehead 1996, p. 22)

Where children are perceived as active participants in the learning process, the curriculum will reflect positive teacher and pupil interactions which recognise the value of the home language. Notices and labels printed in different scripts, dual language texts in the book corner, and recordings of songs and rhymes on audio cassettes can offer a meaningful context for bilingual children in school.

Psychological assessments have tended to ignore the existence of cultural or social contexts, and locate problems in the individual child such as levels of intelligence or motivation. A key issue is empowerment. The social and emotional well-being of the young bilingual can be increased by incorporating the home language and culture into the life of the school. If policies are sensitive to dietary requirements, dress codes and religious observances of bilingual families, children of all backgrounds will be able to see cultural, social and linguistic variation reflected positively in their school.

Children, their families and communities

Parental involvement in school can make a vital contribution to a child's progress, particularly in the early years, and has been encouraged since the introduction of the National Curriculum in 1988. Participation by parents must be carefully planned, so that the process is one of consultation rather than confrontation. Where family members are denied access, power or status, children can become withdrawn, suffer lack of emotional and academic progress, and ultimately feel excluded. With bilinguals, this situation is exacerbated.

The interaction patterns between parents and bilinguals may be different to those in monolingual families. Cultural background affects attitudes to child rearing practices, home environment and motivation for language learning. Children from linguistic minorities can be subjected to societal and parental pressure to become bilingual if the home language has limited official status.

Through home visits and parental involvement in the pre-school setting, educators are aware of the child's experiences and interests, and can use this knowledge to plan appropriate classroom activities, thereby bridging the gap between experience in the home and expectations in the play group or nursery.

Multicultural education is not a National Curriculum subject, but is defined by a cross curricular approach embedded in the quality of relationships within a school and its community. Successful liaison depends on a policy of collaboration. Ashworth and Wakefield (1994) describe three types of community that can support adults working with bilinguals in schools: geopolitical groups (the education authority and local neighbourhood), common interest groups (the family, political and religious groups) and professional groups (the educational psychologists and health care services).

Teachers and care givers need to be informed about religious customs and naming systems in different cultures which can affect children's schooling. Members of the community might be able to offer extra curricular mother tongue literacy classes, or be willing to translate correspondence between school and home.

With the co-operation of child, family and community, it should be possible for early years educators to compile a profile of the young bilingual. Information might include the language used by the mother and/or father, the name of a relative or friend willing to interpret for school or parents, the child's preferred language for communication with siblings, the effects of school life, conducted in English, on social behaviour and interpersonal relationships, as well as academic achievements.

Teachers need to know which languages the child is able to read, write and understand, and whether the child speaks a standard form of first language or a related dialect. Gravelle (1996) addresses the issue of terminology such as first, home, community, heritage, preferred language and mother tongue – all of which are used in the context of education, but which can be inaccurately applied.

Young children living in a monolingual society

It is curious that in the United Kingdom, 'community language' or 'mother tongue' are words used to describe a language other than English, just as 'ethnicity' suggests a reference to minority groups or marginalised people. The terminology affirms diversity yet, by implication, the majority is not a community.

> Foreign languages are regarded in English culture as 'other' – not being, or needing to be, embedded in the lives of the learners – quite literally 'foreign'.
>
> (Meek 1996, p. 126)

Many native speakers of English in the United Kingdom believe their monolingual existence to be acceptable, given the status of English as an international language, yet for a high percentage of the world's population, the multilingual approach to communication is the norm.

> Monolingual pupils should be encouraged to value languages other than their own.
>
> (Browne 1996, p. 272)

Equality of opportunity in education must transcend the tokenist approach to multilingualism, and embrace a new philosophy that will resource the implications of linguistic diversity. By exerting some influence in the micro society of the classroom, teachers can foster qualities such as tolerance and linguistic sensitivity in collaboration with parents of multilingual families who encounter the social reality of life in the community.

The excitement and challenge of multilingualism

In Britain, discussion of bilingualism tends to focus on children from the West Indies, Africa and the Indian subcontinent, yet all bilingual pupils have specific needs which are distinct from those of the indigenous population. According to The Primary Language Record (ILEA 1988), these children reflect the normality of the multilingual experience outside Britain.

Multilingualism is a highly complex field, especially if speech and writing systems are considered separately. Children whose families originate from the Indian subcontinent are aware of close links between language, community and religion.

In a guide for parents, teachers and young people interested in bilingual education, Alladina (1995) shares his experience as a multilingual child:

> When I was a child, we used Gujerati at home. My mother and father used Kachchi, a language related to Gujerati to each other. Sometimes there were visitors in the house, when perhaps Urdu, Hindi or English was spoken. The language of the streets and markets was Swahili. The language of religion was Arabic, and the language of the school was English! At school, I was taught to read and write Gujerati and English and later on, I started learning French . . . This is not unusual – it happens in many parts of the world.
>
> (Alladina 1995, p. 9)

Achievement in the National Curriculum assumes mastery of the English language, and bilinguals are expected to reach the same levels of attainment as their monolingual peers, even though they may be developing fluency at the age of seven in the assessment tasks for Key Stage 1. Ironically, when bilingual children with rich linguistic backgrounds are learning European languages in the secondary school, success in public examinations will also depend on their ability to translate into English.

A European Community

Virtually all of the European Union countries have made a national commitment to foreign language learning in primary schools. Some have been teaching languages to young children for many years: The

Netherlands, Luxembourg, Switzerland, Sweden. These policies tend to begin with children between the ages of seven and eight.

In Scotland, recent government initiatives have led to the provision of a second language within the primary curriculum, and children in Wales have benefited from a national programme to promote the Welsh language. Despite the enthusiasm of interested local education authorities, headteachers and school governors, this subject is omitted from the National Curriculum for children between the ages of five and eleven in English primary schools: 'There is no statutory requirement to teach modern foreign languages at Key Stages 1 and 2' (SCAA 1996c, p. 46).

An early start with modern foreign languages can introduce young children to a different means of communication, the existence of cultures other than their own, and ultimately an appreciation of the fact that language is the key to people and their culture. Language learning needs to be central to the aims, organisation and planning of the school day and the wider curriculum.

Increasing parental demand for language learning facilities has led to a plethora of language clubs aimed at very young children, which are attended as an extra curricular activity after school and at the weekend.

If bilingualism is regarded as a communicative and reflective skill, it should be possible to offer second language learning in nursery and primary schools so that all children are given the opportunity to attain a degree of fluency as potential bilinguals.

A specific learning difficulty or a valuable teaching resource? The principal aim of bilingual, and by extension multicultural, education – that of eradicating ignorance, prejudice and racism – applies to all schools. As teachers or professionals in childcare, we should create an environment which promotes the knowledge and understanding of other languages and cultures, and ultimately removes the traditional ethnocentric perspective.

Language differences in the playgroup or classroom lead naturally to an awareness of diversity within society. It is therefore the duty of all adults working with young children to acknowledge the values and experiences of a multilingual, multicultural community.

> Language issues should be seen in the context of education for racial equality and local education authority language centre resources can often be used to raise the awareness of staff and monolingual children.
>
> (Siraj-Blatchford 1994, p. 49)

It is crucial that children are given the strategies and accurate information to reflect the variations within, as well as between, cultures to question and evaluate a variety of media, and thereby develop a positive, authentic view of the world.

Young children in a multilingual world

A society that seeks to address the needs, resources and potential of all children is one which recognises linguistic individuality yet promotes social and racial equality. Language acquisition is to be encouraged and celebrated in the home and in public, and become part of the organic development of the whole community.

Local authorities need to recognise the diversity of linguistic heritage, and promote foreign languages outside their historical, regional and ethnic boundaries, so that they are available to all citizens regardless of age. For the success of such a policy, resources in both the voluntary and public sectors need to be coordinated so that language centres have status in the community.

Fluency in another language brings not only increased knowledge, but also cultural engagement and extension of thinking. Code switching provides the bilingual with an additional means of expression. 'Observation does show that from about three years old, children do use their two or three languages in appropriate and consistent ways. For them, that is, language choice is no longer a problem' (Harding and Riley 1986, p. 55).

Baker (1995, p. 43) believes that 'the bilingual is a different language creation from the monolingual. For many bilinguals, bilingualism is their language.' Even monolingual children operate a number of linguistic systems, demonstrating changes in register or use of regional dialect. By responding positively to the challenges of multilingualism, parents and care givers can affect the quality of childhood experiences for both bilinguals and monolinguals.

Very few studies have investigated the perceptions of bilinguals:

> It is usually clear when the child has no inkling of the fact that she is bilingual and when she has a clear perception of herself as a bilingual person. It is the period of transition which is difficult to pin down.
>
> (Harding and Riley 1986, p.56)

Perhaps attendance at literacy classes, whether to enhance first language skills or knowledge of English, places them outside the society in which they are encouraged to be active participants. This is not a choice that young people like to make, and there may be situations where a child disavows the language of the family in order to be accepted by the peer group.

Any preoccupation with the teaching of English as an additional language must not obscure the deeper needs of bilinguals. The quality of education for young children will be greatly diminished if success is measured entirely in terms of assessment. Children should be given opportunities for developing positive attitudes towards themselves and others: experiences that promote an awareness of difference and the avoidance of stereotype will help young people to validate their perceptions in adulthood.

A number of challenging questions arise in this highly complex area which transcend the purely linguistic issues: the growth of polyculturalism, the interface between linguistic inheritance and affiliation, and the dilemma of whether to change the experience or the expectations for bilingual children. I recall the words of a bilingual child in an inner London school discussing her family profile: 'Just because I can speak two languages, Miss, it doesn't mean I'm two children . . . I'm just me.'

Issues

1. What assumptions are made about the requirements of bilingual children in school?

2. How are bilingual children best supported?

3. What is the effect of family and teacher expectations on the child entering the education system?

References

Ashworth, M. and Wakefield, H. P. (1994) *Teaching the world's children: ESL for ages three to seven*. Ontario: Pippin Publishing.

Alladina, S. (1995) *Being bilingual: A guide for parents, teachers and young people on mother tongue, heritage language and bilingual education*. Stoke-on-Trent: Trentham Books.

Baker, C. (1988) *Key issues in bilingualism and bilingual education*. Clevedon: Multilingual Matters.

Baker, C. (1995) *A parents' and teachers' guide to bilingualism* p. 43. Clevedon: Multilingual Matters.

Bourne, J. (1989) *Moving into the mainstream: LEA provision for bilingual pupils*. Windsor: NFER-Nelson.

Browne, A. (1996) *Developing language and literacy 3–8*. London: Paul Chapman.

Bullock, A. (1975) *A language for life*. London: HMSO.

Cox, C. B. (1988) *English for ages 5–11: Report of the English Working Group*. London: HMSO.

Cummins, J. (1976) *The influence of bilingualism on cognitive growth: A synthesis of research findings and explanatory hypotheses.* Working Papers on Bilingualism 9.

Gravelle, M. (1996) *Supporting bilingual learners in schools.* Stoke-on-Trent: Trentham Books.

Harding, E. and Riley, P. (1986) *The bilingual family: A handbook for parents.* Cambridge: Cambridge University Press.

ILEA (1988) *The Primary Language Record: Handbook for teachers.* London: Centre for Language in Primary Education.

Kingman, J. (1988) *Report of the Committees of Inquiry into the teaching of the English language.* London: HMSO.

Lyon, J. (1996) *Becoming bilingual: Language acquisition in a bilingual community.* Clevedon: Multilingual Matters.

Meek, M. (ed.) (1996) *Developing pedagogies in the multilingual classroom: The writings of Josie Levine.* Stoke-on-Trent: Trentham Books.

SCAA (1996a) *Teaching and learning English as an additional language: New perspectives.* SCAA Discussion Papers: Number 5. London: SCAA.

SCAA (1996b) *Teaching English as an additional language: A framework for policy.* London: SCAA.

SCAA (1996c) *A guide to the National Curriculum.* London: SCAA/ACAC.

Siraj-Blatchford, I. (1994) *The early years: Laying the foundations for racial equality.* Stoke-on-Trent: Trentham Books.

Whitehead, M. (1996) *The development of language and literacy.* London: Hodder and Stoughton.

11

Spiritual development and religious education

Mike Radford

This is a problematic area of the curriculum. Despite a number of efforts on the part of the NCC (NCC 1993), SCAA (SCAA 1996) and others (Best 1996) spiritual development remains a difficult area to define. The difficulties lie in the nature of the spiritual (i) as distinct and yet containing, at least in part, the moral, aesthetic and cultural, (ii) in its association with the potentially sensitive areas of religion and religious education and (iii) the nature of non or 'extra religious' spirituality. It is recognised in this chapter that there is an area of experience that may be designated 'spiritual', an experience of a non material dimension to human consciousness, connected with, and complementary to, moral and aesthetic awareness but not subsumed under them. It is a difficult area of experience to articulate although there is no shortage of scriptural literature that seeks to do so.

Religious education clearly has a crucial part to play in supporting the identification of this experience since it is through religion that such experience has been primarily articulated. There are sound justifications for religious education in the curriculum, over and above how it might support the definition of the 'spiritual'. Religion is a part of human history and is a central focus of human beliefs and values whether one adheres to any particular religious belief or not. To deliberately exclude this area of human thought and activity, as is the case in some countries including the USA and France, is to neglect exploration and reflection on a fundamental dimension to human development.

From the religious point of view, schools are required by the Education Reform Act 1988 to teach a syllabus that reflects:

> the fact that the religious traditions in Great Britain are in the main Christian, while taking account of teachings and practices of other principle religions represented in Great Britain

> (ERA 1988 Sect 8(3))

At the same time the syllabus must not have as its object any 'design to convert pupils or to urge a particular religion or religious belief on pupils' (Education Act 1944 Sect 26(2)). It is natural to suggest that since we are seeking to establish the boundaries for religious education, the content of this part of the curriculum should be focused on religious practice and forms of expression: however, the situation is more complex. It might not be too controversial to claim that the majority of people in the U.K. are not particularly religious. Many people may have some sort of half formed or semi articulated belief in the non material reality upon which most religious beliefs are based (Kibble 1996), but a relatively small part of the population are practising members of any religious group. Religious education in this context may have some relevance as a socio-anthropological/cultural study, taking a kind of objectivist theological approach and this would be in keeping with the legal requirements as stated thus far.

It may be, however, that we have higher expectations for religious education. Religion provides a framework for the articulation of the spiritual dimension to human experience (as well as the moral and cultural dimensions) and it is a legal requirement of the ERA that we attend to the 'spiritual, moral, (and) cultural ... development of pupils'. If we are not, in accordance with the 1944 Act, to convert pupils to a particular form of religious expression, what alternative kind of framework are we to provide for their spiritual (and moral and cultural) reflection and development? If we are not to seek to offer the pupil, or assume that she has from some other source, experience of the non material reality that is accessed through religious belief, how can we approach religious education? The process might become a bit like science without the experiments or art criticism without the aesthetic experience of art!

A number of official publications have been produced in recent years (NCC 1993; DfE 1994; SCAA 1996) reporting attempts to define the 'spiritual' both within and without a religious context, and to establish a place for religious education insofar as it addresses spiritual matters for the religious and non religious alike. Reading these papers is a bit like reading an account of the proverbial blind men trying to describe an elephant, with references to 'the essence of being human', 'development of the inner life' and 'a response to God', the 'other' or the 'ultimate'. Trying to define 'spiritual' experience is similar to trying to define 'aesthetic' or 'intellectual' experience. These aspects of human experience are multi dimensional with a web of interconnections and potential points of emphasis and it may be vain to search for any specific factor that is identified as at the centre of the experience.

There are, however, still substantially unanswered questions in this sensitive and complex area of human experience.

If there is little more to say in terms of the nature of spiritual experience, than has already been said in the discussion papers mentioned above, it would be superfluous to add another blind person's contribution to the 'elephant debate'. What I would like to do in this chapter is present some key questions and, from the perspective of these, to evaluate certain points raised in these discussions. Having offered such an evaluation it may be possible to re-visit the objectives that 'spiritual' and religious education in this context are designed to meet and make suggestions for the development of the agenda in terms of the continuing debate.

The first question concerns the nature of religious education as an articulation of spiritual experience, as it might be seen by the non religious pupil. For the pupil studying science there is a body of experience that is clearly available to all members of the class and by which scientific statements can be objectively evaluated. One might argue that science is by no means the objectivist study that young people tend to see it (Grimmitt 1987). Scientists work under different 'paradigms' and seek to explain experience in different ways; however, it is more easy to access the body of experiences that underlie these different explanations and scientists can, by reference to such common experiences, bridge the 'paradigm gap' even if debate continues to happen. They are able to speak in a common language and in general there has been a drawing together of perceptions among different peoples towards shared understandings of the experience of the material reality that we all share. This may not be the case in religious understanding. The common denominator of experience, an experience of a non material reality, that lies at the basis of the various religious expressions, does not offer the same degree of accessibility and the claims that are made about this reality are consequently less amenable to debate.

The second question is that of the forms by which it might be considered appropriate to articulate the common experience that has been delineated in the context of religious practice, without actually engaging the pupils in particular practices themselves. One may find oneself 'borrowing' from the religious context. The use of ritual, lighting candles and establishing artefacts that have symbolic significance may serve to lend significance to a situation in which pupils are being asked to reflect on the non material qualities that define human life. Simple rituals perhaps with some theatrical aspect also might contribute to a sense of the occasion as addressing matters of such significance.

It may be generally noted that people warm to such experiences. The setting up of shrines, lighting of candles and laying of flowers at various places on the death of the Princess of Wales took on a 'religious' tone with its ritualistic way of expressing a sense of public bereavement. Rituals of this sort, however, are also used in other contexts and might been seen as particularly potent in the processes by which people come to identify with a particular groups. Religious extremists and political groups of the extreme left and right have recognised the power of ritual as a means to encouraging the suspension of judgement. Ritual may have a place in the educational environment but should always be set in a context of reflective judgement.

A third question pertains to the moral dimension in spiritual experience. We are not so much concerned with how spiritual development supports moral education but with the relationship between the two. Moral education is in part the process of moral reasoning, of the development of sound moral judgement but it is also a process of developing and engaging in relationships. There is an issue here that we may trace back through the history of moral philosophy, that is the view that on the one hand moral behaviour is a matter of reason and enlightened understanding and on the other that it is a matter of feeling, of love and empathy for one's fellow human beings. Certainly moral reasoning will play a part in pupils' moral education but the spiritual dimension in relation to moral behaviour is more closely aligned with that part of feelings in that process. Questions that are raised in the context of spiritual development such as those of personal identity and worth, purposes 'in' and 'of' life and the possibility of 'otherness' (SCAA 1996, p. 6) etc., the environment within which young people develop relationships and the discussion of matters of moral judgement will intimately interact with the development of personal identity and worth.

Thus three questions lie at the basis of our analysis – firstly that of how religious education 'speaks' to the spiritual experience of pupils, secondly what alternative frameworks might be available to the pupil, how else might she be led to articulate this part of her experience, and thirdly what is the relationship between moral and spiritual development?

Experience in spiritual and religious education

There are two broad views that underlie the religious education debate and that reflect fundamental philosophical doctrines, that is, on the one hand the extent to which we see understanding and experience as based on an external reality, i.e. realism, and on the other, the notion of understanding as based primarily on human needs and interests that may be seen to be factors in determining, or at least, focusing experience. This latter view sees reality, at least in part, as a construction. If God, insofar as we might place 'him' at the centre of spiritual experience, or perhaps as a metaphor for spirituality, is a human construction, it might still be appropriate to talk of pupils 'discovering' him as an objective reality just as one 'discovers' the music of Beethoven during one's musical education. Alternatively one might wish to see pupils as constructing their own 'vision' or 'concept' in the context of what others have said about 'him'.

From the realist point of view we may ask to what extent religion describes a reality to which we all have access via experience? The religious minded might say that there is a reality, the reality of God, and that some people's experience of God is more vivid and immediate than others. They may go on to say that all people may experience God through religious teachings and observances i.e. worship and prayer. It may be that access to the 'real' and separate 'truth' of God involves more than the courting of, or surrender to, some kind of experience. David Carr (1994) talks of an 'independent order of reality' though whether this is an experienced reality or a constructed one, he does not make entirely clear. What his 'reality' does offer is an objective 'mind independent' truth, accessed through rational discussion based on religious teachings about human purposes and religious ways of life.

In opposition to this view, others might argue that the 'reality' of God is not experienced or rationally constructed in the same way that we experience material objects or rationally construct forms of knowledge such as mathematics or logic. The 'reality' of God does not yield the same sort of shared perceptions available in the exploration of other realities. For most people, the reality of God is not immediate and for those who approach it through religious belief and observance it is variable. The qualities that believers attach to their experience of God depend on the religious framework through which 'he' is experienced. I am conscious here of referring to God as male, and this reflects the ambivalence in human understandings regarding the nature of the deity. Is God male or female or sexually neutral? The significance that one lays on this question and the answer at which one might arrive reflect the idea that God is a construction upon whom we lay our human preoccupations (for the purpose of ease of style I will continue to refer to God as male). There is then a strong cultural context to people's ideas about God and the qualities that are attributed to him. In this context the question becomes one of how far God is an independent reality that is a source of experience for believers and how far 'he' is a human construction based on some vague sense of a non material reality along with a collection of cultural, social and moral beliefs. Whether God is an external reality, or a human construction, does not necessarily make his 'reality' any less objective. God may have objective reality in the same way as we might assert objective meaning to a work of art. If the intentions of the artist are quite clear and if the meaning that is attached by the viewing public to that work corresponds to those intentions then we might talk of a degree, at least, of objectivity in terms of the meaning of this construction. Having said that, the public meaning attached to the concept of God is by no means shared within our multi faith and to a large extent religiously non aligned society.

Thus if the use of religious practices in order to access the 'reality' of God is controversial how then do we handle this area of experience of the non material dimension to human experience that we term the 'spiritual', outside the religious framework? Is it possible to establish a framework that we can use to access the spiritual dimension to pupils' experience, that is religiously neutral, that enables pupils to discuss the constructions of particular cultural perspectives but provides a common denominator for spiritual reflection and understanding? Religious education becomes 'religious studies' with emphasis on philosophical and psychological considerations. The study thus takes on a cognitive and intellectual emphasis and while such activity can help us to focus on experience and establish constructions within which we make it more understandable, it may only partially be understood to deal with the idea we have of spiritual development. As has been suggested it might be a bit like art criticism without actually enjoying the art. Part of the objectives in terms of spiritual development in the curriculum are more akin to those of drama and other arts, that is to develop feelings and attitudes, to sensitise and promote certain beliefs and values without engaging in practices that could be regarded as indoctrinatory. This might be to define a 'conceptual space' within which pupils can freely construct their own responses to the ideas that are being discussed. I will return to this notion of a conceptual space in the next section.

In order to discuss spiritual development one is led to the question of the nature of spirituality or spiritual experience, which is the one that I have said earlier that I wish to avoid. It may, however, be useful to summarise some of the conclusions of existing reported discussions. The NCC produced a paper in 1993 that centres spiritual development on eight points:

1. the development of *beliefs* including religious beliefs and an appreciation of how these affect one's life and contribute to personal identity;
2. a sense of *awe, wonder* and *mystery* at the natural world, or at human achievement;
3. feelings of *transcendence,* to rise above every day experiences and/or an awareness of the existence of a divine being;
4. the *search for meaning and purpose* in or of life including facing the challenge of suffering, beauty and death;
5. self knowledge, the ability to reflect on one's own thoughts, feelings and emotions along with a sense of personal responsibility and self respect;
6. relationships, sensing the worth of others as individuals and being able to build relationships;
7. creativity as an expression of inner thoughts and feelings and exercising imagination, inspiration, intuition and insight; and
8. feelings and emotions, a sensitivity to beauty or kindness, injustice of aggression and learning how to control emotions and feelings.

(NCC 1993)

Clearly some of these points are appropriately addressed in religious education to the extent that through this subject pupils engage in discussion about their beliefs and those of different religious groups. The literature of religious education offers a rich resource for the discussion of mystery, meanings and purposes in and of life, justice and injustice. Other of the above aspects are addressed in study of history, in the arts and are also 'knitted into' the management of the pupils' behaviour by teachers' attitudes towards work and play and the relationships that are established both between teachers and pupils and between pupils themselves. For some, however, religious belief is fundamental to all these aspects and rather than simply providing a set of literatures, or supporting the discussion of one or two of the issues, religious education might be considered to have a more active role to play.

Discussion in January 1996 under the auspices of SCAA (SCAA 1996) gave rise to the comment that spirituality only becomes meaningful when 'developed within a system of beliefs that gives a coherent understanding of the world'. This is in a sense true of all experience and understanding, that whatever is experienced has to be so in a context or framework of expectations, existing understandings and other experiences. Religions may be seen to provide such frameworks. Within the religious perspective spirituality is not the vague and elusive dimension to human experience that touches various aspects of being as outlined above, but provides a coherent understanding, a bringing of everything together under one form of knowledge, set of beliefs and behaviours. Under this view, schools that are aligned to a particular church or profess a particular religious foundation may see themselves as having less of a problem in addressing the spiritual development of pupils. Others may see such institutions as indoctrinatory and potentially insensitive to the needs of a multicultural and ethically liberal society. In constructing a particular framework for the articulation of this aspect of human experience other possibilities are closed off and in the event of the individual losing her faith in a particular system of religious belief there may be no broader framework within which to locate herself in relation to this dimension to her experience.

Furthermore, religious education is not the process of providing a set of beliefs 'that gives a coherent understanding' of the spiritual dimension to human experience. It is not the induction of learners into particular frameworks of religious belief but rather an exploration of how different groups of peoples have addressed spiritual experience and the ways in which pupils are addressing them, if at all, within their own social and cultural context. Discussion on identity, self respect, relationships and the non material qualities that define human life can be conducted in the context of religious teachings and the accompanying literature and indeed it would be to neglect a fundamental dimension to the development of humankind if this area of reflection and teaching was not used.

Thus religious education is a process of examining ways in which different forms of religious belief have sought to define the non material realities of human life. For the pupils this requires the teacher to take cognisance of the ways in which their life experience brings them to these areas of experience. Religious literature provides a resource for discussion of such matters which are of significance to us all, without engaging us in particular sets of belief or doctrine. Furthermore, these realities can be explored in other areas of the curriculum, especially in social studies, drama and the arts.

Other frameworks for the articulation of spiritual experience

As has been suggested above it might be considered negligent to ignore the role of religious education in the spiritual development of pupils. Religious forms of belief and activity are perhaps the major form in which humankind has articulated this dimension to experience; however, there are circumstances of particular sensitivity in our multi faith society where reference to religious belief is difficult in the context of open discussion. Apart from this sensitivity, it may be that people's experience of religious belief, and the consequent response, varies from wholesale acceptance of particular forms to open antagonism to any form. It is therefore important, if the school is to address the developing spirituality of all pupils, to provide a wider range of points of focus than discussion of religions and their literature. In any case, as was suggested above, spiritual development is as much about coming to understand one's feelings, about attitudes and sensitising pupils to particular values and beliefs which may require more than the cognitively orientated discussion of religious beliefs even if it is accompanied by consideration of the aesthetic qualities of scripture.

As was suggested in the introduction it might be that certain aspects of ritual, normally associated with religious practice, are used in secular contexts: however, such practices can take on an artificiality and unless there is a clear identification of the purpose of the activity it may be of little more than cosmetic value. Lighting candles, laying flowers and ritualising certain events in itself does not lead to a greater understanding of the import of an event. What does it do? It makes the event an object of reverence – it sets the event apart, creates a frame of mind that signals our relationship to the event – a process of self definition – says something about what we feel is really important.

Dennis Starkings (1993) identifies the possibility of spirituality outside the religious framework in terms of 'some wisdom, some humanity, some integration of our life's experience' which support us in the way that we 'define ourselves and the world we inhabit' (p. 14). The arts, he suggests, provide us with frameworks of meaning or what Margaret Boden (1994) refers to as areas of 'conceptual space' (p. 79), which direct or provide a basis for the organisation of our experience in terms of this process. The arts are concerned with the construction of meaning at a number of levels.

At one, perhaps crucial, level they are concerned with the construction of formal aesthetic meanings, exploration that is, of the senses, of form and space. Music is essentially about form and as such has been identified as perhaps the purest of arts. A Bach fugue or a Beethoven string quartet say nothing beyond themselves. There is no reference to anything apart from the pure formal construction that is what they are, no more and no less. This is not to say that such music cannot arouse feelings that are used in the context of religious worship to focus worshippers towards experience of the spiritual. There is, however, some question as to the relationship between what we may term the aesthetic and the spiritual. Aesthetic experience in this purely formal sense is the experience of a non material dimension, an aspect of human consciousness often closely associated with experience of a spiritual nature but not the same. An aesthetically rich curriculum, again in the formal sense, would not necessarily meet the spiritual development of the pupil. There are certainly aspects of the aesthetic experience that coincide with those aspects of spiritual experience identified in Starkings' paper cited earlier. There is a sense in which the arts can 'touch us' in terms of our sense of awe and wonder in the face of human achievement. They may also give us a sense of the transcendent, a sense of otherness, particularly in acts of creation. Artists describe inspiration as coming from without, and the Greeks identified or constructed an idea of divine communication through the arts from the Gods of the Muses. The arts also support the exploration of our feelings and the sense of the self. At this purely formal level i.e. simply concerned with shape and pattern in space, as powerful as the arts may be, there are limitations on the extent to which they can construct meanings of a spiritual nature. A Bach fugue or a Beethoven string quartet, as has been suggested, say nothing beyond themselves.

The situation, however, is complicated by the fact that not all art simply inhabits this formal context. Much art has content insofar as it seeks to comment on the human condition. Literature, dance, drama and the visual arts offer opportunities for the construction of meanings at all levels associated with the spiritual. Nothing belongs beyond the daring, others might say arrogance, of the artist. Some art occupies itself with relatively mundane matters but more often than not the arts concern themselves with exploration of meaning and purpose, the nature of human feelings and beliefs and the nature of God himself; all within the compass of humankind as s/he engages in the arts. If this is the case, why do we need anything more? What are the limitations of the arts in terms of the development of a framework for the handling of spiritual experience?

One difference is that although the arts may support an exploration of moral truths and human relationships there is nothing intrinsically moral about the arts. In some instances one might argue that the arts hijack moral issues to make artistic impact. At a popular level the Lennon/McCartney song 'She's leaving home' uses a moral theme of alienation between generations to create a mood. The song might be used as a starting point to explore its theme, but in itself the song does not move the hearer forward. At the level of 'high' culture, the same may be said of Handel's *Messiah*!

Spirituality is not always set in a social dimension. The 'holy' life has, in most religions, found a socially isolationist form of expression, the individual seen in an individual relationship with God and eschewing human contact, but the framework for the exploration of the spiritual in the educational context is essentially a social one. The seeking of God or spiritual transcendence is hardly something that we could expect pupils to engage in on their own (or even necessarily in company) and those who do engage in this task generally do so from an exalted level of spiritual awareness, within a sophisticated spiritual frame of reference and commitment. Thus the exploration of the spiritual might be seen to necessarily involve consideration of the social dimension. Spirituality says something about human relationships and it is unlikely that we will identify the spiritual outside the context of moral development.

A second difference is one of accessibility. Education in the arts is about skills and competences that pupils acquire with varying degrees of proficiency and we can assess achievement both in terms of pupils' performance and in their appraisal of the arts. By virtue of limitations in terms of ability, not all pupils have equal access in terms of the ability to articulate their ideas in the arts. In the context of spiritual development there are certainly judgements that may be made about this aspect of the pupils' educational attainment. Judgements are made by school inspectors about the spiritual development of pupils based on criteria outlined in the Ofsted Handbook *Guidance on the Inspection of Nursery and Primary Schools* (Ofsted 1995). This refers to such matters as the ways in which pupils articulate their consideration of 'life's fundamental questions', whether they display attitudes of reverence or respect in the context of worship and a sense of self or 'self knowledge'. Attitudes and appropriate states of mind, self esteem and a sense of purpose in life, are not matters of competence but perhaps more broadly matters of what it means to be a person, perhaps matters of human psychology. The inspection of schools is based on the understanding that there are more or less appropriate social relationships, certain values in the school, organisational features and characteristics of the management of behaviour and learning, that make spiritual development more or less likely for all pupils regardless of ability. Spiritual development is not a matter of developing skills and competences as that of establishing a certain mental outlook, a 'mind set' that is secure, socially generous, that recognises the appropriateness of respect and reverence in certain contexts. The NCC guidelines mentioned above talk about a sense of wonder and awe in certain contexts, but it may be that an absence of cynicism, a sense of hope and optimism in relation to one's work and relationships with others, is equally appropriate. These are not matters of competence or skill but aspects of the social discourse in which all individuals are to a greater or lesser extent engaged.

This is not to say that the arts do not have a part to play in this process. The arts help pupils to reflect on these matters and are a central tool in the teacher's armoury but spiritual development is not the same as aesthetic development or development in the arts. The framework for the development of spirituality lies in a much broader context than those provided by religious or arts education. It is a framework that is defined by the ethos of the school, in the human relationships and attitudes that are engendered in all aspects of the school's functioning.

Spiritual and moral development

It has been suggested above that it is unlikely that one could identify a good level of spiritual development among pupils without a similarly good level of moral development. If a dimension to spiritual awareness is the sense of wonder at the nature of living things and the environment that they inhabit, then it may follow that that individual will show respect and some reverence for the natural world and for human beings within it. Other aspects of spiritual experience identified in the NCC document are closely connected to the moral development of the individual. The emotional capacity to share in the feelings of others and to sense justice and injustice are clearly important to moral development.

It may be, however, that some of the other qualities of 'spiritual' experience, such as the sense of the transcendent and the idea of meaning and purpose in life, are not necessarily associated with moral considerations as we would see them. There was a strong sense of the transcendent and similarly of meaning and purpose associated with extremist politics in the 1930s. Pseudo religious frames of reference were used to generate popular support for political movements that appealed to these dimensions of human spirituality. Political leaders such as Stalin, Hitler and Mussolini were invested with a degree of divinity by their followers. Their political ideologies were very strong on purpose and meaning in life and a sense of the transcendence as some kind of 'spiritual' reality that was the political ideal. From an educational point of view the point raised earlier, that ritual and ceremony should always be used in the context of exploration and reflection, takes on great importance from reflection on these historical incidences.

Moral education is about teaching the principles that enable individuals to identify right from wrong. The justification for acting morally may be based on the Greek notion that virtue is a form of knowledge that leads one to the good life thus behaving well becomes a matter of enlightened self interest (Audi 1995, p. 840). In this instance one is not left to rely on human feeling or any sense of wonder at the natural world but rather on a knowledge of duty and order. Moral development is quite compatible with a degree of cynicism in spiritual matters and it may be argued that this is probably a safer way to proceed since feelings are often unreliable in the context of moral behaviour. Socrates argues that we must suborn our feeling and 'spirit' to our reason, that we discover the right way to act through reason and that we must discipline our feelings, or 'school our consciences' towards those ends (Plato, trans. Lee 1955, p. 192).

The objective in this chapter is to explore the possible frames of reference within which spiritual experience is recognised, explored and reflected upon. Central to moral education is knowledge and understanding in relation to acts and their consequences but it is unlikely that these could be considered outside the context of feelings, values and attitudes and there is something of central importance to our sense of self, in terms of the feelings we have and the attitudes and values that we adopt. Moral education should not be incompatible with cynicism in terms of awe and wonder and a degree of reverence and respect for the reality we find around us, but the exploration of moral behaviour in discussion and through the arts, drama and literature can help to generate certain feelings that help us in making good decisions in moral contexts. The danger of spiritually guided moral acts, however, is that of idealism and moral education is concerned with moral behaviour in a non ideal world.

Conclusion

Three questions were presented at the outset to this chapter, first that of how religious education 'speaks' to the spiritual experience of pupils, secondly what alternative frameworks might be available to the pupil for the articulation of this experience, and thirdly that of the relationship between moral and spiritual development. It would be vainly ambitious to hope in a brief chapter to do justice to these questions. There are no fixed answers, merely suggestions and conceptions that might move the discussion on in the attempt to find more satisfying or useful perspectives.

In this chapter it has been suggested that religious education provides a framework or marks out a 'conceptual space' within which pupils may explore their experiences in terms of the dimensions identified in the various papers discussed here. The advantage of this notion of a conceptual space (Boden 1994) is more open than the idea of a framework. It allows individuals a degree of creative licence to develop responses that may make more or less sense given the particular experiences of the social group in which discussion is taking place. It is an arena in which young people can experiment with ideas and explanations in their efforts to define themselves and the non material space that they occupy. A further matter of possible importance in religious education is the opportunity that pupils have to explore and reflect upon the nature of ritual and symbolism, and its place alongside that of judgement in religious forms of activity.

The idea of a 'conceptual space' is derived from analysis by Boden in relation to creativity in the arts, draws attention to the arts as an alternative means of expression within which this dimension to human experience can be explored. It is important to bear in mind the limitations of the arts insofar as, first, access to such expression is marked by the development of skills and competences that might in some instances become barriers to such articulation and, secondly, so that we do not confuse the aesthetic with the spiritual. The concept of aesthetic experience in relation to art and criticism provides a useful analogy for religious education and spiritual development. We cannot teach in the arts without some sense of the aesthetic. It is important that pupils experience the aesthetic qualities of the objects of their attention. Religious education is not a process of inducting pupils into particular frameworks for the experience of the spiritual but it is important that pupils, though they may not adhere to the particular beliefs under discussion, understand how they relate to a dimension in their own experience. Religious education gives some ideas of the boundaries to this area of experience and possibilities for discussion within it.

Finally we addressed the question of the relationship between the moral and spiritual development of the pupil. Moral development in terms of the understandings that underlie moral behaviour occupies space both within and outside that defined by religious discussion. How we understand our behaviour from a moral point of view and indeed how we actually behave, is a part of the way in which we define ourselves in relation to others; however, it is important to recognise that moral education has a significant dimension outside that of self definition, empathy and feelings in relation to justice. Feelings are not always reliable in relation to moral behaviour and the existence of moral principles rationally derived from our needs as members of an ordered society are there in order to insulate us from excesses of feeling.

Issues

Inspectors of nursery provision in the private, voluntary and independent sectors (Ofsted 1998) must judge whether each nursery appropriately fosters young children's spiritual, moral, social and cultural development and learning. What might they use as evidence of appropriate fostering:

1. in the area of spiritual development and learning;

2. in the area of moral development and learning; and

3. how might such evidence be a) similar for the two areas, and b) different for the two areas?

References

Audi, R. (ed.) (1995) *The Cambridge Dictionary of Philosophy*. Cambridge: Cambridge University Press.

Best, R. (ed.) (1996) *Education, Spirituality and the Whole Child*. London: Cassell.

Boden, M. (1994) *Dimensions of Creativity*. London: MIT Press.

Carr, D. Knowledge and Truth in Religious Education (1994). *Journal of Philosophy of Education*, Vol. 28, No. 2, p. 7.

DfE (1994) *Religious Education and Collective Worship* (Circular 1/94). London: Dept. for Education.

Grimmitt, M. (1987) *Religious Education and Human Development*. Essex: McCrimmon.

Kibble, D. G. (1996) Spiritual Development, Experience and Education, in R. Best (ed.) *Education, Spirituality and the Whole Child*. London: Cassell.

Lee, H. (trans.) (1955) *Plato: The Republic*. London: Penguin.

NCC (1993) *Spiritual and Moral Development – A Discussion Paper*. York: NCC.

Ofsted (1995) *Guidance on the Inspection of Nursery and Primary Schools*. London: HMSO.

Ofsted (1998) *Guidance on the Inspection of Nursery Education Provision in the*

Private,Voluntary and Independent Sectors. London: The Stationery Office.

SCAA (1996) *Education for Adult Life: The Spiritual and Moral Development of Young People*. York: SCAA.

Starkings, D. (ed.) (1993) *Religion and the Arts in Education*. London: Hodder and Stoughton.

12

Young citizens: children's development of national identity

Keith Sharpe
with
Patricia Broadfoot, Marilyn Osborn, Claire Planel
and Brigitte Ward

Acquiring a sense of national identity

How do young children develop a sense of the importance of their belonging to the country into which they were born? How do they turn the objective accident of birth into a subjective value which can assume such huge significance that they may eventually be prepared to die for it? How is children's sense of national identity different in different countries? In this chapter findings are reported from a large scale ESRC-funded comparative study of children's perceptions of national identity and citizenship in England and France. These reveal marked contrasts in the attitudes of ten and eleven year old children in the two countries and suggest that during early childhood ideas, attitudes, values and sentiments deriving from the culture of the 'national context' are assimilated through a variety of overt and covert social channels. Analysis of the findings indicates that while formal schooling plays a role in shaping pupils' identity, the 'hidden curriculum' may be at least as important as the curriculum which is actually planned for and taught.

The concept of national identity

Identity can usefully be conceived of as a multilayered construction through which a person locates her/himself in relation to various human groupings. At the core of personal identity are the 'selves' grounded in relationships with 'significant others', family, kinship and friends, and surrounding this inner 'heart' metaphorically speaking are an onion-like series of other layers arising out of self identifications with a diverse range of social organisations concerned with work, leisure, politics, religion, residential location and so forth. Each of these layers is one answer to the question 'who am I?': I am a daughter, a wife, a mother, a friend, a pianist, a doctor, a keen gardener, a lifelong socialist, a regular churchgoer etc. Many of these social role identifications essentially take the form, 'I am this, I am not that': I am an anglican, not a methodist, catholic, or muslim; I am married, not single, separated, divorced or widowed. The broadest level of social organisation at which people have to define themselves is in relation to the whole society in which they feel a sense of membership, 'I belong to this nation and not to that nation'.

The 'onion-layers' metaphor for personal identity does, however, have its limitations. Although it may seem reasonable to view national identity as the 'last social identity', the outside of the onion as it were, in practice national identity permeates all layers and is arguably acquired alongside other constituent identity roles. To understand oneself to be an 'anglican churchgoer', at least for those born and raised in England, is already to have absorbed a considerable degree of 'Englishness'. English people with English friends similarly mediate 'Englishness' to each other through their interactions unceasingly, albeit unintentionally. Children born to French families assimilate 'Frenchness' across the dinner table, in the customs surrounding family celebrations, and through everything exchanged in the mother–child relationship.

In what then can 'Englishness' or 'Frenchness' be said to consist? The term 'national identity' encompasses a number of different elements for which an analysis is suggested in Figure 12.1.

The analytical framework proposed here is based upon two important distinctions. The first is between 'experienced' identity, i.e. how a person 'lives' their national identity from the 'inside', and 'observed' identity, i.e. how another person of the same or different nationality 'recognises' characteristic attitudes and behaviours as signalling 'Frenchness', 'Englishness', 'Americanness' etc. The second is the difference between the cognitive and the emotional aspects of national identity, what it is one has to know and understand to have a national identity as against how one feels about belonging to a particular nation. Using these distinctions as parameters generates the six analytic categories above. The concern here is principally with 'experienced' identity as this is lived by young children in England and France, and the ways in which the national context of the two countries shapes their growing sense of themselves as English or French.

INTERNAL
(experience)

understanding of societal   commitment to social/moral/
membership/citizenship   civic values

self-identification and   feeling of national pride
sense of belonging

COGNITIVE--------- NATIONAL IDENTITY---------EMOTIONAL
(understanding)   (feelings)

'characteristic'   'characteristic'
behaviours   attitudes and opinions

EXTERNAL
(observable)

Figure 12.1. An analysis of 'national identity'

National context and national identity: pupil outcomes in England and France

In order to collect detailed evidence about the ways in which national contexts impinge on pupil experience the 'QUEST' research project, funded by the Economic and Social Research Council, was established by a team of researchers based in Canterbury and Bristol (Osborn 1997). The research was based on a representative sample of 400 ten and eleven year old pupils in England and 400 in France across four regions: Calais, Marseilles, Kent and the Bristol area, with schools from four different socioeconomic catchment areas selected in each region. Qualitative and quantitative methods were used in order to investigate three broad issues:

- level and style of achievement in language and mathematics;
- attitudes to schooling;
- pupil identity including national identity.

Clear national differences were apparent throughout, and some of these are reported elsewhere (Osborn 1997; Broadfoot 1997; Planel 1997). In relation to questions concerning their sense of national identity it was clear that English and French children adopted different approaches. As part of a wider questionnaire concerned with their life in class and at school, pupils in each country were asked six multiple choice questions about their conception of themselves as being English or French. They were asked to agree or disagree with statements intended to assess their feelings of national pride, the extent to which they identified themselves with their country and had a sense of 'belonging' to it, the importance they attach to having a particular nationality, how well they feel their primary schooling has prepared them for future citizenship in their society, the degree to which they have been explicitly taught about the multicultural character of the country, and how far they believe they are part of a country in which everybody is equal. The results are shown in Tables 12.1–12.6, and although they arise out of a study of ten and eleven year olds, it is important to bear in mind that they represent the outcomes of processes underway during the preceding years of infancy and early childhood.

Table 12.1.   Sense of national pride.

'I feel very proud of being French/English'

	Strongly agree	Agree	Disagree	Strongly disagree	Not sure	No answer
England	35%	27%	10%	7%	20%	1%
France	57%	21%	5%	7%	8%	2%

Two features stand out from these figures in Table 12.1. The French pupils appear to have a high level of pride in their nationality, and to be very definite about this, as evident in the difference between strongly agree and agree. The English profile of figures suggests an altogether more diffident attitude, with a more even spread across the four categories of response and the 20 per cent who are not sure.

Table 12.2.   Self-identification and sense of belonging.

'I consider myself to be very French/English'

	Strongly agree	Agree	Disagree	Strongly disagree	Not sure	No answer
England	38%	27%	12%	5%	16%	2%
France	70%	15%	4%	5%	5%	2%

The results in Table 12.2 provide an even starker contrast. French pupils seem unequivocal in their identification of themselves with

France, whereas again the English response is much more restrained and more evenly spread across the response categories, again with a relatively high number of 'not sure' choices. It is possible to see two issues involved in this question: is French identity in itself somehow more certain and sharply defined so that French children have a clearer idea of what it is that they have to associate themselves with, or is it just that, while both populations know what their respective heritages are, more French children embrace theirs more enthusiastically? The discussion of freely written comments below develops this point further.

Table 12.3. Commitment to societal membership.

'I think it matters what country I belong to'						
	Strongly agree	Agree	Disagree	Strongly disagree	Not sure	No answer
England	25%	17%	26%	14%	16%	2%
France	48%	26%	5%	4%	15%	2%

The pattern continues in Table 12.3. Almost three quarters of the French sample agreed that their nationality matters, while less than half of the English sample thought so. Forty per cent actually rejected the idea, something done by only 9 per cent of French pupils.

Table 12.4. Perception of education for citizenship.

'In class I learn about what is expected of me as a future French/English citizen'						
	Strongly agree	Agree	Disagree	Strongly disagree	Not sure	No answer
England	9%	21%	24%	13%	30%	3%
France	32%	27%	10%	10%	15%	6%

The figures in Table 12.4 are broadly consistent with previous responses. There are almost twice as many positive responses from the French sample, and the English pupils are once more 'not sure' in large numbers whether they have learned about their future citizenship. These results do nevertheless raise interesting questions about the extent to which the civic education which is an explicit part of France's primary national curriculum actually impacts upon pupil consciousness; higher French 'agree' figures might have been expected by educational policy-makers in Paris.

Table 12.5. Perception of education for multicultural society.

'In class I learn about the life of children who are not of French/English origin'						
	Strongly agree	Agree	Disagree	Strongly disagree	Not sure	No answer
England	16%	25%	19%	7%	29%	4%
France	27%	28%	14%	16%	13%	2%

In 12.5 too there may be disappointments for policy-makers, this time on the north side of the Channel. Multicultural education is supposed to be an important element in pupils' experience in English schooling, yet the positive response amount to only 40 per cent of the English pupil population, with more than 30 per cent not sure or giving no answer. It is less explicit in the official texts governing French schooling yet more than half of the pupils felt they were getting it in some form.

Table 12.6. Perception of social equality as cultural value.

'In France/England all citzens are equal'						
	Strongly agree	Agree	Disagree	Strongly disagree	Not sure	No answer
England	12%	20%	25%	16%	25%	2%
France	27%	14%	14%	20%	22%	3%

This question in Table 12.6 was included largely because of the thorough permeation of the republican concepts of liberty, equality and fraternity in French society, and because of the increasing use of the words 'citizen' and 'citizenship' in English political and media discourse in recent years. This is the one question where the overall response was similar from both population samples, although there is still the intriguing difference that whatever the French pupils felt they tended to feel it more strongly. The English responses hover around the middle, the French responses gather at the extremes.

National context and national pride

At the heart of the issue seems to be whether children have a strong sense of being proud of belonging to the country they identify with. In addition to the multiple choice questions detailed above children were asked to write a response to the open-ended question:

A good reason for being proud of being English is..........
Cite une raison pour laquelle on peut être fier d'être français..........

This is a difficult question for children to answer. Many adults faced with it would struggle to articulate any kind of meaningful rationalisation for their feelings of national pride and the difficulties for ten and eleven year olds are obviously greater. Nevertheless it was thought to be a worthwhile question to include in the questionnaire on the grounds that characteristic national responses might nevertheless emerge reflecting national differences in experience.

The numbers of children overall not writing anything in response to this question were quite high, but noticeably higher in the case of the French sample. Analysis of the answers that were given by the two national populations possibly sheds some light on why there was a difference in the level of non-response. It seems as if what many of the French children were trying to put into words is an intrinsically harder thing to express than what sprang to mind about national pride for many of the English children. Where they found the words to do so many children referred to their feelings of attachment to and affection for France. English children, by contrast, seemed broadly to interpret the question as an invitation to stand back in imagination, almost as if they could for the purposes of the exercise detach themselves temporarily from being English, and then think objectively of pragmatic reasons why being English is a good thing.

French responses included:

parce que j'aime ce pays. Il y a tout.
because I love this country. There is everything.
parce que j'aime la France
because I love France
il y a beaucoup d'ambience et qu'il y a de beau paysage
there's lots of atmosphere and there's beautiful countryside
car on fait des chose intéressantes et c'est un beau pays
because you do interesting things and it's a beautiful country
pour notre beau pays
for our beautiful country
parce que c'est un beau pays
because it's a great country
parce que c'est bien
because it's great
parce que les français sont bien.
because the French are great

English children tended not to write in quite these affectionate terms. The idea of 'la belle France' seems to figure clearly in the thinking of the French sample; 'Douce France, cher pays de mon enfance' in the words of the famous French popular song seems to be a sentiment continuing to be felt by the *classes de cours moyen* (upper junior classes) of 1996. For many French pupils it seemed obvious that if one was born French one would be proud of being French:

parce que je suis français(e)
because I am French
parce que je suis né(e) en France
because I was born in France
parce qu'on est né en France
because you are born in France

These responses offered by many French children give further indication of a kind of unconditional approach to loving one's country. It is enough to be born there to love the place, just as one does not choose to love one's parents; they are your parents and you love them because of that fact. Some also applied this principle to their town as a part of France:

parce que je suis Marseillais et que je suis né à Marseille
because I am Marseillais and I was born in Marseilles

French children who wrote in this vein seemed to be constituting 'France' as a sort of living being, a lovely being who provokes a warm glow, to whom one responds in an a priori fashion and not on the basis of rational choice. The references to the beauty of France are not perhaps to be taken as neutral assessments of the geography of the place. What these French children know, even in the deprived inner city areas of a sprawling conurbation, is that their country is beautiful both literally and metaphorically. They know that France is a country of freedom and equality, if not of fraternity. One child wrote:

car la France est un pays magnifique et démocratique et accueillant
because France is a magnificent, democratic and welcoming country

but this rather high flown tone about a country of ideals was reflected in the comments of several others:

parce qu'ils sont tous égaux
because they are all equal
pour la liberté et l'égalité
for freedom and equality
parce qu'on est libre
because we are free

car la France est un pays libre, donc nous sommes libres
because France is a free country, so we are free
nous sommes tous égaux
we are all equal.

No English child wrote in these grandiose terms. It is significant that while some of the French responses making references to equality might have been prompted by the inclusion of the statement, 'En France tous les citoyens sont égaux' in the preceding multiple choice agree/disagree section, none of the English children wrote anything about equality even though the equivalent, 'In England everyone is equal' was similarly in front of their eyes in the section above. Taken in conjunction with the *liberté* references what this seems to suggest is that French children have absorbed some of the prevailing themes of their society's culture and the discourse through which key values are mediated. It is arguable that the English responses more readily reflect a child's perspective and the French responses tend often to appear as echoes of adult perspectives. It may, however, be that the real distinction is between the essential pragmatism of much English culture on the one hand and the commitment to idealism inherent in French culture on the other, and that by the age of ten or eleven both sets of children have been pretty well assimilated into the cultural outlooks of their respective societies.

If the predominant tone of French responses can be characterised as expressive, the majority of English written responses adopted a decidedly instrumental tone. What obviously preoccupied the English children most were the practical benefits and achievements associated with the country, particularly in the areas of sport, music and language as the following merely illustrative comments suggest:

because we have good football teams
they are a very good football country
what they have done at most sports
good music, good sports teams
we won the world cup in 1966
Man Utd come from England, so do Arsenal
English is a very well known language and it is known world wide
I can talk to people and they understand
I know one language and no others
you can talk to people in Great Britain easily

Throughout the responses there is much less in the way of passion and emotional commitment for the country as such and much more of a measured and calculating 'weighing up' of the advantages. This was particularly apparent in those responses which compared England with other countries less fortunate in respect of wealth, climate, food, wars and so on:

we are very lucky because we don't live in a poor country
I don't live in slums like in Africa and we don't have a hard life
you have pork, turkey, beef, chicken and lamb (a child who had lived in the Philippines where meat was expensive)
we don't tolerate wars or fighting and you need a licence for a gun
it's not too hot or cold
we can have clean water and food to live on
we have good computers
English people are good and healthy

Behind these sorts of observations lies a sort of cold and irrefutable rationality which posits that there are good countries and bad countries and it is obviously better to live in a good one than a bad one. On the kinds of criteria implied above England comes out quite well and so it's good to be English. It is as if the English children interpret the question as suggesting that they can be independent consumers of nationality, consider the alternatives on offer and then opt for Englishness for specific informed reasons. If the French children can be seen to reproduce the sentiment of 1940s popular songs, the English children's approach is more 1880s Gilbert and Sullivan,

and resisting all temptations
to belong to other nations
he remains an Englishman.

Some responses focused on England's perceived superiority in specific respects:

that we join in with most major world wide matters
we have the hardest language
we haven't been invaded since 1066
lots of special people come from England
we are a strong country for how small we are

There were some references to a sense of national belonging but they tended to be couched in more practical terms than the equivalent French comments:

because you belong to the country
being an independent country
I've been told about the country and that's where I come from
to be with your people

Amongst these English ten and eleven year olds there was no clear idea of having an emotional attachment to your country because you were born in it in the way that several French responses suggested. The nearest a few comments came was the notion perhaps best conceived of as 'belonging where you feel comfortable'. It could be said that to prioritise the country's independent state might be another expression of this view, i.e. the desirability of being separated and free from others who are not like you. The only English observation really approaching emotional declamation was the somewhat enigmatic:

Top weather, top all round place, top buzz

The mentions of English national icons were few and far between with only occasional references to the queen and pubs, and none of them indicating any kind of chest-swelling pride:

because we have a good queen
we have pubs and good football teams

A small number of French responses did also make reference to French national icons, and indeed to French sport. However, there is again a difference of tone in the way these are expressed:

pour les monuments crées en France comme la Tour Eiffel, l'Arc de Triomphe
for the monuments created in France like the Eiffel Tower, the Arc de Triomphe
d'aller au stade vélodrome pour voir l'OM (Olympique Marseille)
to go to the football stadium to see l'OM
quand Marseille gagne
when Marseilles wins
quand un Français ou une Française gagne aux jeux olympiques
when a Frenchman or Frenchwoman wins in the Olympic Games

What these comments emphasise is the active experience of being French. You feel proud of being French when you go to the football stadium and experience the collective emotional high of the football crowd, you feel the excitement of Marseilles winning, you imaginatively stand in the shoes of French sports winners who represent you. Even when you think about the monuments, it's not just a case of 'having them', it is that they were created by one's French compatriots. Ultimately the single most important thing created by one's compatriots through the ages is the society itself and some French children's reasons referred to this:

pour son histoire
for its history
pour savoir tout ce qui s'est passé en France
to know everything which has happened in France

A number of English children actually rejected the question.

I don't want to do this question because there is no point. Being English makes no difference to me. If I was born French I wouldn't want to do this one either.

This is quite a remarkable reversal of the widespread view in the French sample that indeed it does matter into which nation one is born. While the above comment is something of a hymn to national neutrality, other comments were more directly negative about being proud of being English:

I don't agree there is any good reason to be proud of being English
I am not proud of being English because we have a bad reputation
I am not proud of being English
There is nothing to be proud of.

It appears that few French children would make these kinds of observations and indicates perhaps the extent to which it is possible for some English children to detach themselves from the nationality of their birth, to make objective assessments of 'Englishness' and eventually to conclude that it is not a particularly good thing.

Some of the children from ethnic minority backgrounds in both samples expressed negative views of the nation within which they were living:

I am not proud because I am a Muslim
Je ne suis pas fier parce que je suis italien/tunisien
I am not proud because I am Italian/Tunisian
Je ne suis pas très d'accord avec les français (child with arabic name)
I am not very much in agreement with the French

Because of the greater prevalence of multicultural approaches in English primary education it might prima facie be expected that children with strong ethnic minority cultural identification would be less likely to be disaffected in England than in France where there is a much stronger emphasis on assimilationist approaches. Although there are some indications that this is not so in the QUEST national samples there is no specific data in the project, and this would need to be the subject of another project.

Why do these differences exist? The significance of 'national context'

A simple answer to the question of why these differences exist is that the cultures of France and England into which young children are socialised are very different in important respects. These cultural differences are evident in the divergent ways in which the formal systems of schooling developed in the two countries. Between 1833 and 1870 systems of elementary education emerged on both sides of the Channel largely in response to changing economic needs, but equally with a concern to provide appropriate moral education for the growing urban industrial working classes. There is a tendency in some educational discussion to talk about 'education' as if it were a some kind of naturally occurring single phenomenon, as if it were possible to remove it from the social context in which it emerges and is lived out daily in schools, as if it were somehow 'neutral'. This might be called the fallacy of neutrality. Education is impregnated with value orientations at every turn. Fourez (1990) comments:

> Les valeurs, les idéologies et l'éducation à la vie sociale sont partout présentes dans l'enseignement. On peut notamment les analyser dans les contenus, les motivations proposées, les relations, les structures institutionelles (quoted in Vinuesa 1996, p. 8)
>
> *Values, ideologies and social education are present in every aspect of teaching. They can be analysed through the curriculum, the systems of reward and punishment, relationships and institutional structures.*

The contrasting development of primary schooling in England and France clearly illustrates the importance of cultural values and beliefs underpinning the institutional structures in which teaching and learning are embedded. Whereas the French state assumed overall responsibility for the education of 'the people' into a common national culture built around republican values, in England the government funded local initiatives to supplement what was already provided privately. And ever since the two systems of primary education can, underneath surface changes, be seen to have promoted divergent but characteristically national values through all the various reforms inaugurated by ministers of education in each country feeling the exigencies of social, economic and political pressures up to the present day preoccupation with assessment and accountability.

It is perhaps useful at this point to attempt to distil out from these different cultural value orientations key contrasting emphases in order to draw attention to the ways in which pupils are 'treated differently' by their respective national systems of schooling. Five contrasts are of particular importance.

1) *universalism (F) – particularism (E)*

The goal of French education is to offer the same education equally to all pupils as an entitlement due to them as future citizens of the French republic, irrespective of who they are, where on the national territory they live (including French colonies), and as far as possible irrespective of any disabilities they may have. As Vinuesa (1996) observes:

> On peut donc suggérer que l'universalité de l'enseignement française est révélatrice de l'héritage républicain et d'une certaine conception de l'éducation comme base de l'égalité des citoyens. (Vinuesa 1996, p. 15).

> *It is fair to suggest that the universalism which characterises French teaching arises out of the republican heritage and out of a certain conception of education as foundation for the equality of citizens.*

While the French system is geared up in every respect to respond to what is universal about children, English primary schooling aims to respond to everything that is particular, local and different: a particular school 'ethos' with rituals, badges and uniforms, classes named after particular teachers, and differentiated work to meet the individual needs of particular children.

2) *collectivism (F) – individualism (E)*

The republican project has always been anxious to make committed French citizens of whoever attends its schools. Education in France is always 'L'Education Nationale' ('National Education') and the categories used to mark progress through the ladder of schooling are always national – the *petits, moyens, grands* sections of the *école maternelle*, the *cours préparatoire*, the *cours élémentaire* and the *cours moyen* of the *école primaire* and the various numerical levels, *sixieme, cinquieme* etc. of the secondary cycle. The child's success is measured by the capacity to master the prescribed knowledge and skills for each rung of the ladder. In this way French children succeed by embodying the national identikit for the stage they are at. English preoccupation with the individual by contrast stresses 'developmental' approaches, with each child presumed to have a 'unique' nature to be brought out and 'nurtured', and so children are expected to develop 'at their own pace'. Even after ten years of the 'national curriculum' in English education, differentiation, wide variations in achievement at the same age, and the lack of any clear sense of a national structure of progress amongst primary pupils are the norm. As Broadfoot *et al.* noted in 1995:

> fundamental teacher values and practices remain substantially unchanged, English teachers' perceptions of education still emphasiasing individual development and the whole child, French teachers' perceptions of education still focusing on the acquisition of skills to standardized national levels.
>
> (Broadfoot *et al.* 1995, p. 6)

3) *specificity (F) – diffuseness (E)*

In France teachers and pupils relate to one another in clearly defined and bounded ways. They relate as teacher and pupil with the roles of each being closely circumscribed. The teacher is there to teach the prescribed curriculum and the pupil is there to learn it. In English primary education teachers' and pupils' roles are much more diffuse, with the teacher seeing herself as responsible for all aspects of the child's development – social, moral, cultural, spiritual, physical, aesthetic as well as intellectual/cognitive.

4) *ascription (F) – achievement (E)*

In France the pupil's identity is largely an ascribed one: if he or she is in the *cours préparatoire* then he or she will be treated as a *cours préparatoire* pupil, the same as all the others, wherever they are in France. It is predominantly an identity ascribed on the basis of a given social category. Individual characteristics which mark this particular child out as different in personal terms are largely treated as irrelevant. In a real sense this is arguably a preparation for citizenship in that a key principle of republican citizenship is that citizens are, or are treated as, homogeneous with no fear or favour being accorded to individual differences. In England pupil identity (and teacher identity) is a much more open business, with opportunities to acquire a range of positions within the class according to the vagaries of individual behaviour, attitudes and performance. In the absence of clearly defined national educational statuses everything is open to negotiation between pupil and teacher in the particular local circumstances obtaining within the class, the school and the local area.

5) *affective neutrality (F) – affectivity (E)*

Teachers in France treat their professional obligations in a contractual manner (Broadfoot and Osborn 1993; Sharpe 1997a). They have a specific duty to discharge on behalf of the French state, and they deal with the objects of that duty in an affectively neutral manner. It is not expected that they will develop personal relationships with their pupils. In England, by contrast, the rich diversity of teacher–pupil interaction is meant to facilitate deeper relationships through which social, moral, emotional and spiritual values can be developed.

The argument being advanced here is that these two sets of values are institutionalised in English and French schooling and they influence pupil identity both explicitly and implicitly. Almost 100 per cent of French three year olds are in formal schooling and the national policy is to extend this to all two and a half year olds. At the point of entry they become part of this huge national system which has been the common experience of their parents, and their parents' parents and for several generations back all over France. Progressing from the *cours préparatoire* to the *cours élémentaire*, reciting *leçons*, preparing for regular dictation tests are all examples of shared national experience which are part and parcel of the taken for granted discourse of everyday life to which children are exposed at home, in the neighbourhood and through the media. Only in a country like this could two hours of prime time television on a Saturday night be devoted each year to National and International Dictation championships.

Few two and a half year olds are in any kind of educational establishment in England and formal primary education starts years later. In the primary classroom children confront a smiling teacher who is interested in them as persons. Each child finds her own individuality celebrated and her own creations valued and displayed. She is encouraged to make choices and to reflect on what she has learnt. She is expected to do her best and to develop her potential. She is encouraged to identify with her class and with her teacher, and beyond this with the school as a local moral community based on respect for individuals. She learns that it is most important to be a nice person. As that most English of English educationists, Sir Michael Sadler, observes:

> The German is apt to ask about a young man, 'What does he know?'
> The American to ask, 'What can he do?'
> The Frenchman to ask, 'What examination has he passed?'
> The Englishman's usual question is, 'What sort of fellow is he?'
>
> (Sadler 1906)

The kinds of national identity these two approaches to schooling engender are evident in the responses of the children reported above. On the one hand there is a the high profile sense of national belonging characteristic of the French pupils. It is possible to see a parallel between this and the open-ended responses to the question Broadfoot *et al.* (1988) asked in an earlier study focusing on English and French primary teachers, 'how would you characterise your teaching style?' For many French teachers teaching was not something about which such questions made any real sense. Teaching is teaching, it is unproblematic, given and obvious. Similarly for many French pupils their French identity and national pride are in the same way apparently both givens. For responders, and almost certainly also for a large number of non-responders in the French sample, it appears to be self-evident that if one is born French one will be proud of being French and there is little or nothing more that needs to be said. By contrast, just as the English teachers in the earlier study felt able to articulate sometimes lengthy, considered answers about the exact implications of the various strategies they employed in their overall teaching style, children in the English sample were much more willing to take the question at face value and attempt to offer sensible, itemised 'reasons' for being proud of being English, and even in some cases to volunteer reasons for not being proud of being English.

Can national identity and pride be taught?

The issue of teachers' responsibility for fostering young children's sense of national identity has assumed considerable significance in the English policy context over recent years. In particular, Nicholas Tate, chief executive of the School Curriculum and Assessment Authority (now the QAA: Qualifications and Assessment Authority), has forcefully argued for the importance of schooling in shaping national identity:

> The proposals for British history, standard English and the English literary heritage are designed to reinforce a common culture. A national curriculum, we imply, is more than just a recipe for meeting economic needs, vital though these are; it is more than just the means to facilitate the infinitely varied life choices of collections of isolated individuals. It also plays a key part in helping society maintain its identity.
> *(Times Educational Supplement* 29 July 1994, p. 5)

At a SCAA national conference on 'Curriculum, Culture and Society' he contended that

Education is about developing the individual within a community, and individuals' sense of identity with the communities to which they belong. It is especially about developing pupils' sense of civic and national identity.

(SCAA 1996, p. 14)

The question is, however, whether, or to what extent, national identity is actually something easily amenable to being affected by overt educational policy. The evidence from the above research suggests that the kinds of national identity apparently developed in English and French nursery and primary schools have more to do with basic values institutionalised in the culture of the wider society than with explicit teaching of programmes of study in a national curriculum. Indeed, another contributor to the same SCAA conference, Evans (1996), drew attention to the importance of the work of the historian Linda Colley, who has argued that at the time of the 'forging of the nation' in the seventeenth and eighteenth century England's fundamental value commitments derived from Protestantism (notably particularism and individualism in opposition to the universalism and collectivism apparent across the Channel), and that the strength of national identity is fundamentally related to perceptions of 'threat' from a more powerful 'other' nation/group. Interestingly in the light of the overwhelming preoccupation of the English pupil sample with football, Evans also observed that :

National identity in the twentieth century is revealed by sporting allegiance. Most sporting enthusiasts evince much less support for England than they do for their local, or regional, clubs.

(Evans 1997, in SCAA 1997)

It is certainly true that there are differences between the curriculum offered to French pupils and the present form of the primary curriculum in England. In particular there is the complete absence of religious education in France, which has always been banned in state schools, and the inclusion of civic education right from the beginning stages of elementary education. The situation in England is of course the reverse. It is arguable that the effect of this difference lies not so much in the overt 'content' of RE syllabuses on the one hand or civic education programmes on the other, but rather more in the implicit values which the two channels mediate: the one emphasising the moral development and spiritual awareness of each individual child, the other stressing the rights and duties of 'the citizen', whoever, whatever, wherever they may be. In other words, what shapes children's growing conceptualisation of their national identity are all the messages received about what the environning society believes in, holds dear, and takes for granted as obvious. Apart from the alternative message conduits of family, neighbourhood, peer group and the media, school itself communicates important messages through channels other than direct teaching. Indeed, direct teaching may itself communicate unintended or undesired (by teachers) messages. Where there is pupil resistance, disaffection or opposition (an anti-school culture) direct teaching of values may be ineffective or counter-productive. It is significant in this connection that the QUEST project found much higher levels of pupil identification with teacher intentions in France than in England, where the existence of resistant peer cultures appeared widespread.

At the end of the recent SCAA conference it was noted that 'If citizenship education is introduced, there are resourcing issues and teacher training implications'. If the above analysis is valid, and if 'citizenship education' is intended to go beyond factual instruction on democratic procedures, legal responsibilities and the like to attempt to foster an enhanced sense of national identity it is likely that the teacher training and resource implications will be far from a simple matter.

Issues

1. Reflect on your own sense of national identity, and discuss:
   - How strongly do you feel it?
   - How does it relate to other aspects of your personal identity?
   - How do you think you acquired it?
2. Do any of the findings in this chapter surprise you? Why, or why not?
3. What do you consider to be the proper role of parents and teachers in promoting a sense of national identity in young children?

References

Broadfoot, P. and Osborn, M. with Gilly, M. and Paillet, A. (1988) What Professional Responsibility Means to Teachers: national contexts and classroom constants. *British Journal of Sociology of Education*, 9, 3, 265–87.

Broadfoot, P. and Osborne, M. (1993) *Perceptions of Teaching*. London: Cassell.

Broadfoot, P., Osborn, M., Planel, C. and Pollard, A. (1995) *Systems, teachers and policy change: a comparison of English and French teachers at a turbulent time.* Paper Presented to the European Conference on Educational Research, Univerity of Bath.

Broadfoot, P. (1997) *A comparative Study of Pupil Achievement in England and France*. Paper presented to the British Educational Research Association conference, University of York.

Osborn, M. (1997) *Learning, Working and Climbing the Ladder: Pupil Perspectives on Primary Schooling in England and France*. Paper presented to the British Educational Research Association conference, University of York.

Planel, C. (1997) *'Il était une fois' and One Fine Day in Wallopville': The impact of learning culture on children's approaches to story writing in England and France*. Paper presented to the British Educational Research Association conference, University of York.

Sadler, M. (1906) Lecture agiven on the occasion of a visit of professors from the University of Paris to the University of London, in 1906. Quoted in Vinuesa q.v.

SCAA (1996) *Curriculum, Culture and Society* – Conference Report. London: SCAA.

Sharpe, K. (1997a) English – and not very proud of it. *Times Educational Supplement* 23/05/97.

Sharpe, K (1997b) The Protestant Ethic and the Spirit of Catholicism: ideological and institutional constraints in English and French primary schooling. *Comparative Education*, 33, 3.

Vinuesa, M (1996) *Transmission Culturelle par le Curriculum Caché – La socialisation des enfants de 5 à 7 ans à l'école publique en France et en Angleterre*. Unpublished doctoral thesis Université de Paris XIII.

13

Changing childhoods, changing minds

Tricia David and Sacha Powell

Time, place and childhood: constructions of childhood and societal values

Much of what we take for granted in our lives as in some way fixed is in fact a social construction. The millennium itself is occurring because our ancestors decided to call what they conjectured to be the year of the birth of Christ as year zero – hence we end up celebrating the year 2000. Events such as this are seen by some as having mystical significance. However most of us view the millennium, it can be the catalyst for reflection on how our society has been, and is, developing. Among other debates, it can cause us to pause and consider our country's attitude to and treatment of the youngest children in our society.

What is a child? According to both the UN Convention on the Rights of a Child (United Nations 1989) and the UK's Children Act 1989, a child is a person aged between birth and eighteen years. In this chapter, as in this book as a whole, we are considering the earlier years of childhood, from birth to eight, which is internationally recognised as 'early childhood'. However, once infancy is past, chronological age may not accord with sociocultural behaviour, as Allison James points out (1998). Once it had been realised that expectations about

> the abilities and competencies of 'the child' had been shown to vary cross-culturally and over time, it was suggested that biological development must be seen as contextualising, rather than uneqivocally determining, children's experience.

(James 1998, p. 47)

What happens to, or is thought to be 'right' for, young children in

204

any society or subcultural group is related to the childhoods constructed by that society (Nunes 1994; Tobin *et al.* 1989; see also Keith Sharpe's chapter, 'Young citizens', in this book). Once we become aware of the ways in which childhood itself is constructed in different societies or at different times, we also begin to ask ourselves why children are treated in certain ways, why particular curricula are considered appropriate for children at different stages in their lives and what all this tells us about that society.

For many years babies and young children were not accorded the powers psychologists now acknowledge. For example, Deloache and Brown (1987) and Singer (1992) have documented the ways in which developmental psychology, because of its underlying assumptions and methods, failed to access those powers.

It was probably the ground-breaking paper 'The American child and other cultural inventions' by William Kessen (1979) which challenged many of the notions held by both developmental psychologists and created a climate in which psychologists began to liaise with others, such as historians and sociologists (see for example, Elder *et al.* 1993; Panter-Brick 1998). Kessen could see that childhood is defined by a particular society at a particular time in a particular way. What Kessen, who in the mid-1970s participated in a delegation visiting educational settings for children in communist China (Kessen 1975), was really highlighting was the question of why different societies construct childhood in particular ways and why certain childhoods are assigned to particular children. By claiming that one version of childhood is a correct or true version and by demanding conformity, developmental psychologists and early years practitioners appear to have operated in a culture- or context-blind fashion. We must ask if in defining stages in development and in seeking to protect young children, we also limit their achievements.

'That children have certain characteristics, that adults have others, and that it is natural to grow from one to the other, are messages that we receive from all forms of mass communication' (Morss 1996, p. 29). In each of his challenging studies Morss (1990 and 1996) questions the taken-for-granted nature of developmentalism in Western/Northern thinking about children. He cites Harré's (1983, 1986) argument that

> stage-based accounts of childhood make the pretence that a sequence of stages unfolds through some natural process. ... The world or worlds of the child, Harré argued, have to be described not as if biologically determined but more as forms of culture.
>
> (Morss 1996, pp. 33–34)

Another member of Kessen's delegation to China, Urie Bronfenbrenner (1975 and 1979), attempted to bring together context and biology in his ecological theory of child development. He proposed that each child's 'ecological niche' is unique because each will experience the relationships and processes of interaction between home, nursery, wider world and the ideology in which all these are embedded. He also argued that children themselves, like the others around them, actively influence this 'ecological niche'. Since that time the idea that members of a group or society co-construct particular childhoods and that children are active participants in that construction has provided a powerful challenge to decontextualized theories of child development. More recently, Bronfenbrenner (Bronfenbrenner and Morris 1998) has further developed his ecological theory of child development into a bioecological model, because of his recognition of even more complexity throughout the lives of human beings. Bronfenbrenner has become especially aware of the omission, and importance, of personal characteristics, of processes, and of time as factors which have an impact.

As Bronfenbrenner and Morris (ibid.) point out, in the past, a research finding which did not 'fit' a tight model, with many of the 'variables' in a child's life 'controlled', would have been seen as 'wrong/ a mistake' rather than challenging the research and theory design. By opening up to other disciplines with other theories, researchers such as Kessen and Bronfenbrenner have shown how much more can be learnt about the focus of our attention and about the way our cultural assumptions can lead us to inappropriate, narrow conclusions, for 'the disciplines have different stories to tell' (Elder *et al.* 1993, p. 175).

It may be that alliances between early years professionals from a range of fields and disciplines will move us on even further in our ability to comprehend and respond reflectively to young children. For this reason, those of us in the education field need to look more widely at the ideas and research from a range of other areas of study. Stimulating new ideas concerning the complementary nature of genetic and epigenetic factors in children's brain development are being researched by psycho-physiologists such as Lambert (1996) in Paris. He suggests that contrary to the notion that babies and young children have to wait for their nervous connections to grow and for interaction with the environment to stimulate that growth, there are in fact many connections already in existence and it is through the complementarity of biology and experience that just one nervous connection (for a particular muscle action let's say) survives – the others die off. We can see how such a theory makes sense in the way human babies display all the sounds necessary to speak any language – but by around twelve months of age a child will begin to lose all the sounds not used in the home language or languages. Similarly, it makes sense in relation to the influence 'significant others' have on the meanings children attribute to objects and events in their lives, for it is through these significant others that children's early attempts to make sense of their world are mediated – their co-construction of their world is determined by the ability of those around them to both aid that co-construction by being able to 'see from the child's point of view' and to understand that world themselves (see Mike Radford's chapter 'Co-constructing reality' in this book).

Now Gardner (1983) has added a further dimension to the questioning of assumptions about childhood, by questioning assumptions about what kinds of achievements we nurture through our education systems. Gardner proposes (ibid.) the idea of multiple intelligences, most of which we in the West appear unable to foster because we cannot 'see' and do not value many of those 'intelligences'. As he explains,

> The time has come to broaden our notion of the spectrum of talents. The single most important contribution education can make to a child's development is to help him (*sic*) toward a field where his talents suit him best, where he will be satisfied and competent. We've completely lost sight of that. Instead, we subject everyone to an education where, if you succeed, you will be best suited to be a college professor. And we evaluate everyone along the way according to whether they meet that narrow standard of success. We should spend less time ranking children and more time helping them to identify their natural competencies and gifts, and cultivate those. There are hundreds and hundreds of ways to succeed, and many, many different abilities that will help you get there.
>
> (from an interview quoted in Goleman 1996, p. 37)

The dominant discourses concerning 'the very young child' in the UK have tended to be based on limited and out-dated theories and beliefs. In the past, ideas about maternal deprivation and children's emotional needs (Bowlby 1953) were used as arguments against the provision of nursery education (see David 1990). Further, the idea that young children are active learners capable of constructing their own view of the world, or rather co-constructing it with knowing others around them, and that they are capable of participating in the creation of knowledge was not used to inform a coherent policy for our youngest children. Although the present Government's requirements relating to local authority nursery and daycare plans are an improvement on any previous national strategy to date, conceptual difficulties related to these powerful discourses seem almost insurmountable. For standards of achievement to be raised, the birth to five age-phase needs to be thought of as one 'cycle' in the education process, the six to eleven years primary 'cycle' the second and Key Stage 4 as the third. At present, children under five in Britain experience numerous changes of settings during those first five years, some even spend time in two different edu-care settings within a single day, in order to cover their parents' work hours. Further, there is a notion that the learning achieved in the first five years is not 'real education' and that the purpose of nursery provision is to prepare children, to lick them into shape in a number of ways, so that 'the reception class can begin the proper process of education' (*The Times* 1995, p. 17).

Earlier this century professionals in the UK who worked with babies and young children were told that newborn babies do not feel pain, that young children cannot understand the world from another's viewpoint, that they cannot communicate or interact with others. However, recent research suggests that children come into this world 'programmed' to make sense of the situation in which they find themselves and to communicate with other human beings (Trevarthen 1992) and that they learn more in their first five years than in all the other years of their lives.

The ways in which we think young children should be treated and educated today is not only influenced by our national, local and family histories, it is influenced by the ideas with which we have come into contact. However, we are constantly becoming more aware of the ways in which ideas, like childhood itself, are shaped by the time and place in which they are 'born'. For example, Ariès's (1962) idea that childhood was not regarded as a separate phase of life in Western Europe during the Middle Ages, and the idea that because so many children died early in life their parents would not care about them, together with Postman's (1985) claim that childhood was invented with the printing press, have been challenged (James 1998; Pollock 1983).

Recent research indicates that babies and young children will live 'up or down' to societal and family expectations, that they will try to please the adults around them in order to be valued, loved and accepted (e.g. Bruner and Haste 1987; Trevarthen 1992). So the curriculum we decide on for young children, both its content and its teaching approaches, may have crucial long term consequences for our society. We have to decide what kind of people we want our children to be and to become. We have to ask ourselves how they will cope with a world we will not be here to see and experience, and above all we have to remember they may be small but they are not our possessions. They are people who are actively trying to make sense of their world.

Childhood in contemporary Britain

British family policy has been permeated with the belief that 'an Englishman's home is his castle' to such an extent that state intervention in the family is thought an intrusion and a diminution of rights. Compared with other European countries, Britain's approach to family policy has been described as 'implicit and reluctant' (Fox Harding 1996, p. 205) and as 'pro-family and non-interventionist' (Gauthier 1996, p. 205), which means, for example, that while there is no discouragement to both women and men to go out to work when they have small children, their childcare arrangements are their own responsibility. In previous centuries, children would have been seen as their parents' possessions (or more correctly, the possessions of the senior male member of the family) and, perhaps because most policy makers throughout history, certainly until recently, would not have spent much time with babies and small children, they may have contributed to the notion that 'real learning' begins at school and that babies are rather like parcels which can be left to be looked after anywhere. Unfortunately, developmental psychology in its early days did little to dispel this myth, because observations of small children in unnatural laboratory situations doing meaningless (to them) tasks were doomed to show them as fairly incompetent. The views and observations of those most familiar with small children, their mothers, nannies, carers and nursery workers would have been discounted as uninformed and unscientific. Developmental psychologists too are recognising that earlier research underestimated children's powers (Deloache and Brown 1987).

One of the main influences on our understanding and assumptions about babies and small children in the UK would have been the church. Perhaps an advantage of the Protestant Church of England's assumptions, compared with Roman Catholic assumptions, as far as children are concerned, would have been the relative unimportance of original sin. However, a key disadvantage would have been the inculcation of the Protestant work ethic – even little children being expected to take life seriously and not waste time on joy and idleness.

Perhaps this belief has led to notions such as 'if it isn't hurting it isn't working', and the mistaken view that play and fun are not conducive to learning. Thus there may be a feeling that the education process should be painful, rather than a delightful, challenging adventure (although Keith Sharpe's 1997 conclusions about the comparative harshness of French primary education would contradict this idea – see his chapter on citizenship in this volume).

Yet it seems strange that in a country where not only would both churches have taken Jesus Christ's teaching as the basis for action, most politicians and educators too would have claimed Christian credentials. Presumably they acknowledged his call:

> Let the little children come unto me. If any man harm one hair on the head of one of these my little ones, it were better for him if a millstone were hung around his neck and he were cast to the bottom of the sea

as a principle, so one is left wondering about their interpretations of this aspect of his ministry.

Unfortunately, the way in which we, in the UK, treat young children does not appear to be always underpinned by the philosophy enshrined in Christ's statement. Using both international comparisons with other Western/Northern nations and comparisons with our own national records, we find that during the last few years:

- the reported infant mortality rate is higher in the UK than in Sweden, Norway, Switzerland, and the Netherlands and higher proportions of the UK population live in relative poverty than in those countries – and the divide between rich and poor has increased during the last fifteen years;

- the UK and Denmark have the highest percentages of lone parents in the European Union (EU) and there are links between lone parenthood and poverty (Utting 1995);

- studies have shown that there is evidence of a decline in average reading standards unaffected by teaching methods but related to the rapid increase in relative deprivation (Wilkinson 1994) and achievements (or lack of them) in the later years of school are also related to socio-economic factors;

- more than half the children in London's poorest boroughs are entitled to free school meals (Brindle 1994) and the growing differentials in access to a healthy environment and diet carry risks such as increased risk of early death (Kumar 1993);

- the UK has the fastest increase of maternal employment outside the home yet more than a third of fathers of children aged between birth and nine years work more than 50 hours a week – the highest levels in the EU (Cohen 1990). The result can be little time to spend together as a family – yet we have known for many years that isolation can lead to parental depression;

- meanwhile, parental anxiety about the potential for child physical abuse as a result of the stress caused by unemployment has been documented by the NSPCC – the UK has the second highest proportion of unemployed fathers of children under nine in the EU (Moss 1996);

- the risk of homicide for babies under one year old is four times that of any other age group. We have the fifth highest rate of infant homicide in the European Union (Butler 1996).

Thus the childhoods experienced by children in different areas of the UK, or from different family backgrounds, are not the same. We now know that diet casts a long shadow forward, but so too does the family and community's ability to provide emotional, social and intellectual stimulation. Such evidence of the links between poverty and failure has been borne out in a recent analysis of Ofsted's own data (Pyke 1998).

Of course, the list above paints a particularly gloomy picture. Most of our children are thriving, well-cared for and well-educated. But all too often we assume that Britain offers 'the best' to all its citizens – including the youngest – and since this is presumably what we would wish to achieve we must evaluate the areas where we clearly do not offer 'the best'.

Another country which has made tremendous strides during the last few decades in terms of its ability to deal with famine and other natural disasters, together with the devastation caused by war and a turbulent history, is China. Since William Kessen's delegation visited the country over twenty years ago, naturally much has changed. Although, as we stated above, many different childhoods must be currently extant in contemporary Britain alone, as China is a country with a different ideological perspective from that of the UK, it is thought provoking to explore the similarities and differences between the two, in order to recognise and reflect upon some of the influences which only become 'visible' in one's own society by investigating one which is very different. It is to this overview we now turn.

Childhood in contemporary China

To build a single picture representing the lives of children at any given time in a chosen country is at best difficult, and at worst guilty of over-generalisation. Faced with the People's Republic of China as that chosen country, it is vital not only to recognise that this nation contains some 22 per cent of the world's population spread over a vast geographical area, but also that within that figure there exist 55 ethnic minorities whose cultural heritage and traditions, spoken language, environment and daily lives can differ greatly from one to the next (Gladney 1994), and by comparison with the majority of urban-dwelling (Han) Chinese people, upon whose situation this account is focused.

Childhood, as a social phenomenon, is well-chronicled (Kinney 1995) as far back in Chinese history as the Han Dynasty (206 BC–AD 220) and some of the forces which play a part in piecing together the contemporary jigsaw of childhood can be traced back to these premodern times, while others are the product of a recently transformed society.

Some of the most enduring of Chinese native traditions stem from the writings of the early philosopher and scholar, Confucius. His teachings were mainly concerned with the family as a social unit, and the hierarchies to be found within that unit. For centuries, Chinese children have been brought up in accordance with the principles which taught that they should honour and respect their parents, ancestors and 'ruler'. Bound up with the hierarchies and the pervasive practice of ancestor-worship came a predilection – or indeed necessity – for families to desire to bear sons in preference to daughters. Although the way of life prescribed by Confucius is not one which always fits with the modern Chinese urban family, and should not be seen as the single religious or philosophical tradition influencing current Chinese child socialization (Lau 1996), evidence points to an abiding desire among Chinese couples to have a son.[1]

During the leadership of Chairman Mao Zedong (1949–1976), the Confucian values which advocated respect for parents and teachers were sidelined as the Cultural Revolution (1966–1976) thrust political ideology to the fore, and respect for the Communist Party became paramount, with the additional emphasis upon aspiring to emulate the ways of the workers and peasants. The present leadership maintains its ideological hold upon the people by organising community- and work-based political meetings on a regular basis.

China's moves towards economic modernisation and its espousal of a greater openness towards international exchange (in trade, education, culture etc.) are also factors in the construction of childhood in China today. Guanzhou, Shanghai, and Beijing are just three of the now many, rapidly changing, ever more cosmopolitan cities in China where consumer goods fill the shelves of entrepreneurs' shops and stalls, and where cars are replacing bicycles on the busy streets (see Christiansen and Rai 1996).

Education in China is highly valued by the government and the people, and facilities, resources and standards are constantly being improved. In spite of such improvements, demand for preschool provision still outweighs supply. The decline of the extended family group in China has exacerbated this problem. In the current economic climate, where both parents need to work to maintain a reasonable standard of living, the small nuclear family is unable to handle childcare and so looks to kindergartens and pre-primary classes (run by neighbourhood committees, the place of work, the state or private institutions). Although the preschool curriculum is standard throughout the country, the quality and quantity of such childcare is not uniform, and children in remote areas tend to come off worst in the equation. Similarly, shortages of funds and training mean that some institutions would be seen as grossly understaffed by comparison with UK ratios. Further, many of the staff have few qualifications, particularly in the more isolated communities (Ebbeck and Wei 1996).

Perhaps the most significant factor in modern Chinese childhood has been the enforcement of the One Child per Family Policy, which the Chinese government introduced with severity in the late 1970s in order to stabilise population growth, so that the country's modernisation drive might have a greater chance of success. Draconian punishments for non-compliance began to be imposed, particularly in the cities, and incentives or honours were offered to couples who adhered to the policy.

While the most obvious result of the plan is that many Chinese children have no siblings, it has also led to problems in relation to the desire for a son (and failure to have one), and has produced a national anxiety about spoiling. The '4-2-1 syndrome' (Tobin *et al.* 1989) where grandparents and parents lavish their attentions upon an only child led to such children being dubbed 'Little Emperors' whose alleged wilful ways and brattish natures were frequently reviled in the Chinese media, since such children did not fit the picture of the model Chinese citizen, dedicated to the good of the community. The concern among parents is such that even greater pressure has been heaped upon preschools to provide an antidote to spoiling at home, and the curriculum places great emphasis upon altruism and collectiveness.

In spite of the problems associated with the One Child Policy, it does also have its merits. Where family finances are limited, there are fewer mouths to feed, and the child may benefit from more parental free time. The decrease in the population growth, and the increase and improvements in child care and other facilities provide children with better education, health and welfare.

Childhood UK 2000: a vision for the future

As a nation,the UK has signed up to the UN Convention on the Rights of the Child (United Nations 1989). Furthermore, we have the Children Act 1989, which requires we act in the best interests of the child, heed the child's views, support parents in their role as responsible carers and, as professionals involved with children and their families, work together effectively to these ends. As Louise Sylwander, Children's Ombudsman for Sweden, has pointed out, 'the Convention is something which has to be lived' (Sylwander 1996, p. 49). The way we think of and, as a result, treat children, especially those in their earliest years, has consequences. In the end, we get the children we deserve. *The Child as Citizen* (Council of Europe 1996) reminds readers that children form one of the largest groups in society but they do not form a lobby and are rarely represented in decision-making processes.

Furthermore, we cannot disembed the economy from the polity. Valuing children, both nationally and globally, the inheritance of a 'civic covenant' which includes a moral responsibility for the generations which follow us, is John O'Neill's (1994) argument in *The Missing Child in Liberal Theory*. He suggests that the power of the global market must be restrained, that capitalism has always been dependent upon moral and political restraints to keep it from destroying itself.

The constant reminders that our education system is failing our children always seem to omit the fact that we do not, as a society, pay enough attention to the very earliest years. It may also be worth noting that the Government is constantly reminding us that our education system must do better in order that we may *compete* on the world stage – whereas surely we have reached a point in history where we wish to have an education system which is second to none in order that our citizens may *cooperate* with other nations to promote health, well-being and peace?

We might also ask if we pay enough attention to the 'needs' and rhythms of young children (David 1996). In an age when some parents may have plenty of time but no resources and others no time and a sufficiency of resources (Handy 1994), we need to debate the issues of working hours and social justice as they impact upon children. Further, the African proverb 'It takes a village to raise a child' urges us to take stock of who is responsible for children – only parents or the whole of society, and what are the responsibilities?

Collaboration across services and settings is a goal for the future, but we might also think about the benefits, the developments in our knowledge base which could be derived from a more collaborative model for research in this field. We have already seen examples of this, where parents have 'told their stories about their children' as part of a project (Athey 1990). So much research in the past has been based on data collected in restrained settings by 'strangers', whereas observations by those who know the children well are more likely to be infused with a more intimate understanding of the meanings the child attributes to particular behaviours and events.

Additionally, we still need greater coherence, a more holistic view of what the services should be for as far as the children themselves are concerned (Penn 1997). In many of our European partner countries what happens to the children, the kind of curriculum offered, the services provided, are subject to evaluation and communal debate (Dahlberg and Asen 1994) and a recent EU Recommendation called for all member states to take measures to ensure the provision of childcare facilities for working parents and that those services should combine 'reliable care with a pedagogical approach' (Moss 1996, p. 48).

In the majority of our European partner countries, there is much more widespread support for parents in the form of childcare services, parental leave and recognition for public responsibility towards the children of working parents, thus alleviating and sharing the challenges of bringing up small children in today's rapidly changing world. Many of the new UK Government's policies (for example: requiring local authorities to provide plans concerning future development of provision for all under fives (DfEE 1997); the £540 million programme to tackle social exclusion from the earliest years (Ghouri 1998) have created a climate in which young children, their learning and achievements are at last recognised as of great importance and these beginnings are the foundations on which those of us in the field of early years and primary education can build.

Most importantly, many of the new policies have demanded discussion among educators, parents and politicians but perhaps the most important debates to be initiated concern our constructions of early childhood and the values exposed by those constructions, for it is the ideas and discourses concerning 'the child' which shape educational provision, as one of the social institutions of childhood in our own and other societies.

When we ask whether our society values young children, we would do well to remember it is these babies and young children now trying to make sense of their world who will be tomorrow's citizens and as the poet Kahlil Gibran writes:

> You may give them your love but not your thoughts,
> For they have their own thoughts . . .
> For life goes not backwards nor tarries with yesterday.
> You are the bows from which your children as living arrows are sent forth.
>
> (Gibran 1926, in the 1994 edition, p. 20)

Issues

1. What effect might China's One Child Policy have upon parents' expectations for their children, and upon the children's lives as a result of such expectations?
2. How might Chinese children themselves be influencing educational or social policy?
3. How are children in the UK influencing educational and/or social policy?

Note

[1] In the 1980s, the Chinese government ran an advertising campaign which extolled the merits of having daughters, and proclaimed them equal to sons. The extensive reporting in the international press of widespread abortion, some female infanticide and neglect of baby girls also bear witness to the urgency (to have a son) which Chinese couples often feel.

References

Ariès, P. (1962) *Centuries of Childhood*. London: Jonathan Cape.

Athey, C. (1990) *Extending Thought in Young Children: A Parent–Teacher Partnership*. London: Paul Chapman.

Bowlby, J. (1953) *Child Care and the Growth of Love*. Harmondsworth: Penguin.

Brindle, D. (1994) Poverty highlighted by school meals survey. *The Guardian* 31.1.94.

Bronfenbrenner, U. (1975) Reality and research in the ecology of human development. *Proceedings of the American Philosophical Society*, 119, pp. 439–69.

Bronfenbrenner, U. (1979) *The Ecology of Human Development*. Cambridge Mass.: Harvard University Press.

Bronfenbrenner, U. and Morris, P. (1998) The ecology of developmental processes, in W. Damon (ed.) *The Handbook of Child Psychology Vol. 1: theoretical models of human development* (5th edition). New York: John Wiley and Sons.

Bruner, J. and Haste, H. (eds.) (1987) *Making Sense*. London: Methuen.

Butler, A. J. P. (1996) Review of Children and Violence. *Child Abuse Review*, 5 (4), pp. 297–98.

Christiansen, F. and Rai, S. (1996) *Chinese Politics and Society*. Hemel Hempstead: Prentice Hall Europe.

Cohen, B. (1990) *Caring for Children: the 1990 Report*. London: FPSC/SCAFA.

Council of Europe (1996) *The Child as Citizen*. Strasbourg: Council of Europe.

Dahlberg, G. and Asen, G. (1994) A question of empowerment, in P. Moss and A. Pence (eds.) *Valuing Quality in Early Childhood Services*. London: Paul Chapman.

David, T. (1990) *Under Five – Under-Educated?* Milton Keynes: Open University Press.

David, T. (1996) Their right to play, in C. Nutbrown (ed.) *Children's Rights and Early Education*. London: Paul Chapman.

Deloache, J. S. and Brown, A. L. (1987) The early emergence of planning skills in children, in J. Bruner and H. Haste (eds.) *Making Sense*. London: Cassell.

DfEE (1997) *Excellence in Schools* Cm3681. London: The Stationery Office.

Ebbeck, M. and Wei, Z. G. (1996) The importance of preschool education in the PRC. *International Journal of Early Years Education*, 4 (1), pp. 27–34.

Elder, G., Modell, J. and Parke, R. (eds.) (1993) *Children in Time and Space: Developmental and Historical Insights*. Cambridge, Cambridge University Press.

Fox Harding, L. (1996) *Family, State and Social Policy*. London: Macmillan.

Gardner, H. (1983) *Frames of Mind: the Theory of Multiple Intelligences*. New York: Basic Books.

Gardner, H. (1993) *The Unschooled Mind*. London: Fontana.

Gauthier, A. H. (1996) *The state and the family*. Oxford: Clarendon Press.

Gibran, K. (1926) *The Prophet*. London: William Heinemann.

Gladney, D.C. (1994) Ethnic Identity in China: The New Politics of Difference, in W. A. Joseph (ed.) *China Briefing 1994*. Boulder, CO: Westview Press, pp. 171–92.

Goleman, D. (1996) *Emotional Intelligence*. London: Bloomsbury.

Ghouri, N. (1998) Start-right cash to combat exclusion. *Times Educational Supplement* 4283, p. 7.

Handy, C. (1994) *The Empty Raincoat*. London: Hutchinson.

Harré, R.(1983) *Personal Being: A Theory for Individual Psychology*. Oxford: Blackwell.

Harré, R. (1986) The steps to social constructionism, in M. Richards and P. Light (eds.) *Children of Social Worlds*. Cambridge: Polity Press.

James, A. (1998) From the child's point of view: issues in the social construction of childhood, in C. Panter-Brick (ed.) *Biosocial Perspectives on Children*. Cambridge, Cambridge University Press pp. 45–65.

Kessen, W. (1979) The American child and other cultural inventions. *American Psychologist*, 34 (10) pp. 815–20.

Kessen, W. (ed.) (1975) *Childhood in China*. New Haven USA: Yale University Press.

Kinney, A. B. (ed.) (1995): *Chinese Views of Childhood*. Honolulu: University of Hawaii Press.

Kumar, V. (1993) *Poverty and Inequality in the UK. The Effects on Children*. London: NCB.

Lambert, J.F. (1996) *Des règles et du jeu*. Paper presented at the European Seminar of OMEP, UNESCO Paris 24–27 October 1996.

Lau, S (ed.) (1996) *Growing Up The Chinese Way*. Hong Kong: Chinese University Press.

Morss, J. (1990) *The Biologising of Childhood: developmental psychology and the Darwinian myth*. Hove: Lawrence Erlbaum Associates.

Morss, J. (1996) *Growing Critical: alternatives to developmental psychology*. London: Routledge.

Moss, P. (1996) Perspectives from Europe, in G. Pugh (ed.) *Contemporary Issues in the Early Years*. London: Paul Chapman pp. 30–50.

Nunes, T. (1994) The relationship between childhood and society. *Van Leer Foundation Newsletter*, Spring, pp. 16–17.

O'Neill, J. (1994) *The Missing Child in Liberal Theory*. London: University of Toronto Press.

Panter-Brick, C. (ed.) (1998) *Biosocial Perspectives on Children*. Cambridge: Cambridge University Press.

Penn, H. (1997) *Comparing Nurseries*. London: Paul Chapman.

Pollock, L. A. (1983) *Forgotten Children: parent–child relations from 1500 to 1900*. Cambridge: Cambridge University Press.

Postman, N. (1985) *The Disappearance of Childhood*. London: Comet/W. H. Allen.

Pyke, N. (1998) Ofsted figures support failing schools poverty link. *Times Educational Supplement* No. 4283, 31.7.98, p. 3.

Sharpe, K. (1997) The Protestant ethic and the spirit of Catholocism: ideological and institutional constraints in English and French primary schools. *Comparative Education*, 33 (3) pp. 329–48.

Singer, E. (1992) *Child Development and Daycare*. London: Routledge.

Sylwander, L. (1996) Why we need an Ombudsman for children, in Council of Europe, *The child as citizen*. Strasbourg: Council of Europe.

The Times (1995) Three kind mice. (Editorial) *The Times* 12 September 1995.

Tobin, J. J., Wu, D. Y. H. and Davidson, D. H. (1989) *Preschool in Three Cultures:*

Japan, China and the United States. London: Yale University Press.

Trevarthen, C. (1992) 'An infant's motives for speaking and thinking in the culture, in A. H. Wold (ed.) *The Dialogical Alternative.* Oxford: Oxford University Press, pp. 99–137.

United Nations (1989) *The Convention on the Rights of the Child.* New York: United Nations.

Utting, D. (1995) *Family and Parenthood: supporting families, preventing breakdown.* York: Joseph Rowntree Foundation.

Wilkinson, R. G. (1994) *Unfair Shares.* London: Barnardos.

Index

For enquiries or renewal at
Quarles LRC
Tel: 01708 455011 – Extension 4009